Mythical Monsters in Classical Literature

Polyphemus, Acis and Galatea
by Giulio Romano (see p. 177).

Mythical Monsters
in
Classical Literature

Paul Murgatroyd

Duckworth

First published in 2007 by
Gerald Duckworth & Co. Ltd.
90-93 Cowcross Street, London EC1M 6BF
Tel: 020 7490 7300
Fax: 020 7490 0080
inquiries@duckworth-publishers.co.uk
www.ducknet.co.uk

A catalogue record for this book is available
from the British Library

ISBN 978 0 7156 3627 5

Typset by Ray Davies
Printed and bound in Great Britain by
MPG Books Limited, Bodmin, Cornwall

Contents

Contents

Illustrations

For Isla

Preface

This book grew out of my first-level myth course, and many of the topics, translations and interpretations in it were tried out on McMaster students over several years. It is aimed at similar myth classes, and also at the general reader interested in monsters and mythology. Like my course, it has its scholarly aspects, but is also meant to be stimulating and entertaining (telling most of the variously appealing stories about Classical monsters and, I hope, making those stories really come alive). All the translations from original sources are my own.

The consideration of these creatures from a literary standpoint is a perfectly valid one, and also a new one, which fills out the picture and makes for a more balanced view. As many of my readers may not know all that much about literary criticism, I have been at pains to introduce that element slowly and to build up gradually to quite sophisticated literary analysis in the final few chapters. The point of all this is to enhance readers' appreciation and plain enjoyment of the ancient versions of these myths. As users of this book may well browse, I have made each chapter suitable for independent reading (explaining references again rather than assuming that explanations given earlier in the book have been seen and digested). The index should also make this a useful reference work.

The pleasant task of recording my thanks remains. First I must thank one of our graduate students, Allison Kennedy, who kindly looked through an early draft of several chapters, picking up typographical errors and making various helpful comments. And I owe a particular debt of gratitude to my good friend Dr Bridget Reeves, who read the typescript with real perception and painstaking care, was extremely supportive, and contributed many valuable suggestions and criticisms.

The Head of Medusa by Peter Paul Rubens (1577-1640) and Frans Snijders (1579-1657). Kunsthistorisches Museum, Vienna.

Introduction

Since earliest times monsters have awed, terrified and enthralled us, and they have figured in the myths, stories, poetry and prose of numerous cultures down the ages.[1] There are thousands of poems and passages about them in Classical (i.e. ancient Greek and Latin) literature, ranging all the way from the horrific to the humorous. This book will acquaint you with the most famous monsters mentioned by the authors of Greece and Rome and show you the many ways in which they are employed by those poets and prose writers. As well as finding stories about these creatures which are highly entertaining in themselves, you will acquire a basic grounding in literary criticism which will enable you to read narratives about monsters (and other narratives) with more perception and more enjoyment. You will also learn much about Greek and Latin literature, see and engage in comparative study (tracing monsters in various civilizations and media down to the twenty-first century), and probe some of the darkest, deepest and most ancient fears of the human race. But first some preliminaries are necessary.

For a start we need to establish what exactly is meant by 'monster'. The word is derived from the Latin *monstrum* (which is connected with *moneo*, meaning 'advise, warn'). *Monstrum* originally denoted a supernatural phenomenon (like a rain of blood) which constituted a portent or omen sent by the gods, but it came to be applied to any uncanny person, creature or thing (especially someone or something wicked and menacing). The English 'monster' has a much wider application (for instance, we use it of any person of whom we disapprove), which results in a certain vagueness. The definition of 'monster' is a tricky business, but in this book the word will cover mythical, fabulous and imaginary creatures which are extraordinary, alien and abnormal. They are often malformed, having multiple limbs (such as three heads) or combining elements from different forms (e.g. a man's body with a bull's head), and sometimes they can change their shape (like a werewolf). Frequently they are of vast size, and very powerful, at times supernaturally so (they breathe out searing flames etc.). Usually they are terrifying, malevolent, savage and evil; but there are also harmless and beneficent monsters (see, for example, Chapter 7 below).[2] Sometimes in a search for precision scholars attempt to classify these beings in categories based on size, form, function, habitat and so on,[3] but such classification does not work too well, because monsters notoriously cross boundaries.[4]

1

Then there is the fascinating issue of origins. Where *did* such weird creatures come from really? This question has exercised many critics, and many solutions have been proposed. For instance, some argue that errors of perception were to blame (so baboons were seen as dog-headed people) or exaggeration and tall tales (told by travellers to distant lands in particular). Others point out that some monsters will actually have existed: there are such things as men of gigantic size and one-eyed babies and huge sea-beasts.[5] A recent book maintains that the ancients must have seen the bones of dinosaurs and other enormous animals (like elephants) and identified those fossils with giants and other monsters.[6] In the case of just one particular being (the snaky-haired Gorgon whose gaze turned men to stone) there is a whole set of theories. The etymological explanation is that the Gorgon represents thunder and lightning because the name is derived from the Sanskrit *garj* meaning 'noise'. Others claim that the Gorgon came from a real animal which it resembled (a lion, gorilla, squid or octopus) or is a personification (of fear). Then again the origin may be meteorological (the Gorgon = the moon or the sun), and so on.[7] Such speculation about monsters is all very intriguing, and there is probably something in most of these theories, although no one of them will explain all of the bizarre creatures.

Monsters also reveal a lot about the cultures that produce them. The fact that there were so many Classical monsters makes it clear that they filled a need for the Greeks and Romans, for example by providing a safe thrill and scare. They show us what the ancients feared and also found fascinating, what worried them, and what (in contrast to monstrosity) was felt to be good and normal. They give us insights into a view of the human situation – the trials and horrors of life, and how they are overcome (or not); the terrifying powers of wild nature; the dangers of miscegenation and the transgression of borders. Modern research concentrates in particular on 'the other', discussing how monsters by being alien validate one's own civilization and demonstrate the unacceptability of external civilizations, and how enemies and foreigners and their gods are represented as monstrous.[8] For the postmodern critic monsters stand for the outcast and the revolutionary who threatens society and they stem from the need of the majority to vilify the different minority. For Marxists they symbolize predatory and destructive capitalism. Anthropologists speculate variously (such creatures represent a threat to a community's integrity and moral order etc.), as do psychologists (seeing the beast as phallic, a target for castration and so on).[9]

These are the kinds of issues that serious studies of monsters have addressed, and (for fullness) it was necessary to raise them in this introduction. But they will not provide the main thrust of this book. I do not feel that the world needs a lengthy rehash of such theories or yet another theory (of my own) explaining the origins of these beings or relating them to their cultural milieu. But I do feel that I can usefully fill a gap by covering purely literary aspects, which have been largely ignored by scholars so far.[10] The area on which I have opted to focus is both important and interesting, as I hope you will see when you read the chapters that follow. Many of the best Classical writers expended much thought and effort on accounts of monstrous creatures, and their work deserves and repays close attention.

Vampires, Werewolves and the Living Dead

We tend to associate vampires and werewolves with Eastern Europe and the living dead (zombies) with the West Indies, and people often think that these standard monsters of contemporary books and films are fairly recent phenomena. However, precedents can be found for them in the literature of ancient Greece and Rome. This chapter will investigate the more striking of these precedents and will also look at some of the basic techniques involved in conveying horrific details and telling a good horror story.

Furies, Keres, Empusa and strix

The precise definition of a vampire is somewhat disputed, but most would accept that it is a malignant, preternatural creature (most often a dead person reanimated) that sucks blood to nourish itself and to inflict harm.[1] Although we do not find in antiquity some of the by now customary paraphernalia (garlic, crucifixes etc.), there were then various creatures which were definitely akin to vampires. For example, when the Greek hero Odysseus, seeking information about his voyage home from Troy, visits the Land of the Dead in book 11 of Homer's *Odyssey*, he digs a trench and cuts the throats of some sheep that he sacrifices over it, so that the dark blood pours into it. In an eerie scene the dead are attracted to the blood and come flocking to it in large numbers. Those allowed by him to drink the blood acquire somehow the ability to recognize him, speak the truth to him in answer to his questions and ask him about their own dear ones still in the land of the living. Similarly in one of Euripides' plays the Greek warrior Neoptolemus sacrifices Polyxena, a daughter of the king of Troy, and offers her blood to the ghost of his father Achilles to drink, while in another play of his the god Death himself consumes blood from offerings made at tombs.[2]

The Erinyes (or Furies) were dread avenging goddesses of the Underworld who had black bodies, blood dripping from their eyes and snakes twined in their hair. They especially punished crimes by humans against other members of their families and so went after Orestes when he killed his mother. In plays connected with that myth the Greek tragedian Aeschylus depicts them as imbibing gore to embolden themselves and drinking the blood of sinners to punish and weaken them, prior to hauling them off to the Underworld for more retribution.[3] So at *Eumenides* 264ff.

they have tracked down Orestes and address him, claiming him for punishment:

> In atonement you must let us suck the red clotted
> blood from your body while you are still alive. Let   265
> me feed on you – a repulsive drink! While you are
> still alive, I'll drain you dry and carry you off to the dead
> to suffer agony in punishment for murdering your mother.

Their eager anticipation and the way in which they gloat and go into grim detail there is thoroughly unpleasant, and there is a disturbing combination of justice and (in its agents) vampiric horror. Somewhat similar are the Keres, ghosts or sprites which brought evils (such as disease, old age and death) and dragged off warriors who fell in battle to suck their blood.[4] They feature notably (together with the three goddesses of fate) at lines 248ff. in an epic poem called the *Shield of Heracles*, where there is a description of a marvellously ornamented shield carried by that superhero. On one part of it were depicted men at war, watched in fear by their aged fathers and by women screaming out and tearing their cheeks in grief:

> The men were engaged in combat, and behind them,
> gnashing their white teeth, were the dark Keres,
> a daunting sight, grim-faced, bloody and terrible.   250
> They fought each other over the fallen. For they were all
> longing to drink dark blood. As soon as one of them seized
> a man lying on the ground or wounded and falling, she
> closed her great claws around him, and his soul went down to
> chill Tartarus in the Underworld. When they were sated with   255
> a human's blood, they would fling that man behind them
> and rush back into the fray and din of battle.
> Clotho and Lachesis stood over them, and so did the
> divine Atropos, not as tall and not large,
> but superior to the others and the eldest of them.   260
> The Keres all fought fiercely over one mortal, glaring
> evilly at each other with eyes of fury and making
> identical attacks on one another with hands and claws.

As well as the callous attitude to the dead, there is impact in the appalling fighting among the Keres over victims, the sating of themselves with blood (which implies that they gulp down a lot of it) and the piling up of powerful adjectives at lines 249-50.

In Philostratus' *Life of Apollonius* 4.25 we find a story about a female monster with supernatural powers and a taste for human blood. She is called an Empusa and is also identified with the monsters called Lamia and Mormolycia.[5] Philostratus (late second to early third centuries AD) wrote a fabulous and dubious biography of a certain Apollonius. The latter

6

may not have actually existed, but was said to have been a Greek philosopher, mystic and holy man of the first century AD who as a wandering teacher and sage visited remote and exotic lands, and whose miracles became so famous that he was worshipped as a god. Philostratus' chapter on the Empusa is not there simply to frighten. In fact its main point is to give a full account of the best known tale about Apollonius and to put across his wonderful prophetic skill and perceptiveness, his care for his pupils and his complete superiority over the awesome Empusa.[6] But in doing all that Philostratus produces an unsettling and uncanny narrative (not a tale of terror; something more like *The Blair Witch Project* or *The Mothman Prophecies*). Here it is (set in the Greek town of Corinth):

In Corinth at that time there was a teacher of philosophy called Demetrius, who combined in his doctrines all the strongest points of the Cynics' system, and who subsequently received honourable mention in several of Favorinus' works. He reacted towards Apollonius exactly as they say Antisthenes did to the wise Socrates: he followed Apollonius, keen to become his pupil and devoted to his words, and converted his more illustrious acquaintances into adherents of Apollonius. Menippus from Lycia was one of them. He was 25 years old, intelligent, had a good physique and looked like a handsome, well-born athlete. Most people thought that his lover was a foreign woman, and she seemed to be beautiful and very delicate, and was said to be rich; but absolutely none of this was so, it was all an illusion. For, when he was walking alone along the road to Cenchreae, a spectre had come across him and changed itself into a woman. She grasped his hand and said that she came from Phoenicia and lived in a suburb of Corinth, naming a particular suburb. 'If you go there this evening,' she added, 'I will sing for you and you'll have wine like none that you have ever drunk. There won't be any rival for you to worry about, and we will live together, two beautiful people together.' The young man was ensnared by all this (he was a good philosopher, but susceptible to passion) and visited her in the evening. After that he spent most of his time with her (as if she was his girlfriend), as yet unaware that she was a spectre.

Apollonius looked at Menippus as a sculptor does and traced an outline of the young man; then he observed him closely and formed his judgement. He said, 'You are a handsome man, and you are chased by beautiful women; but you are cherishing a snake, and the snake is cherishing you.' Menippus was amazed, and Apollonius added, 'For this woman is no wife for you. How could she be? Do you imagine that she loves you?' Menippus said, 'Yes, because she treats me as if she loves me.' 'And would you marry her?' 'Yes. It would be lovely to marry a woman who cares for me.' So Apollonius asked, 'When will the wedding take place?' 'Soon. Perhaps tomorrow.'

Apollonius kept an eye out for the wedding banquet and just after the guests arrived went up to them and said, 'Where is the delicate bride who brought us here?' 'Here,' said Menippus, getting up from his seat and blushing. 'Which of you two owns the silver and gold and all the other things adorning the banquet-room?' Menippus said, 'She does,' and then pointed to his threadbare cloak, adding, 'This is all I own.' Apollonius said, 'Do you people know about the trees that hang over Tantalus, how they exist and yet don't exist?' They replied, 'Yes, we know of them from Homer, not having gone down to the Underworld ourselves.' 'You must realize that this finery is the same. These aren't real things, they just seem to be things. Let me prove that I am talking the truth: this fine bride is one of the Empusas, who most people identify with Lamias and Mormolycias. These females do love; they love sex, but above all human flesh, and they use sex to allure men they want to eat.'

The bride said, 'Be quiet and leave!' She pretended to be appalled at what he had said and was quite critical about philosophers for always talking nonsense. But when the golden goblets and the vision of silver were proved to be as insubstantial as wind, and everything flitted away out of their sight, and the wine waiters and cooks and all the other servants vanished on being proved to be fake by Apollonius, the spectre seemed to weep, and it begged him not to examine it and force it to confess what it was. But when he pressed and wouldn't let it go, it said that it was an Empusa and was fattening up Menippus with delicacies with a view to devouring his body, for it was its habit to feed on beautiful young bodies, as their blood is pure.

This is the best known story about Apollonius and I had to tell it at length because many people know of it and that the events occurred in central Greece, but they have only heard in outline that he once overcame a Lamia in Corinth and don't know what it was up to and that he did it for Menippus' sake. I have based my version on Damis' account.

In this story there is an unpleasant combination of the erotic and the horrific, the perverse and the predatory, typical of classic vampire tales; and the Empusa is like a standard female vampire – alluring, insidious, sinister, menacing and attracted to blood. All the names and details (especially at the start, to incline us to believe what follows) impart a feeling of solidity and realism; so too the citation of the source at the end adds some corroboration, and the philosophical connection together with the absence of lurid sensationalism gives the narrative a rather muted and scholarly flavour and so makes it seem more acceptable.[7] A distinct sense of unease is created by the presence of so many eerie details, and by the fact that some of them are really telling (such as the oddness of Apollonius sketching Menippus in outline and somehow just knowing about so many things, like the wedding plans; the disturbing notion of the monster especially craving the blood of the young; and the chilling intelligence of the Empusa, which launches a concerted attack, enticing by means of beauty, sex, song and wealth, all of which are well aimed at its impoverished and amorous victim).

There is a careful manipulation of material as well, with an effective build-up. After a slow and lulling start Philostratus gradually winds up the tension. We are induced to be sympathetic towards Menippus by being told of his youth, intelligence, and so on, and so we feel misgivings when he is ensnared by the spectre. We can't be sure that its aims are evil (for example, it could just want some love and affection), until Apollonius calls it a snake. Then comes the worrying news that Menippus intends to marry, at once. That is rapidly succeeded by the wedding and the weirdness of all the false finery and the horror in the revelation of the bride's true identity and voracious nature. Then the mysterious disappearance of all the illusory trappings is succeeded by the crowning horror of the Empusa fattening Menippus up in order to devour him, habitually preying on beautiful young bodies and having a particular fondness for their pure blood. A diminuendo in the final paragraph winds down the tension, although one still goes away with a shiver over how very close Menippus came to being eaten up.[8]

Writing shortly before the birth of Christ, the Latin poet Ovid produced a rather more shocking passage about the *strix* (an undetermined type of screech-owl, a bird of the night associated with magic, death and ill omen, which made vampire-like attacks on people, sucking their blood and sometimes eating them too). The passage occurs in Ovid's *Fasti* (6.131ff.), a poetic calendar which is much concerned with deities, cults and festivals, and which often recounts illustrative tales. Again the author is not trying simply to terrify; and again the primary point of the story is to celebrate someone (the goddess Cranae), but achieving that involves distinctly frightening elements (as Ovid builds up the screech-owls as formidable opponents for the goddess). He tells how the birds attacked an early Italian king called Proca when he was a baby, and how Cranae used against them (amongst other things) a twig of whitethorn which repelled harm and was given to her by the god Janus. Ovid had just explained (at 6.105ff.) that the beautiful but mischievous Cranae had had many suitors who went up to her in the countryside and propositioned her, and she had always agreed to sleep with them if they would go ahead of her to a secluded cave; but when they trustingly set off she would hide behind their backs in the undergrowth and could not be found anywhere. But one day she was approached by Janus, the god with two faces (the usual one looking forwards, and also one behind looking backwards). She tried the same trick with him, comically somehow unaware that he literally had eyes in the back of his head. He saw where she hid behind him, went back to her and made her keep her promise to have sex with him; then in return he made her the goddess of hinges and gave her the powerful whitethorn. Immediately after that comes the narrative about the screech-owls:

> There are voracious birds – not the ones that cheated Phineus'
>   throat of food, but they are descended from those.
> They have large heads, goggling eyes, beaks made for rapine,
>   grey in their feathers and hooks on their claws.
> They fly at night and attack children without a nurse,   135
>   snatching them from their cradles and mutilating them.
> Men say they tear the flesh of unweaned babies with their
>   beaks and drink down the blood till their gullets are full.

9

They are called screech-owls – so called because of
   their habit of screeching horribly at night.   140
So then, whether they are born birds or become so by magic
   (turned from old women into fowls by a Marsian spell),
they entered Proca's nursery. There Proca, a child five
   days old, was fresh prey for the birds.
They drained the blood from the infant's chest with greedy   145
   tongues; the poor boy wailed for help.
His nurse ran up, terrified by her baby's cry,
   and found his cheeks raked by rigid claws.
What should she do? His face was the colour that autumn
   leaves usually have when nipped by an early winter.   150
She went to Cranae and told her. Cranae said, 'Don't be afraid
   any more: your nursling will be safe.'
Cranae went to the cradle. The mother and father wept;
   she said, 'Stop crying, I'll make him well.'
At once with arbutus leaves three times in due order she   155
   touched the doorposts and marked the threshold.
She sprinkled the entrance with medicated water and held
   the raw inwards of a pig two months old
and said, 'Birds of night, leave the boy's inwards alone:
   this small creature is sacrificed for the small child.   160
I pray, take its heart for his, its entrails for his.
   I give you this animal's life for a better life.'
After this offering she set the inwards in the open and
   forbade those present at the rite to look back at them.
The twig of whitethorn that Janus had given her was placed   165
   where a small window let light into the nursery.
They say that after that the birds did not violate the cradle
   and the boy recovered his former complexion.

The depiction of the screech-owls at lines 131-40 is powerful in itself. It is lengthy and full and has many vivid and arresting details. Then there is the reference to Phineus, who for offending the gods was punished by means of the Harpies (birds with the heads of girls and faces pale with hunger, which swooped down on his food whenever he tried to eat and rendered it inedible by befouling it with their droppings and infecting it with their disgusting stench). By that allusion Ovid at the very start puts the screech-owls on a par with the notorious and dread Harpies of myth and epic poetry, and economically implies that the screech-owls were similarly repulsive and relentless enemies of mankind, horrific spoilers hard to drive off. The description gains further impact from the sudden and stark contrast with the light-hearted story (about Cranae deceiving her suitors) that preceded it. This is the literary equivalent of the shock we get from the abrupt and unexpected appearance of a monster in a film (as in *Alien*). At 141ff. Ovid maintains the horror, injecting magic and mystery into the birds' origins, dwelling on their appalling and damaging attack on a tender baby (an ancestor of his Roman readers), and picking up from 131-40 (and so stressing by means of repetition) their greed, rapaciousness and violence. In addition he adds drama (the tense 149) and pathos (146, 147 and 153). As a result of all that we are really involved in the narrative and feel great relief and real admiration for Cranae when she intervenes, swiftly reassuring and completely effective (both in banishing the birds and in restoring Proca's health). There, with a lively development and an interesting tonal mix, what began as a tale of terror gives way to solemn ritual and ends on a note of quiet triumph.

Werewolves

The wolf had various uncanny associations in the ancient world (for example, its appearance was usually an evil omen; a small tuft of hair in its tail was said to contain a love potion; and if a wolf saw a man before the man saw the wolf, he was supposedly struck dumb[9]). Still more uncanny was the human who mutated into a wolf and then back again into a human. In Greek and Latin literature we find several definite examples of such werewolves,[10] and there are various brief references to them and longer stories about them.[11]

Among the shorter allusions, the Greek historian Herodotus (fifth century BC) at 4.105 tells of a tribe called the Neuri (beyond furthest Scythia, on the edge of the known world) who were said to change into wolves once a year for a day or two and then to turn back into men again.[12] There were also supposed to be werewolves in mainland Greece itself, and they were particularly connected with the area in southern Greece called Arcadia. A secret sacrifice to Zeus took place on the peak of Mount Lycaeus there (a strange place where nothing ever cast a shadow, and any unauthorized person who entered died within the year). We are informed that anyone who tasted human flesh in that sacrifice was fated to become a wolf; that a man always turned into a wolf at that ceremony but after nine years returned to his original form if he had not fed on a human as a wolf (if he had, he stayed a wolf for ever); and that a boxer called Damarchus or Daemenetus tasted the entrails of a child sacrificed to Zeus and duly metamorphosed into a wolf, but nine years later became a man again and went on to become a victor in the boxing at the Olympic Games.[13] There was also a report that someone from the clan of a certain Anthus would be chosen by lot and taken to a lake in Arcadia, where he hung his clothes on an oak, swam across the lake and went off into the wilds, transformed into a wolf; there he associated with real wolves for nine years, and if he had not partaken of human flesh in that period, he then swam back across the lake, recovered his human shape and got back his clothes.[14]

There is a longer account in one of the many fables dubiously attributed to Aesop.[15] For a change there is some cleverness and a deliberately comic aspect (as the werewolf superstition is craftily exploited) and also a didactic element (in the message added to the tale). The removal of clothing as a necessary preliminary to mutation into a wolf is a standard detail; the howling by the werewolf is also found elsewhere in the tradition; and the number three was supposed to be a particularly powerful one, closely linked to magic. Here is the fable:

> A thief stayed at an inn, remaining there for some time in the expectation of stealing something, but without success. One day he saw that the inn-keeper had put on a fine new tunic (as there was a festival) and was sitting in front of the inn's door, with nobody else around. The thief went up to the inn-keeper, sat down by him and began to chat with him. After they had chatted long enough, the thief yawned and together with the yawn howled like a wolf. The inn-keeper asked him why he did that, and the thief replied, 'I'll tell you now. But please look after my clothes, which I'm going to leave here. Sir, I don't know what causes these yawns of mine, I can't tell if they are punishment for the wrong I have done or happen for some other reason. Anyway, whenever I give three quick yawns I become a wolf, a man-eater.' With that he yawned a second time and howled again, as before. The inn-keeper believed what the thief said and was frightened; he stood up, eager to get away. The thief grabbed hold of his tunic and appealed to him: 'Sir, wait and take my clothes, so that I don't lose them!' As he said this, he opened his mouth and began to yawn a third time. The inn-keeper, afraid that he was going to be eaten, ran into the inn, leaving his tunic behind, and locked himself up safe inside. The thief took the tunic and left.
> This is what happens to those who believe in lies.

The most famous werewolf story in antiquity appears in the *Satyricon*, a satirical novel by a first-century AD Roman author, Petronius. In one episode a lavish and tasteless dinner party is put on by Trimalchio. This former slave who had become a millionaire is desperately keen to impress (with his wealth and supposed style, learning, wit, etc.) and win the affection and respect of his guests. They are for the most part equally uneducated and unsophisticated ex-slaves, and often they are actually taken in by Trimalchio's absurd antics. Petronius presents there a comic picture of an ignorant and vulgar foreign upstart making a ludicrously unsuccessful attempt to ape high society by means of a hopelessly incompetent version of a smart dinner party (complete with a dog-fight, a violent row between host and hostess, constant and obvious showing off by Trimalchio, and so on). Petronius thereby satirizes the host's stupidity, social ineptness, pretentiousness, ostentation, and so on (and also criticizes the guests for being gullible and similarly unpolished).

At one point in the party (chapter 61) we are presented with Trimalchio's idea of intelligent and civilized dinner conversation. He turns to a guest called Niceros, complains that he used to be better company at a party and asks him to tell them all about an adventure that he'd once had. This is the story told by Niceros in response:

1. Vampires, Werewolves and the Living Dead

'When I was still a slave, we lived in a narrow street. The house belongs to Gavilla now. There, as heaven willed, I fell in love with the wife of the inn-keeper Terentius. You knew her – Melissa, from Tarentum, a really lovely little peach. But it really wasn't a physical thing, I wasn't interested in her for sex; no, it was her nice nature. If I asked her for anything, she never refused me. Whatever cash she got, I got half. I put all I got into her pocket and was never cheated.

'One day her husband died, at his master's place in the country. So I hatched up a scheme and moved heaven and earth to get to her (you know, a friend in need is a friend indeed). It so happened that my master had gone off to Capua, to attend to some odds and sods. I seized my chance and persuaded a guest in our house to go with me as far as the fifth milestone. He was a soldier, brave as hell. We buggered off about cock-crow, the moon made it bright as noon. When we reached the bit of the road with tombs on either side, my friend began to make for the gravestones. I sat down, singing a song and counting the gravestones. Then, when I looked round at him, he stripped off and put all his clothes at the side of the road. My heart was in my mouth, I stood there like a dead man. But he pissed in a ring around his clothes and suddenly turned into a wolf. Don't think I'm joking, I wouldn't make this up no matter how much I was paid. But, as I was saying, he turned into a wolf, then began to howl and ran off into the woods.

'At first I didn't know where I was, then I went to pick up his clothes, but they'd turned into stone. If ever a man died of fright, it was me. But I drew my sword and hacked at shadows all the way to the house where my girl was. I entered like a ghost, almost at my last gasp, with sweat pouring down my crotch, my eyes like a dead man's. I don't know how I ever recovered. My Melissa was amazed at me walking around so late and said, "If you'd come earlier, you could at least have helped us. A wolf got into the grounds and attacked all the sheep, it was like a butcher's shop, blood everywhere. But it didn't have the last laugh, even if it did get away – one of our slaves put a spear through its neck."

'After I heard this there was no way that I could close my eyes and go to sleep. As soon as it was broad daylight, I ran to my master Gaius' house like an inn-keeper after thieving guests. When I came to the spot where the clothes had turned to stone, all I could find was blood. But when I got home, my friend the soldier was lying in bed like an ox, and a doctor was seeing to his neck. I realized that he was a werewolf, and after that I couldn't have shared a meal with him, not if you killed me. Others can decide for themselves what they think about all this, but if I'm telling lies, may your guardian angels strike me down!'

As an eerie story this has distinct merits. It is told at just the right length, neither too short (although it is brisk) nor too long (although Niceros does ramble a bit in the first paragraph, in just the expansive way that a man might reminisce about a former girlfriend). He begins by giving us an adequate amount of information about the background situation, and at the start of the second paragraph sets the scene well for what follows. The fact that Niceros represents himself as so closely involved in the events means that they have greater immediacy, and their impact on the reader is heightened by the way in which the narrator relates his own reactions (of shock, fear, etc.). And there is an effective bit of relief with a brief lessening of tension in the latter half of the second paragraph (before it is screwed up again): there apparently Niceros first imagines that his companion has gone off to relieve himself (as people often did among tombstones at the side of the road) and so carefully looks the other way and occupies himself while waiting; and then when the soldier strips, Niceros fears that he is going to be raped by him. In general the story is never boring, and it is full of action and detail, including some graphic small details and several spooky ones. The reader is further involved and helped to suspend disbelief by various realistic points (in addition to those already mentioned, there is the colloquial style, the adulterous relationship with Melissa, so typical of low life, the slave's understandably mercenary attitude at the end of the first paragraph, and his very human responses to events after setting off with the soldier).

Within the context of the party Niceros comes out with his anecdote simply to awe and frighten his listeners, but Petronius uses it for satirical purposes. The guests and host are all thunderstruck with amazement, a highly entertaining reaction to such guff. But Petronius is not only mocking their gullibility, superstitiousness and lack of sophistication. He also uses this incident to satirize Trimalchio's eagerness to make an impact and goes on to show how *not* to tell a frightening story. For the host cannot bear to be left out, with someone else stealing the show, and so after a few remarks to repay Niceros for responding to his request he hastens (without any invitation) to recover attention with a (rather less effective) tale of his own:

> Trimalchio said, 'I pick no holes in your story. Take my word for it, my hair stood up on end, because I know that Niceros never talks nonsense; no, he's reliable and doesn't run off at the mouth. Anyway I'll tell you a horror story myself, as strange as an ass on a roof. When I still had long hair (for I lived a soft life from being a boy), our master's darling among the slave-boys died. God, he was a pearl, a pretty boy, perfection. So while his poor mother was crying over him and several of us were deeply upset, suddenly witches started to screech – it sounded like a dog was after a hare. At that time we had a man from Cappadocia with us. He was tall, really brave and strong – he could lift an angry bull up off the ground. He drew his sword and bravely rushed outside, after carefully wrapping his cloak around his left hand for a shield, and ran one of the women through the belly, just about here – may no harm come to the part of my body that I'm touching! We heard a groan and (to tell the honest truth) didn't see the witches themselves. Our strongman came in and threw himself on his bed. His body was black and blue, as if he'd been flogged – because, of course, an evil hand had touched him. We closed the door and went back to work, but as the mother put her arms around the body of her son, she touched it and saw that it was just a little

bundle of straw. It had no heart, no insides, no nothing – of course, the witches had swooped on the boy and put a straw doll in his place. Please, you've got to believe me, there really are night-hags, who are too clever, who turn everything upside down. But that tall strongman of ours never got his normal colour back; no, a few days later he died raving mad.'

This anecdote does contain quite a lot of incident, and some of the details are quite disturbing, but it falls rather flat when compared with Niceros' story (and as it comes right after that, such comparison is inevitable). Trimalchio's tale is shorter and simpler, and certainly no better. In fact, its subject (witches) and kernel (theft of a corpse) were less unusual (and so less unnerving) than the werewolf. It also loses immediacy and impact because the narrator was not as intimately involved as Niceros was and does not recount the effect on himself of these events. Similarly (perhaps in his haste to get the story out) Trimalchio does not set the scene very well (for instance, he leaves us ignorant of the hour and the location, points which might well have contributed to the atmosphere). The effectiveness is also lessened by the fact that many of the details in this passage have already been encountered in the previous one (e.g. a death occurs early on, the narrator was then young and a slave, there is an uncanny noise, a mysterious metamorphosis and a manly type who ends up lying on a couch). Finally, Trimalchio's yarn contains a serious and glaring logical flaw, which undermines it completely: after specifying the precise spot at which one of the witches was run through, he immediately goes on to claim that they were invisible. So laughably the grand host, competing with a lesser mortal, comes off second best. In addition, since Trimalchio asks Niceros to tell his story and seems conversant with it, he may well have deliberately set up his guest so that he could go one better; if this is the case, then his plans go sadly awry and his failure is even greater and funnier.

The living dead

As for the living dead, although there are no actual zombies in ancient literature, we do find there corpses brought back to life for a time, to serve the purposes of sorcerers. This is what happens with nekyomantia, when the dead are reanimated and made to produce prophecy based on knowledge gained in the Underworld. So in Lucan's first-century AD epic poem called *The Civil War* on the eve of a great battle the son of a Roman general approaches a dreadful and powerful witch called Erichtho, wanting to know how the civil war will turn out. At 6.624ff. she selects a fresh corpse and drags it to a dank and dark cave sheltered by dense trees. She pierces its breast and pours in hot blood mixed with various poisons (derived from the froth of rabid dogs, a hyena's hump, an Arabian flying serpent, dragons' eyes and so on). She utters a spell consisting of discordant and inhuman sounds (the bark of a dog, howl of a wolf, hiss of a snake, shriek of a screech-owl, and more), and then she orders the powers of the Underworld to send up to her the soul of a dead soldier. When she sees the soul beside the body, hesitant to enter it, she furiously beats the corpse with a live serpent and commands the nether gods to make the soul go into it. Suddenly the blood grows warm, the limbs quiver and the corpse leaps up from the ground. Its mouth hangs open, its eyes glare and it looks more like a dying man than someone restored to life. It is still pale and stiff, and is stunned by its return to life. It cannot speak until told to do so by Erichtho, and then it prophesies terrible carnage in the war. When it has finished speaking, more potions and spells are employed so that it can die again, and it is cremated on a funeral pyre by the witch.[16]

A more elaborate and a darkly comic account of the living dead occurs in a second century AD Latin novel written by Apuleius (*Metamorphoses* 1.5ff.). A certain Aristomenes while away from home on business in Thessaly comes across a friend of his called Socrates (but this Socrates is far more degenerate and far less philosophical and wise than the famous fifth-century BC philosopher of that name). Aristomenes asks his friend (who looks like a beggar) what has happened to him, as he had disappeared and his wife thought that he was dead (actually in this story he soon *will* be dead!). Socrates replies that Aristomenes is clearly unaware of the reversals and shifting attacks of fortune (unfortunately for him, in this tale he soon becomes intimately acquainted with them). Aristomenes takes his friend to an inn, gives him food and drink and then learns his story from him.

Socrates explains that he was on his way to watch some gladiators fight in a show when he was attacked and robbed by brigands. We note that, ironically, while going to view violence he became the subject of violence himself; and also that comically things went from bad to worse. For Socrates then stopped with an inn-keeper called Meroe, who was an old but attractive woman, and who took him to her bed, and thereby ensnared him. He says that as a result of that one act of sex he became involved in a disastrous relationship and this fine new wife of his exploited him mercilessly, taking his remaining clothes and the wages that he earned by low manual labour, until he was reduced to his present wretched state.

Aristomenes is outraged and says that for getting involved with that old whore Socrates deserves the most extreme punishment (actually he soon gets it). Socrates warns his friend not to criticize Meroe (having just done exactly that himself!), in case she overhears them and takes revenge. Aristomenes (who will in fact shortly find out all about her power) asks incredulously what kind of a powerful inn-keeper this Meroe is, when Socrates reveals that she is a highly accomplished witch. To prove this, he tells of some of her magic feats, which, ominously enough, were punishments of people who had offended her – like a former lover, who was turned into a beaver (because when hunted it escapes from its pursuers by biting off its own genitals), and the local citizens, who decided to stone her to death because of such outrages and were magically prevented from leaving their homes (unable to unlock or open their doors) until they relented.

After hearing this, Aristomenes becomes afraid that Meroe may be able to overhear them (which, of course, she does). In criticizing Meroe and scoffing at her powers Aristomenes had been rather unguarded, but from now on he makes a series of decisions which are clearly wrong and comically inept (because he is not very bright and also because he is increasingly afraid). The tension rises when Aristomenes suggests to Socrates that they should leave (as well he might), but instead of getting out of there at once, he decides to go to sleep and rest that night and then leave before dawn the next day. Socrates falls asleep, and Aristomenes takes precautions by shutting and locking the door (after just hearing about Meroe's power over doors and locks!).

He cannot sleep at first for fear but is finally nodding off when the door is smashed off its hinges and flung to the ground, knocking him out of bed and his bed on top of him. In comes the dreadful Meroe and another witch, carrying (intriguingly and disturbingly) a sword and a sponge. Meroe berates the sleeping Socrates for insulting her and wanting to leave her, and then turns on Aristomenes for advising that course of action, threatening that he will soon really regret it. Her friend gleefully suggests dismembering him or castrating him, but Meroe decides that he should survive to bury Socrates' corpse with a little earth. She then plunges her sword into Socrates' neck down to the hilt, rummages around inside the wound and finally brings out the heart. Her friend then stops up the wound with the sponge, saying, 'Sponge born in the sea, don't cross a river.' After that the two witches squat over Aristomenes and piss in his face, completely soaking him with their filthy urine. They then leave, and behind them the door springs back into place, now undamaged.

In a panic in case he is accused of the killing, Aristomenes foolishly decides to flee (which would, of course, be taken as a virtual confession of guilt), without even hiding the body to give himself more of a chance to escape. And yet he could have shown the sponge and the heart removed (not normal concomitants of the standard murder), and Socrates' stories have made it clear that the locals know all about Meroe's magic powers (over doors, etc.) and her vindictiveness towards lovers (so that they would probably have accepted his defence). But the incompetent Aristomenes cannot even manage to flee (and the tale now takes on a nightmarish quality). The sleepy porter refuses to let him out at such an hour because of dangerous brigands outside, and when Aristomenes unwisely antagonizes him by calling him a fool, he replies that for all he knows Aristomenes could have killed the friend in his room and be trying to escape. Aristomenes doesn't counter this suggestion and doesn't try to explain why he wants to leave, but just goes back to his room (more or less ensuring that he will be suspected). He foresees death by crucifixion as his punishment for murder, so tries to escape that by committing suicide! He can't get that right either. He tries to hang himself from a beam, but uses an old, rotten rope, which breaks, pitching him on top of the corpse of Socrates.

At this point the porter rushes in shouting, and Socrates promptly sits up, complaining about the noise waking him out of a very sound sleep. Delighted to be able to show the porter that he is not a murderer, Aristomenes embraces his friend, who pushes him off because he reeks of urine. As it is by now morning, the two friends leave and head off out of town. Aristomenes can see no wound in Socrates' neck, so decides that he must have dreamed the whole incident with the witches (forgetting or wilfully ignoring the thorough soaking in urine of his head, which he could not have done himself). When he says that he had had a bad dream last night, Socrates replies that he had too. He had dreamed that his throat was cut and his heart torn out, and he now feels weak and ill and is staggering and in need of some food to restore him. Such a coincidence of the two 'dreams' would seem to most people inexplicable (making it very probable that the witches must have been real), but at this supremely creepy and disturbing moment Aristomenes ... suggests breakfast. He gets Socrates to sit down under a tree and offers him bread and cheese (a man whose throat has been cut and plugged with a sponge).

As Socrates eats, Aristomenes sees that he is getting much worse (going pale, shrivelling up, failing); he thinks again of Meroe and fears that his friend will die there and he will be suspected of murder. But in spite of all that, when Socrates complains of being thirsty, Aristomenes actually suggests that he drink from a nearby river (completely forgetting the witch's words about the sponge not crossing a river). He thus sets himself up for an accusation of murder and partly justifies that accusation, because when Socrates tries to drink from the river, the wound in his neck gapes open, the sponge drops out and he falls down dead (again). Aristomenes promptly inters his friend's body beside the river bank (thereby validating Meroe's words about him surviving to bury Socrates with a little earth) and then flees for his life.

APPENDIX

Non-mythical monsters

The monsters discussed in this book are mythical, apart from some of those just mentioned in this chapter. There are some more non-mythical monsters which also deserve mention, and which are best handled briefly in an appendix. They fall into four main categories – those connected with Alexander the Great; those present in travellers' tales and parody of such tales; those introduced into historical epic poems; and those treated by scholars in works on natural history.

Alexander the Great invaded the Persian empire in the east and swept all before him, conquering and subjugating vast numbers of the enemy as far as the ends of the known world until his death in 323 BC. You might think that this would be enough by way of achievement, but reality can always be improved on, and a later Greek novel of doubtful authorship (attributed to pseudo-Callisthenes) called *The Alexander Romance* attaches to Alexander a number of encounters with fabulous humans and creatures in distant regions (2.32ff.). So he meets a crab the size of a breastplate with pincers six feet long, three-eyed lions, birds that burst into flame when touched by his troops, and two birds with human faces that told him to turn back (speaking to him in Greek, helpfully). He saw men with straps for legs, and others with six hands, men with the heads of dogs, and others with the faces of bulls and lions, and yet others with no heads at all who had their eyes and mouths on their chests. He tells of a baby like Scylla, which was human in its upper part, but from the thighs down had the heads of lions and wild dogs. He also came across giants. Some of them had round bodies and fiery faces and looked like lions. Another one had a body entirely covered with hair and glared savagely. Alexander had a naked woman brought to the giant to see what he would do with her. He promptly started to eat her.

At least some of these stories will be travellers' tales grafted on to Alexander's adventures. Greek merchants, mercenaries and colonists pushed out from early times into the world beyond Greece, and tall stories came back. For instance, there were the Shadyfeet, supposedly men who lived in a scorching desert and had enormous feet, and who, when things became too hot for them, lay on their backs with their feet in the air to provide shade for themselves.[17] These stories were apparently widely believed, as a later Greek called Lucian wrote a send-up of them, wickedly entitled *A True Story*, recounting how he and some companions sailed off west out of the Mediterranean into the Ocean. At one point they met some men rather like the Shadyfeet: these are the Corkmen, who can run across the sea because they have feet of cork. At another point Lucian and his men encountered some women-vines, which had thick stems lower down but were perfectly formed females in their upper parts. They were very friendly vines and kissed some of the men (who promptly became reeling drunk) and wanted them to have intercourse with them. But when two of the men did so, they found themselves caught by the genitals and became one with the plants and took root with them. Later Lucian's ship was swept up by a violent whirlwind and carried off to the moon. The inhabitants of the moon are rather unusual. Apart from the fact that they are all men and males copulate with males, using an orifice behind the knee (with the foetus growing in the calf of the younger man), they have beards almost down to their knees, only a single toe on each foot (with no toenails) and a long green cabbage leaf for a tail (their noses run with honey instead of mucus, and they sweat milk, from which you can make cheese by mixing in the honey-mucus, if you really want to). Lucian and his men got drawn into a war between the men of the moon and their enemies on the sun, and the opposing armies formed a striking spectacle: troops mounted on great fleas, and on huge three-headed vultures, and on birds that have grass instead of plumage and wings like lettuce leaves are matched against soldiers on winged ants 200 feet long, and dog-faced men on flying acorns, and Cloud-Centaurs (a combination of winged horse and giant). Back on earth again, Lucian's ship was swallowed whole by an enormous sea-monster, and so on and so forth.

Several Latin poets wrote epics about events in Roman history (like the war between Rome and Carthage and the civil war between Caesar and Pompey). Most epics concerned myth and contained a rich array of mythical figures, such as gods and heroes and monsters. As a way of injecting this type of sensational material into their historical epics some poets included monstrous creatures not taken from myth but supposedly found in the real world.[18] So Silius Italicus mentions a snake that was about 300 feet long (unfortunately its length meant that it experienced some difficulty when trying to bathe in its local river, since before it could immerse its whole body it would find that its head was already out of the water and resting on the opposite bank). In Lucan the Roman general Cato and his army come into contact with even nastier specimens while marching through an African desert. Some of these were just horrific snakes rather than actual monsters, like the dipsas (whose bite so dehydrated one of the soldiers that he hacked open his veins and gulped down his own blood) and the javelin-snake (which killed a man by launching itself at him from a tree and passing through his temples) and the prester (whose bite got one Roman swelling to enormous proportions, making his breastplate pop off and the rest of the army flee in terror before he went out with a bang). But there were also dragons, glittering with the sheen of gold, inhaling so strongly that they drew down passing birds into their throats, and using their tails to flog to death bulls and elephants.

Other authors referred to monstrous animals in what were intended to be works of serious scholarship, thereby giving evidence of their neglect of personal observation and uncritical acceptance of sources.[19] Among snakes there is the amphisbaena (which has a head at either end of its body) and the basilisk (which can kill other serpents with its smell and men with a mere look). Among aquatic creatures there is the nautilus. This lives in the sand, but quite often rises to the surface of the sea face down, flips on to its back, sticks two feet up into the air, runs between them a fine membrane for a sail, simultaneously (and rather acrobatically) keeping its two other feet under the water to act as rudders, and then goes wind-surfing. But my personal favourite is the cucumis (cucumber-fish), which looks like a cucumber, and, more startlingly, smells like a cucumber too. Among birds there is a Caspian bird mentioned by Aelian, which is as big as the largest cockerel and gay with many colours, and which (for some reason best known to itself) flies along just above the ground, upside down, with its legs in the air, making a sound like a puppy. There are strange land-animals too. I am also very taken with the achlis, a kind of reindeer with a very large upper lip; in fact its lip is so large that when grazing the achlis has to walk backwards, because if it went forwards it would step on its own lip and trip up. Finally, let me describe the mantichora. You may never meet a mantichora, and if you do it is unlikely that you would mistake it for anything else; but you never know when this type of information may come in handy. The mantichora is as big as a lion and has the body of a lion, with two triple rows of very sharp teeth, an overall blood-red colour, grey eyes, a tail armed with scorpion stings, the face and ears of a man, and a voice that resembles the sound of a trumpet blended with a pan-pipe, and (last but not least) it has a special fondness for the taste of human flesh.

*

Finally, a study in horror. Establish the essential features of ancient vampire types (for which see the start of this chapter). Next examine a modern film (like *Van Helsing*) or novel (from Bram Stoker to Anne Rice) about vampires and isolate the elements that are added there to the ancient features. Then consider how exactly those additions heighten the terror (or fail to because they are clichéd and predictable).

2

Impact

We are all familiar with the various techniques employed to ensure that monsters in film have an impact on us. For example, there is the gradual and suspenseful build-up, when we are shown just traces of the monster, fleeting and partial views of it, the aftermath of its attacks and so on; there is the sudden, unheralded appearance of it on screen doing something really horrific (such as savaging a victim), accompanied by shockingly loud noise; there are repulsive details (like drooling and squelching) caught vividly; and there is the reaction shot, whereby we are presented in close-up with the face of somebody (often female) reacting with revulsion and terror to the monster and its actions off screen. Literature uses some of these techniques too, such as the reaction. But when we are reading we cannot be startled by the abrupt entrance of a monster or by sound or stunning special effects, so in place of these cinematic stand-bys (or clichés) a literary treatment employs other (often more subtle and sophisticated) methods of getting to an audience. Because we are so used to visual narrative (cinema and TV) we have become mentally lazy and want to sit back and be shown things rather than picturing them for ourselves, and so we often fail to get all that we could out of a piece of writing. We have to make a bit of an effort with it, but it is usually well worthwhile,[1] and authors generally give us some help. To increase your critical appreciation and plain enjoyment of monsters in literature, this chapter will build on the last one and analyse in more depth some of the main ways in which writers achieve impact (some of them shared with cinema, some purely literary). Readers are affected simply by what authors say and also by how they say it. Let us begin with the former.

Films seldom concern themselves with a monster's origins, but mention of its parents can be a good way of increasing the menace and horror. So Earth gave birth to the Gigantes (Giants) because she was so enraged with Zeus and the other Olympian gods (and the Gigantes duly went on to attack them with tremendous violence). Sometimes the monster has a divine parent, which means that the creature itself is mighty and has a potent ally. Polyphemus, a savage, one-eyed giant, was the son of the sea-god Poseidon, and when the Greek hero Odysseus blinded him in his single eye, Polyphemus complained to Poseidon, who pursued Odysseus remorselessly thereafter. Sometimes one or more of the parents are monstrous, so that there is a great concentration of dreadfulness, repulsiveness, and so on.

For instance, at Hesiod *Theogony* 306ff. the two monsters Typhos and Echidna mate and produce three equally monstrous beasts (among them Cerberus, the dreadful watch-dog of the land of the dead):

> They say that Typhos, that lawless and overbearing terror,
> made love to Echidna, the girl with the darting eyes.
> She conceived and bore hard-hearted offspring:
> she gave birth firstly to Orthus (Geryon's dog),
> and then to irresistible, unspeakable Cerberus who devours   310
> raw flesh, Hades' brazen-voiced hound,
> fifty-headed, relentless and hard;
> thirdly she gave birth to the evil-hearted Hydra
> of Lerna.

An effective literary account will also really reach readers by bringing out the physical and mental nature of the monster itself. There are good monsters (see Chapter 7 below), but the bad ones come across much more strongly. The writer can usefully highlight horrible and awesome aspects of the creature's appearance, such as immensity, malformation and unnatural combinations. So Hesiod underscores the alien nature of Echidna at *Theogony* 295ff.:

> In a hollow cavern she gave birth to another   295
> irresistible monster quite unlike mortal men and immortal
> gods – divine Echidna, the cruel of heart, who is in one half
> a dancing-eyed nymph with beautiful cheeks, but in the other
> half a monstrous, speckled snake, a dread, massive creature
> that devours raw flesh down in her lair beneath the holy earth.   300

Similarly he stresses the misshapen, hybrid form of the Chimaera and the abnormal admixture of fire at *Theogony* 319ff.:

> She bore the Chimaera that breathed forth irresistible fire,
> an awesome creature – massive, swift-footed and strong.   320
> It had three heads: one was that of a flashing-eyed lion, the
> second was a goat's, the third was that of a powerful serpent.
> It was in its fore part a lion, in the rear a snake, in the middle a
> goat, and it breathed out the awesome might of blazing fire.

It is daunting to be told how much stronger and better armed these beasts are, and that some of them are invulnerable and almost invincible (so the lion of Nemea had a hide that just could not be penetrated by weapons, and the Hydra of Lerna had nine heads, of which one was immortal, while in the case of the other eight if one head was chopped off two grew back in its place). A skilful author will also put across how evil the monster is – ferocious, aggressive, malevolent, vindictive, voracious,[2] etc. Particularly unsettling (for me at any rate) is the notion that the creature has intelli-

Etruscan bronze Chimaera from Arezzo, Italy, late fifth century BC.
Archaeological Museum, Florence.

gence. So the bird-like females called the Sirens tried to lure passing sailors to them by their beautiful and seemingly innocent singing, so that they could butcher them in their meadow filled with rotting corpses and bones.[3] And Apuleius at *Metamorphoses* 8.19ff. recounts how an enormous snake preys on some travellers when it disguises itself as a weak and weary old man with a walking-stick and makes a chilling psychological attack on them, arousing pity by weeping profusely and begging them to rescue a beloved grandson who has fallen into a pit nearby and, in danger of dying, is calling again and again to his dear grandfather. When one of the travellers goes off into the bushes to help, he is promptly killed and eaten by the snake.

For impact literature also shows monsters in action (especially unpleasant and sensational action). They can lurk in a sinister silence, or make a terrifying uproar (so Cerberus gives great barks from his multiple heads, protecting the realm of the dead, while the snakes on his necks hiss menacingly[4]). They can be underhand too. They may operate in darkness, like a monster mentioned by Statius[5] which glided into bedrooms by night, snatched new-born babies from the breast and gorged on them, clawing at

2. Impact

their hearts and innards with hooked talons and iron nails. So too Cerberus played a nasty game with souls who came to the gates at the entrance to the land of the dead, as Hesiod explains at *Theogony* 769ff.:

> on guard there is a terrifying and pitiless
> dog that has an evil trick. He fawns on those who $\qquad$ 770
> enter, wagging his tail and pricking up his ears, but he does
> not let them back out again. No, he keeps watch
> and devours whomever he catches going out of the gates.

Literary monsters also make sudden, unannounced attacks, and hurt, maim and kill their victims (often emotive victims like women and children). They also maltreat corpses (triggering deep-rooted and ancient fears of our bodies being eaten, dismembered and otherwise violated). In Valerius Flaccus' *Voyage of Argo* 4.177ff. the giant Amycus (who forces visitors to box with him) plays with those he has killed and puts together a macabre display of severed arms still wearing boxing-gloves, mouldering bones and skulls nailed to trees in a row as a grisly sort of border.

A plurality of monsters can also be deployed to good purpose. There is a genuinely nightmarish feel to *Aeneid* 3.675ff., where Virgil depicts a great mass of Cyclopes (one-eyed giants like Polyphemus) thronging the shore at the foot of Mount Etna, their heads towering into the sky and all their single eyes glaring at some heroes who are sailing away – a staggering sight, if you take a moment to picture it in your mind's eye. Aeschylus at *Prometheus Bound* 790ff. has the god Prometheus predict the dangers in store for the persecuted nymph Io as she journeys on from him. The accumulation of monsters (in remote and mysterious regions) becomes more and more unsettling and intimidating and brings out the great extent and extreme nature of Io's sufferings, as the list progresses from the weird Graeae (three women who were born old and shared a single tooth and eye between them) to the savage Gorgons (whose gaze turned men to stone), and then on to the fierce griffins (which had the body of a lion and the head and wings of an eagle) and the Arimaspians (humans with one eye in the centre of the forehead). Here is what Prometheus says to Io:

> After crossing the stretch of water that bounds the continents, $\qquad$ 790
> travel east (to where the sun rises in fire),
> passing over a waveless sea, until you reach
> the Gorgonian plain of Cisthene, where the
> daughters of Phorcys live – three swan-like and
> aged virgins, who possess one eye in common $\qquad$ 795
> and a single tooth, and who are never seen
> by the sun with his rays or the moon of the night.
> Near them are their three winged sisters –
> the snaky-haired, human-hating Gorgons,

25

the sight of whom means death for mortals.   800
Be on your guard against these, I warn you.
Now for another grim sight – listen to me.
Watch out for the griffins (those sharp-beaked, unbarking
hounds of Zeus) and the one-eyed Arimaspians,
the horde mounted on horses who dwell on the   805
banks of the gold-bearing river Pluton.

As the above passage has just demonstrated, setting can also be important. Many of these creatures lived in (familiar) Greece, Italy and Asia
Minor (modern Turkey). But most often their lairs were in aptly wild,
lonely and dangerous areas of those countries. They might live in woods (a
gloomy enfolding kind of place suitable for lurking and sudden sorties); on
mountains (massive, dwarfing, hard, beyond the reach of civilization); in
a (sinister, treacherous and repulsive) marsh; on islands (which are set
apart); and especially in caves (which are dark and frightening, and are
often entrances to Hell). There is a typical combination of island, mountain
and cave for the home of some serpents in Quintus Smyrnaeus *Posthomerica* 12.449ff.:

Under a rugged crag there was a cave, murky
and inaccessible to mortals. Inside it lived   450
terrifying monsters of accursed Typhos' stock,
in a mountain-cleft on the island which people
call Calydne, out at sea, opposite Troy.

Still more atmospheric and gripping are remote areas that are beyond
our ken (and so are alien, savage and enigmatic). A snake guarded the
Golden Fleece in the land of Colchis in the distant east, while the triple-
bodied Geryon lived on an island far off in the west. Odysseus' adventures
with Polyphemus, the Sirens and so on took place in a never-never land
of unknown location. Another common setting is the ultimately mysterious Underworld, the ugly realm of death, decay and darkness beneath
our own world where the souls of the departed end up when their lives
are over.

What we have been looking at so far is essentially subject matter –
details whose simple inclusion of itself has impact. It is now time to
examine how those details are put across by authors and how their
inherent force is increased for the reader. Various methods are employed
in this connection.

First impressions are important, and when and how a monster is
introduced is often significant. An early and unheralded arrival can be
arresting, but it can also be effective to hold back the beast and build
gradually to its appearance. We can see both types of approach in the case
of Amycus, when he was encountered by some famous Greek heroes (Jason
and the Argonauts) on their quest for the Golden Fleece.

2. Impact

At the end of the first book of his epic poem *The Voyage of Argo*, Apollonius of Rhodes told how the Argonauts sailed up to the land of Bebrycia at sunrise. He begins his second book like this:

> Here were the cattle-stalls and farm of Amycus,
> the arrogant king of the Bebrycians. The son
> of the Bithynian nymph Melie and Poseidon Genethlius,
> he was the most insolent and massive of men.
> He had actually laid down the disgraceful law that   5
> no visitor should leave before testing his skill at
> boxing, and in this way he had killed many of his neighbours.
> Then too he went to the ship, disdained to ask what
> the purpose of their journey was and who they were,
> and had the effrontery to say to them all without preamble: 10
> 'Listen, you sailors. There's something you should know.
> It is the law here that no stranger who comes
> to Bebrycia can go off on his way
> until he has put up his fists against mine.
> So choose the best man out of the crew   15
> to box with me here and now. Believe me,
> if you ignore my law and trample on it, you'll be
> sorry, and you'll be made to obey it by force.'

Amycus is mentioned in the very first line of the book, intruding and bulking large from the start (aptly so for a protagonist). After learning his name in 1, we are given a sudden flurry of information at 2-4, ominous information about his insolence and power that arouses expectations of trouble. That is rapidly succeeded at 5-7 by concrete details to reinforce and sharpen the picture of his evil nature. Then at 8ff. he is brought on stage (we hear of his insolence for a third time here, which makes for real stress) and he speaks, coming alive for us more in this way and (in corroboration) actually showing his arrogance, uncivilized inhospitality, bullying menace, etc. So within eighteen lines this important character dominates the narrative, is clearly sketched and gets the action under way with his challenge to the Argonauts. This makes for drama and anticipation (of a tough boxing match, which duly ensues, and is in fact won by the Argonaut who faces Amycus).

Centuries later a Latin poet, Valerius Flaccus, in his *Voyage of Argo*, took a rather different tack. He relates the Argonauts' encounter with the monster in his fourth book at lines 99ff., but this time Amycus' actual entrance is held back for 100 lines, so that there is a distinct build-up to it and even more anticipation, as our appetite to see him is constantly whetted. Before his arrival on the scene Valerius Flaccus describes him, in more lurid terms than Apollonius, as a truly terrifying and monstrous enemy (a sadist who preys on much inferior boxing opponents and hurls other strangers into the sea from a cliff), and gives him formidable helpers as well (his subjects, who hunt down victims for their king). Valerius also introduces a young man who is in mourning for a friend killed by the giant. In his terror he is desperate for the Argonauts to escape while they can. He tells them about Amycus' slaughter of visitors in general, and in a very emotional account he depicts the killing of his friend in particular: Amycus didn't even wait until the man was ready to box but pounced on him with brutal suddenness and with one punch shattered his forehead and knocked out his eyes. He then takes them to Amycus' cave with its horrific display of the remains of his prey. Because of all this we really want to meet this monster in the text, and we really want to see him beaten and punished. In this way his eventual appearance at line 199 is given great impact.

Narrative pace is also relevant. By that term I mean the relative speed with which action is put across. The pace is slow if nothing actually happens or the author takes a lot of time to recount the little that does happen. This can produce a quiet, muted effect and (when we are given lots of detail) a clear picture of the events. The pace is fast if there is a lot or quite a lot of action and if the action is conveyed in just a few words or lines. The result of that is energy and excitement.

A good example of the importance of all this in connection with monsters is provided by *Odyssey* 10.80ff., where Homer tells how Odysseus and his fleet (on their way back to Greece after the fall of Troy) arrive at the land of the huge and savage cannibals known as the Laestrygonians. Initially in this episode the narrative pace is slow. When we reach Laestrygonia, Homer pauses: he stops the action, spends several lines telling us about the strange local phenomenon whereby there is in effect no night, and then takes up a few more lines describing the harbour (ringed by cliffs). This is all very expansive. After that Homer resumes with action, but for quite a while there is not much action: Odysseus' other ships are tied up in the harbour (whereas he shrewdly moors his own ship outside it at the end of a promontory); he surveys the country from the top of a headland; he then sends three men inland to reconnoitre; they meet a girl drawing water, and she directs them to her father's house. There is no sense of urgency or danger here, and the reader is lulled by this relaxed pace. But this is merely the calm before the storm. Suddenly things start happening, horrible things, and they happen in quick succession within a few lines of text: the men enter the house and encounter the appalling queen of the land; she calls her murderous husband, who grabs one man for his supper; the other two Greeks flee in terror to the ships. The contrast with the former leisurely pace increases the drama here. Then the other Laestrygonians follow and kill all the men in the harbour. But, whereas I have just said that in a few words, Homer takes a lot longer and slows things down again, with another efficacious contrast in pace. Here is Odysseus' account of what happened at 10.119ff.:

2. Impact

> The mighty Laestrygonians came rushing up from different
> directions, thousands of them, not like men, like Giants.   120
> They hurled from the cliffs great boulders too big for a man to
> lift, and an appalling noise started up among the ships, the
> combined din of men being killed and ships being smashed.
> They speared the men like fish and carried them off for a
> repulsive meal. While they slaughtered them in the deep   125
> harbour, I drew my sharp sword from the scabbard at my
> hip and cut the cables of my dark-prowed ship.

Homer here dwells on the slaughter, showing us the masses of enormous Laestrygonians all around up above and the dwarfing rocks that rain down on the Greeks, letting us hear the men groaning and the timbers splintering, and letting us see the Laestrygonians harpooning the men like fish (gasping, wriggling, helpless, etc.) and carrying them off to devour. This is the climax of the whole episode and the poet wants to do it justice, so he slows down to bring out the drama and the horror. In this way we see in some detail and quite vividly the creatures' deeds and their devastating consequences. So thanks to the narrative pace the actions of the monsters here really come home to us.

Description of monsters and their habitats also deserves quite close consideration. The selection of details in this connection and the manner in which they are presented affect our reaction substantially. A vivid, lively and pointed sketch comes across much more strongly than a flat and colourless listing of features, and it can achieve various effects.

With such descriptions writers aim most often at evoking shock, horror and revulsion, but sometimes they have other ends in mind. They may go for an intriguing mysteriousness, as Homer does with the Sirens (see p. 45). There may be frivolous teasing. So Ovid in the eighth book of his epic *Metamorphoses* by means of his depiction of the Calydonian boar and the fighters who gather to hunt it creates anticipation of a massive struggle with that beast, only for that to be followed by a ludicrous comedy of errors when the combat with the boar actually gets under way (see pp. 84ff.).[6] Then again Ovid in the first book of the *Metamorphoses* tells how Jupiter, the king of the gods, raped the nymph Io and, when his wife grew suspicious, changed Io into a beautiful heifer. His wife, still suspicious, asked for this heifer as a present and, to ensure that her husband could not get up to anything with it, set a guard over the animal/nymph. The guard was the monstrous Argus, who is described as follows at 1.625ff.:

> All around Argus' head were a hundred eyes,   625
> which rested and went to sleep in turn, two at a time,
> while the others stayed on guard, keeping a lookout.
> Whatever position he took up, he was looking at Io;
> even when turned away, he had Io before his eyes.

Ovid is trying to entertain his readers with this bizarre, imaginative (626) and amusing (629) picture. He is also trying to involve them by setting a puzzle – how could you beat such a guard? He deliberately withholds the solution for many lines, and when it comes it is darkly comic. At Jupiter's request the god Mercury approaches Argus disguised as a goatherd, plays on his pipes to him to put some of his eyes to sleep, tells him a boring story (about a rape!) to put the rest of the eyes to sleep, and then promptly chops Argus' head off.

You should also be alert to the fact that there are different types of description and different methods are used to describe persons and things. There is not space in this book to cover all the modes, but the next few paragraphs will highlight several of the most common approaches and techniques.

In book five of his *Astronomica* the Latin poet Manilius tells how the Greek hero Perseus rescued the princess Andromeda, who was chained to a cliff to be devoured by a sea-monster. On his way home after securing the head of Medusa, he catches sight of the exposed Andromeda, immediately falls in love with her and decides to save her. He goes to her parents and promises to save her in return for her hand in marriage. Then he returns to the princess on the shore, as the monster makes its appearance:

> He returned to the shore. By now a heavy surge had begun
> to rise, and in a long line wave after wave was fleeing from   580
> the thrust of the mass of the monster. As it cleaved the ocean,
> its head emerged, spewing spume; it bore along in its jaws
> swirling water, and the sea seethed loudly about its teeth.
> Behind it rose its massive coils in an immense chain, and its
> back covered the deep. The waves everywhere were in uproar,   585
> even the cliffs and crags were terrified as it rushed up.
> Poor girl, although you had such a splendid defender,
> there was then absolute horror on your face, you panted in
> quick gasps and went pale all over, as from the hollow
> in the rocks you saw with your own eyes your doom –   590
> the avenging sea-beast swimming towards its tiny prey
> and driving ocean before it.

Expectation is aroused, and excitement and terror are created as Manilius switches to Perseus' adversary and includes some remarkable and sensational elements. He utilizes an economical form of description – not the full and detailed portrayal, but the sketch that leaves the reader to fill out the picture and stimulates the imagination with a few bold strokes (here highlighting the creature's vastness, monstrousness and menace). Manilius gives the beast prominence by making it (here, as later) by far the loudest character and by employing hyperbole (the exaggeration in 586), which brings out the notion of a truly awesome, epic opponent for Perseus. The poet also puts us in the (dangerous) position of the hero and

30

heroine, helping us identify with them and share their experience, as is clear from the order in which items are perceived. So in 579-80 from their vantage point we see first the sudden and unsettling swell of the sea, far out – hence the long column of waves. Next, with 'the mass of the monster' (581), we are aware of the vague general bulk of the beast. Then we make out more specific details. First we realize that it is in motion ('cleaved' in 581) and glimpse its head among the waves (582). Later in 582 we discern the water spewed out, and in 583 the sound reaches us, and we pick out the water swirling in its open mouth, and also the teeth. Then beyond the awful head (which would naturally take the attention first) we observe the huge coils rising up, and they prove to be so immense that they cover the whole sea. At 585-6 the noise abruptly becomes deafening and we realize that the thing is now moving towards the shore rapidly ('rushed up' is left to the end for climax). After that comes the cinematic 'reaction shot' at 587ff. (whereby Andromeda's horror is meant to evoke the same feeling in us) and in 591 the pointed contrast between huge predator and tiny prey to stress the princess's vulnerability and the sea-beast's might.

Some other standard ploys are well illustrated in a description of setting. Earlier in this chapter I mentioned the giant Amycus, who forced strangers to box with him and killed them all, until Jason and the Argonauts arrived. This son of Poseidon/Neptune (the god of the sea) had a cave on the coast where he had set up a gruesome display of the remnants of his victims and his own victorious boxing gloves. Here is Valerius Flaccus' depiction of that (4.177ff.):

> On the tip of the coast was seen an enormous cave,
> covered by trees above and an overhanging ridge,
> a terrifying abode which didn't let in the divine gift of the
> sky's light, and which vibrated with the roaring sea.   180
> On the crag's edge were various horrors – severed arms of men
> who'd been whirled away, dead arms still wearing the gloves,
> disgusting, decaying bones, and among the pine trees an
> appalling line of heads, unidentifiable and featureless
> due to blows to the face; and in the midst were Amycus' gloves,   185
> reverently consecrated and placed on his great father's altar.

This time, instead of giving us a sketch with a few bold touches, the author does much of the work for his readers by providing a lengthy and full description with lots of concrete detail (including small touches which enhance the clarity). There is a concentration of lurid material in the above passage, and in particular there is cumulative impact (as grisly item after item is added) in the long sentence at 181ff. (where there is forceful repetition of the elements of damage and death). The unearthly vibration of the cave in 180 and the surreal touch of the gloves still on the arms in 182 are individualizing and telling details. Vividness is often achieved by means of an appeal to many or all of the senses, and here with a little

The Dragon Devouring Cadmus' Companions by Hendrick Goltzius
(1558-1617). Kolding, Koldinghus.

imagination you can see, hear, feel and smell things. Sometimes setting for monsters is misleadingly inappropriate (they can be found in beautiful countryside, for example), but in this case it is apt, doubly so – for the maiming and killing that Amycus has done so far and will shortly suffer himself in the boxing bout this time.

If you bear in mind the remarks in this chapter when you encounter monsters in your reading, your appreciation will be more informed and you will get much more out of them. Appended below is a passage for you to practise on, looking for the techniques mentioned above and seeing how they increase the impact of the creature. In book 3 of his *Metamorphoses* Ovid tells how Cadmus and some other men from the city of Tyre went into exile (after failing to carry out their king's orders) and were shown a place to found a new city. When Cadmus sent the others off to get water for use in a ritual, they unwittingly violated a sacred grove and disturbed an enormous snake of Mars (god of war). Cadmus, by the way, eventually killed the beast after a terrific fight.

> Before sacrificing to Jupiter, he asked his attendants to go
> and look for fresh water from a spring for libation.

2. Impact

There was an ancient wood, never defiled by an axe, and
in its midst was a cave, overgrown with branches and twigs;
its rocks came together to form a low arch, and an abundant   30
stream gushed from it. Concealed in the cavern was
a serpent of Mars, with a remarkable golden crest;
its eyes flashed fire, its whole body was swollen with venom,
it had a flickering three-forked tongue and three rows of fangs.
When the Tyrian refugees reached this grove on their ill-fated   35
quest and made a noise by dipping their pitchers into
the water, the dark snake thrust its head out
of the deep cave and emitted horrific hisses.
The pitchers slipped from their stunned fingers, they went pale
all over and their bodies suddenly started to shake.   40
It twisted its scaly coils in writhing knots and abruptly
reared up, curving itself into an enormous arc. With more than
half its length raised into the thin air, it looked down on the
whole grove (its full extent, if you could see it, was as long as
the Serpent constellation between the two Bears in the sky).   45
Immediately it seized and killed the men (as they made ready
to fight or flee, or were too frightened to do either),
biting some, crushing others in a long embrace
and breathing the deadly taint of its venom on the rest.

3

Laocoon and the Sea-Snakes

This chapter examines the impact of monsters within a broader context, concentrating on a pair of them that act together in concert and have a momentous impact on human affairs. They appear in book 2 of a famous epic poem (the *Aeneid*) by Virgil, one of Rome's major poets (died 19 BC). We will examine not only the actual passage in which the monsters figure but also the role of this incident in the book as a whole (Virgilian epic works on a large scale, and the poet went in for complex and long-range links and effects).[1]

The *Aeneid* is concerned with the myth of the Trojan War. When the Trojan prince Paris seduced and carried off the Greek queen Helen, a huge army of Greek warriors went and besieged the city of Troy (in modern Turkey) in an attempt to get her back. For ten long years they battled against the Trojans and their allies, but could not break them down, and they only managed to capture the city in the tenth year thanks to a cunning ruse. In book 2 of the *Aeneid* one of the Trojan survivors, the great hero Aeneas, tells the story of the fall of Troy, of how the trusting Trojans, largely abandoned by the gods, were tricked by Greek treachery, saw their fine city captured and destroyed and were butchered in large numbers. This is one of the high points of the poem, a narrative filled with drama, excitement, pathos and horror, a tale of doom and disaster, a tragic and dark book.

Aeneas tells how the Greeks sailed off one day, apparently back to Greece, but actually just to hide on the nearby island of Tenedos, leaving behind a huge wooden horse with warriors hidden inside it. The deluded Trojans came out of their city, joyfully viewed the deserted Greek camp and gazed in amazement at the great horse. They were debating whether to destroy it or take it into their city, when the priest Laocoon rushed down from the citadel, shouting that it was a Greek trick, and hurled his spear into its side. He had nearly won over the Trojans when the Greek Sinon appeared, pretending to be a deserter. A fine actor and a very plausible liar, he maintained that the horse was a religious offering to the goddess Minerva; if the Trojans harmed it, destruction would fall on them, but if they took it inside their city, they would conquer Greece. They were already inclined to believe him when something horrific happened to strengthen that inclination – two monstrous snakes suddenly swam up across the sea and killed Laocoon and his two sons, before disappearing under the statue of Minerva on the Trojan citadel. Men concluded that this was punishment for sacrilege on Laocoon's part (hurling his spear into the side of the horse) and shouted for the horse to be dragged inside the city. They dismantled part of their walls so that the huge wooden structure could be taken in and joyfully installed it on their citadel.

That night, while the Trojans slept, the Greek fleet sailed back and Sinon set free the warriors hidden in the horse, who killed the guards and welcomed their comrades at the now open gates of the city. The slaughter began. Aeneas fought bravely and in the course of the fighting got on to the roof of the palace of Troy's king Priam, where he helped send a tower crashing down on the Greek besiegers. But more Greeks came on and he could only watch in helpless horror as they streamed into the palace in large numbers and massacred the inhabitants. Pyrrhus cruelly killed one of Priam's sons right in front of him, and then murdered the old king himself in a pool of his son's blood at an altar.

After Priam's death Aeneas caught sight of Helen and wanted to kill her, but his mother, the goddess Venus, appeared, reminded him of his family back home, offered to guide him there safely and removed the mist from his eyes, so that he could see that the gods, not Helen, were responsible for the fall of Troy (and an extraordinary vision it was – of awesome divinities smashing down the city walls and summoning more Greeks from the ships). Aeneas went home and managed to persuade his old father to leave Troy only when he received some divine signs – a harmless tongue of flame licking the hair of Aeneas' young son, and a shooting star. As the conflagration engulfing Troy bore down on his house, Aeneas escaped in the dark with his family, carrying his old father on his back and leading his son by the hand through the menacing shadows, only to discover when safely outside the city that his wife had disappeared in the confusion of their sudden flight from suspected attackers. He plunged back into the captured town to find her, actually calling her name aloud, until an apparition of her came to him and told him to stop grieving uselessly; she was kept at Troy by the Mother of the Gods, and he had to sail off to a new land without her. When Aeneas rejoined his father and son, it was to find that many more Trojans had survived and flocked to them. Finally the morning star rose, ushering in daylight after all the darkness and amounting to a symbolic glimmer of hope. (And after several years Aeneas reached Italy, where he established his people and built a settlement there that eventually led to the glorious city of Rome.)

Book 2 of the *Aeneid* breaks down into three sections (summarized in the three paragraphs above), each of which ends darkly and aptly with loss – the deception of the Trojans and killing of Laocoon and his sons, resulting in the horse being taken into Troy; the fighting in Troy that culminates in the murder of king Priam; and Aeneas' escape and the disappearance of his wife. The whole Laocoon-Sinon episode is framed by the inappropriate joy of the Trojans (when they first come out of the city, thinking the Greeks have gone, and later when they pull the horse inside their walls). And Laocoon's appearance begins and ends with the citadel of Troy, from which the priest rushes down at the start, and on which the snakes conceal themselves at the end (the citadel where the Trojans' enemy Minerva has her shrine, and where the wooden horse will shortly be situated). Such massive structural architecture is typical of the *Aeneid*.

Laocoon and the snakes are major players in section one. Virgil seems to have been the first to make him a central character in the fall of Troy and the first to have him fling his spear into the horse, where it judders and makes the structure groan (an effective way of concentrating attention on this all-important artefact). When he initially appears his intervention is sudden and dramatic, and all his rushing and shouting intimates that something important is going on. In contrast to the other Trojans wondering what to do with the horse, he is decisive and vigorous, and he launches into a brisk, urgent and powerful speech which comes tantalizingly close to alerting them to the reality of the trick being played by Ulysses and the rest of the Greeks.

> Then, at the head of a great crowd of people, 40
> Laocoon came blazing down from the top of the citadel,
> shouting from far off: 'You poor fools, are you mad? Do you
> really believe the enemy's sailed away? Do you think there's no
> trickery in a Greek gift? Don't you know Ulysses better?
> Either this wood has Greeks concealed inside or it's 45
> some siege-equipment designed for use against our walls,
> to spy on our homes and attack the city from above, or there's
> some other hidden deception. Trojans, don't trust the horse!
> Whatever it is, I fear Greeks even when they offer gifts.'
> So saying, with his great strength he hurled a huge spear 50
> into its side, into the curved timber of the beast's
> belly. The weapon stuck there, quivering; the interior gave a
> loud groan, as the enveloping womb reverberated.
> If divine destiny and our own wits had not been against us,
> he'd have driven us to hack open the Greeks' lair, there'd still 55
> be a Troy and you, lofty citadel of Priam, would still survive.

The narrator (Aeneas) is clearly sympathetic to Laocoon, which encourages similar sympathy in us. In addition, the priest really comes alive as a character here: he is a strong, vigorous and passionate man of action, impatient, energetic and blunt, one who promptly backs up his words with deeds (50ff.), confidently and courageously (we will also note below the love for his sons that makes him face even the monstrous serpents attacking them). All of this means that his coming death should be really felt by us.

This richly layered narrative contains some symbolism too. Laocoon blazing down from the citadel in line 41 is an early instance of the frequent fire imagery in book 2, and here Trojan fire (unlike the fire that the Greeks will employ) achieves nothing. Similarly his subsequent speech and spear-cast suggest the ineffectiveness now of Trojan vigour and strength and the futility of resistance, while the hurled spear quivering harmlessly in the wood is a visual representation of Laocoon's vehement speech doing no harm to the Greek stratagem.

The passage also has impact on a broader front. In it there is an early heightening of the drama and the emotional level, prior to the still more dramatic and emotional aftermath. The flinging of the weapon in line 50 is the first instance of violence in this generally violent and weapon-strewn book. So too the groan of the horse in 53 looks forward to groans by Greek warriors and Trojan women (in 413, 486 and 679). And in line 54 there is an early mention of the gods' malevolence and abandonment of Troy (developed at much greater length at 602ff.).

After these 17 lines Laocoon abruptly drops out of the text, as Sinon is suddenly introduced and tells his lying tale, dominating lines 57-198. The brevity of the priest's first appearance (especially beside the much longer passage devoted to Sinon) and his dismissal from the poem for over 140 verses, subtly convey a picture of Laocoon being displaced and upstaged and his viewpoint very largely forgotten. And if Sinon's intervention started to undermine Laocoon's position, a second intervention under-mined it completely and made the Trojans accept the Greek's claim at 189ff. that the horse if harmed would bring destruction and if taken into Troy would bring success. At 199 Virgil unexpectedly returns to Laocoon and depicts the slaughter of the priest and his sons in lines of great power and pathos (appealing to all five senses, filled with sensational and grue-some touches, sketching the monsters with a few bold strokes, so that we are left to fill in the rest, and putting us in the position of the Trojans, so that we make out more and more detail as the serpents bear down on us). Virgil only now mentions Laocoon's priestly status, to highlight the horror of his death. He also has Laocoon offer sacrifice – we are not told why, but most obviously someone so suspicious of the horse would be praying for divine help to foil the Greeks. If this was the case, a brutal response from heaven immediately ensued.

> Now we poor, blind Trojans were exposed to something much
> more momentous and frightening, something deeply disturbing.   200
> Laocoon, who had been chosen by lot as a priest of Neptune,
> was sacrificing a large bull at the ceremonial altar.
> Suddenly from Tenedos across the calm sea (I shudder as I
> tell you this), arching their immense coils, twin snakes
> breast the deep and make for the shore side by side.   205
> Erect among the waves, their fore-parts and bloody crests
> tower over the water; the rest of them skims the ocean
> behind, their immense backs undulating sinuously,
> making the sea foam noisily. And now they're on land,
> their blazing eyes shot with fire and blood,   210

Laocoon and his sons struggle with the sea-snakes. Early imperial Roman statue, thought to be a copy of an earlier work. Vatican Museums, Rome.

their hissing mouths licked by flickering tongues.
We pale at the sight and scatter. They go unerringly
for Laocoon. First the pair of serpents embrace
and entwine his two sons' little bodies,
biting and devouring the poor boys limb by limb.   215
Then they seize Laocoon himself (as he comes to help, weapon
in hand), binding him with their enormous coils. They
embrace his waist twice, wrap themselves around his neck
twice, and then their scaly heads and throats tower over him.
His priestly headbands are drenched with gore and black   220
venom; while his hands strain to tear away the knots,
he sends up into the sky appalling shrieks,
like the bellows of a wounded bull running from

3. Laocoon and the Sea-Snakes

the altar and shaking from its neck a badly aimed axe.
Afterwards the two snakes glide away to savage   225
Minerva's shrine high up on the citadel, and there under
her statue's feet and round shield they conceal themselves.

The intriguing puzzle of who or what is behind this attack by the snakes is finally solved at 226f., where the fact that they move off to Minerva's shrine and statue and go into hiding there shows that she sent them. This assault reinforces Sinon's speech, because the Trojans after his claim at 189ff. misinterpret the deaths as punishment for the sin of casting the spear at the horse (whereas in fact they are punishment for the sin of interfering with heaven's plan for the destruction of Troy and a very effective way of ensuring that the plan goes ahead unhindered). There is something particularly unsettling here, in the careful ordering of events, which shows how calculating the goddess is, manipulating the Trojans and craftily encompassing their ruin. She could have sent the monsters at once to kill the priest (and his innocent children) as soon as he speared the horse. Instead she waited until Sinon turned up and explained the horse as an offering to her, so that Laocoon's act appeared to be sacrilegious, and then employed the serpents to provide immediate corroboration of Sinon's words in an arresting and terrifying way (if Sinon had turned up with his explanation after the attack, it would not have had the same impact and it might well have looked as if he had made it all up to suit the incident).

It is also quite possible that another powerful divinity is ranged against the Trojans here and is acting in concert with Minerva. Neptune, the god of the sea, may well be involved too. Neptune is brought into the narrative and connected with Laocoon at 201, and then the snakes come through the sea (his element); and Neptune is one of the gods later seen by Aeneas collaborating with Minerva in the destruction of Troy (at 608ff. Venus says to him: 'Over there, where you see masses of stone scattered about, rocks wrenched from rocks and eddying smoke mixed with dust, Neptune with his mighty trident is shaking and dislodging the walls and foundations, is tearing up the entire city from where it stands. Over there Juno, cruellest of them all, is in the forefront, holding the Scaean Gates, armed with a sword and furiously calling for support from the ships. Minerva (look round!) sits on the citadel's summit, glittering in a stormcloud, the grim Gorgon's head on her breastplate. Jupiter himself gives the Greeks courage and the strength to win, he himself rouses the gods against the warriors of Troy.').

When one bears all this in mind, as well as seeing menace and tragic inevitability in connection with the actual death of Laocoon and his sons, one also experiences wider foreboding and comes away with a sense of remorseless doom for all of Troy, as this opponent of heaven's plans is mercilessly crushed. So too in the lines that follow, as the horse is pulled into Troy, it halts at the gate four times, making the weapons of the warriors inside clash loudly, but the Trojans are impervious to all this, and

39

a prophetess foretells the coming doom of Troy but is disbelieved by the citizens, who actually thank the gods. And in the passage quoted above the unease is reinforced by the simile of the bull at 223f.: in addition to bringing out the dark irony of the priest sacrificing to heaven when he is about to become a victim himself and be killed by heaven, it shows human plans going awry and a sacrifice turning out unfavourably (bellowing and flight by the sacrificial animal was a bad omen), so that things look grim for the people of Troy.

Also ominous is the symbolic significance of this incident, which escaped the Trojans at the time but which we can see with hindsight. The snakes concealing themselves at Minerva's shrine provide a clear link for us with the Greeks concealed at Tenedos and in the wooden horse (an artefact inspired by Minerva, as we are informed in line 15). But there is much else here that foreshadows the coming attack by the Greeks and the fall of the city. For example, the serpents come suddenly across the calm sea from Tenedos and land at Troy, exactly as the Greeks will. Their huge size and their immense backs undulating behind them conjure up a vast fleet with ships sailing behind each other in a long line. The fire and blood connected with the monsters look forward to all the fire and blood involved in the fall of Troy. The Trojans in 212 pale and scatter at the approach of the snakes, and in the same way there will be general panic and flight and little resistance when the enemy appear later. The creatures also attack and kill, as the Greeks will, and Laocoon's resistance proves futile, as will that of the few Trojans who stand up to the invaders. There is more precise anticipation too: for instance, Laocoon trying to protect his boys is echoed by Aeneas protecting his boy as he flees from the city, and the priest being killed near an altar beside his two boys is picked up by the murder of Priam at an altar next to his son. There are more parallels, and the fact that there are so many of them and they are so close is eerie and unsettling.

Links of this kind also play a significant and quite complex structural role in the overall architecture of book 2 of the *Aeneid*. The second group of lines on Laocoon takes up the important motif of violence from the first passage and develops it greatly, and like the first passage the later lines also raise the drama and heighten the emotional level, but do so to a much greater extent, as part of a build-up to the gripping and moving fall of Troy. The Laocoon episode also first highlights the book's major themes of treachery, deception and human blindness (in connection with the horse, Sinon, the snakes and the interpretation of Laocoon's sin).[2] Divine intervention, another important element in book 2, is also given early prominence by means of this incident: the heavenly hostility and destructiveness here is much expanded in the vision later granted to Aeneas of deities lending a hand in the downfall of Troy; and then on the brighter side comes Venus' help for Aeneas and the divine signs that persuade his father to leave (gods do bring about the end of Troy, but also ensure the survival of some Trojans, resulting eventually in the rise of Rome).

3. Laocoon and the Sea-Snakes

There is also the related imagery of the flame and the serpent which runs all through the second book. In connection with Laocoon we have seen the priest blazing down (*ardens*) from the citadel in 41 and the snakes at 203ff., with their blazing eyes shot with fire (210). Subsequently in 240 the wooden horse glides into the city (like the gliding serpents of 225), and in 253 sleep embraces the unsuspecting people of Troy on the fateful night (like the monsters' embrace in 213 and 218). As the Greek fleet returns, one of the ships raises a beacon light for Sinon (256), and as Troy goes up in flames two Greeks are compared to serpents (at 379ff. and 471ff.), while Priam's killer is said to be blazing (*ardens*) in 529. But as well as providing a linking thread this imagery also undergoes dynamic development. At 682ff. Aeneas' father is persuaded to leave Troy by the heaven-sent signs of the fiery shooting star and the flame licking (like the snakes of 211) the hair of Aeneas' son. So we see this imagery now in the transition from darkest despair representing the bright hope of Troy's rebirth rather than her destruction and the violence of the Greeks.[3]

Comparison of another account of this event in a later Greek poet, Quintus of Smyrna, will sharpen the focus further for Virgil's version.[4] Look for differences in details, emphasis and mood, and consider aspects such as impact, economy, restraint and taste (is either version at all guilty of being overlong, overdone or overly sensational?). In book 12 of Quintus' *Posthomerica* Sinon makes a speech about the horse being an offering to Athena (Minerva) and after that Laocoon urges the Trojans to set fire to it at once, to see if it contains anything. Then:

They would have obeyed him and escaped destruction	395
if Athena (who was angry with him and the	
Trojans and their city) had not made the vast	
earth quake beneath the feet of Laocoon.	
That daring man was immediately seized by fear and	
trembling, his strength was shattered and black night was	400
poured over his head. Appalling pain fell on his eyelids,	
making his eyes swim under the shaggy brows.	
The pupils were convulsed by stabs of agony to	
their very roots, and the ache in his eyes made	
them roll. The excruciating twinges even penetrated	405
as far as the membranes and base of his brain.	
At one point his eyes were very bloodshot, at another	
point they were firmly fixed in a glare.	
Often there was a discharge from them, like the water	
clogged with snow that trickles from a rugged mountain-crag.	410
He was like a madman, he saw everything double and	
gave the most awful groans, but still urged the Trojans,	
ignoring his anguish, so the goddess deprived him of his	
precious eyesight.	

The Trojans felt pity for Laocoon, but also feared Athena, so they led the blind man into Troy, and also dragged the wooden horse inside. Still Laocoon urged them to burn it, and although they would not listen to him, Athena punished him for that:

> The great-hearted goddess Athena brought about something
> even more horrendous, something directed at his poor sons.
> Beneath a rugged crag there was a dark
> cavern, inaccessible to mortals, the lair   450
> of dread monsters, descendants of deadly
> Typhon. It was in a ravine, on the island
> called Calydna in the sea before Troy.
> She summoned mighty serpents from that cave and sent
> them to Troy. At her command they sped off, making the   455
> whole island quake. As they came on, the sea roared
> and its waves parted. They swept along with fearsome
> flickering tongues; the creatures of the deep shuddered,
> the river-nymphs (daughters of Xanthus and Simois)
> wailed aloud and on Mount Olympus Aphrodite was filled   460
> with sorrow. They swiftly reached the spot where Athena
> wanted them, whetting their murderous fangs with ferocious
> jaws for use on the poor boys. The Trojans panicked and fled
> when they saw those awful monsters inside their city.
> None of the warriors dared stand their ground, not even those   465
> who'd been fearless before. They felt pity but were all quite
> terrified and tried to escape the beasts. The women screamed,
> and some forgot their own children as they tried to escape an
> appalling death themselves. Troy groaned as her people
> ran away. As they rushed together into the same places,   470
> many had skin torn from their bodies. They jammed streets,
> cowering everywhere. Laocoon was left all on his own,
> with his sons: deadly Doom and the goddess chained them
> to the spot. The boys were afraid to die and stretched out
> their hands to their beloved father, but the serpents seized   475
> them both in their deadly jaws, and he was not able to
> defend them. All around the Trojans were in tears,
> watching from afar, stunned. The two snakes eagerly
> carried out Athena's command (so hostile to Troy)
> and disappeared underground. A marker is still   480
> visible where they went into Apollo's shrine
> on the sacred citadel. In front of it the men of Troy
> gathered and built a cenotaph for Laocoon's sons who had
> been so cruelly killed. Their father shed tears on it
> from his blind eyes. The mother kept on wailing   485
> and shrieking around the cenotaph, groaning at the
> catastrophe caused by her husband's folly, fearing the wrath
> of the gods and expecting something even worse to happen.
> As a nightingale in a shadowy valley circles her
> empty nest wailing, in deep distress because a grim   490

3. Laocoon and the Sea-Snakes

snake with powerful jaws has destroyed her
young fledglings before they had learnt to sing aloud,
and she in an agony of absolute anguish cries
and screams on and on around her empty home,
so the mother groaned over her sons' dismal fate   495
and screamed around their empty tomb. There was also
for her the terrible disaster of her husband's blinding.
She howled for her dear, dead children
and her husband deprived of the light of the sun.

4

Sirens

The monsters known as Sirens are ultimately an enigma (like much in Classical mythology), and a fascinating enigma at that. Their exact origins, nature and import are still debated, and especially because they were not clearly and fully defined in ancient literature they readily lent themselves to adaptation by later authors. This chapter will look at the main literary evidence concerning Sirens in Classical times and then touch on various high (and low) points in their subsequent development down to our own day, tracking them down through about three thousand years of poetry and prose.

In Homer's Odyssey

The earliest surviving references to them are to be found in Homer's epic poem, the *Odyssey* (eighth century BC). The Greek hero Odysseus, on his way home after fighting at Troy in the Trojan War, is warned by the divine sorceress Circe of some of the terrible dangers ahead on his voyage. At 12.39ff. she tells him:

> First you will come to the Sirens, who
> enchant every single man who comes to them.   40
> If anyone draws near to them in ignorance and
> hears the Sirens' voices, there is no homecoming
> for him, no wife and little children beaming at his side.
> Instead he's enchanted by the clear, sweet song of the Sirens,
> who sit in a meadow, surrounded by a great heap of rotting   45
> men – skeletons with shreds of shrivelling skin on them.
> But you must row past them, and to prevent your crew
> from hearing them, soften some honey-sweet wax and
> plug their ears. If you want to listen yourself,
> get the others to lash you upright to your swift   50
> ship's mast, binding you hand and foot, so you can
> listen to the two Sirens' voices to your heart's content;
> but if you beg and order your men to release you,
> then they must tie you up tighter with even more rope.

Odysseus sails off and duly tells his men what Circe has said. As they approach the isle of the Sirens, the gentle breeze that is bearing their ship along suddenly stops blowing and there is a calm, as some divine power lulled the waves. The crew begin to row, Odysseus plugs their ears with

44

wax and then is himself bound to the mast. We are told by Odysseus that, when they were offshore as far as a man's shout can carry, this is what happened (12.182ff.):

> ... They noticed the approach of the
> swift-speeding ship and broke into clear, sweet song:
> 'Come here, illustrious Odysseus, great glory of Greece,
> beach your ship, so you can listen to our voices.   185
> For nobody has ever sailed by on his black ship
> without listening to the honeyed words on our lips
> and then going on his way a happier and wiser man.
> We really do know everything that the Greeks and Trojans
> suffered on Troy's broad plain through the will of the gods,   190
> we know everything that happens on this fertile earth.'
> So they sang with their lovely voices. From the bottom of my
> heart I wanted to listen, and I ordered my crew to release me,
> nodding and frowning; but they put their backs into rowing,
> while Perimedes and Eurylochus got up at once and   195
> tied me up much tighter with even more rope.
> When they had rowed past the Sirens and we couldn't
> hear their songs or their voices any more,
> my faithful crew immediately removed the beeswax
> plugging their ears and untied the ropes that bound me.   200

The reader passes by the Sirens quite quickly, as Odysseus and his crew did, and just as the men were too far off for a close look, so we don't get a clear picture of the Sirens either. Although we cannot tell how much (if anything) Homer's original audience already knew about them, it seems very likely that Homer here tried to make them intriguingly (or bewitchingly) mysterious, as so many questions about them immediately suggest themselves – for example, who are they actually, what do they look like, where is their island, why do they beguile and kill men, exactly how do they kill them, and how do they know so much? These Sirens are figures to conjure with, figures endowed with all kinds of reverberations (suggesting the appeal and deadliness of the female, the sea, flattery and knowledge). They also represent a striking combination of the fabulous, the beautiful and the otherworldly with the macabre, the horrific and the sinister (evident in the eerie calm keeping the men within range, the heap of mouldering bones (and lack of burial was particularly appalling to ancient thought), the awareness somehow of Odysseus' identity and history, the insidious lie in line 188, the cunning appeal in their song to both the intellect and the senses, so well aimed at the curious, music-loving Odysseus). With a singular touch, Homer makes his Sirens at once attractive and repulsive.

Mythical Monsters in Classical Literature

In Apollonius of Rhodes' Voyage of Argo

Only snippets survive of what was written about the Sirens by authors
after Homer until Apollonius of Rhodes (third century BC). In his epic
Voyage of Argo (4.891ff.) he tells how Jason and his crew (the Argonauts)
on their way back to Greece after winning the Golden Fleece also had an
encounter with the Sirens, and how this time the monsters were foiled
thanks to one of the Argonauts, the poet and musician Orpheus, who deftly
employed his lyre (a stringed musical instrument). Typically Apollonius
has an eye to Homer's account, picking up details from it, but also reacting
against it.

A gentle wind carried the ship onward and they soon sighted
the lovely island of Anthemoessa, where the clear-voiced
Sirens, daughters of Achelous, enchanted with their sweet
songs and then destroyed whoever moored there.
Achelous fathered them on beautiful Terpsichore, one 895
of the Muses. In the past they had attended Demeter's
stately daughter, when she was still unmarried, and they
had sung for her in chorus, but now they were
partly like birds and partly like girls in appearance.
They kept a constant lookout from the viewpoint above 900
their fine harbour, and thanks to them many, many men
wasted away and died, deprived of a honey-sweet
homecoming. At once the Sirens started to direct their
lily-like voices at the Argonauts too, who were on the
point of mooring at the shore until Oeagrus' son, Orpheus from 905
Thrace, picked up and strung his Thracian lyre and gave
a lively, ringing rendition of a rippling melody,
sweeping the strings to fill their ears with the
sound. His lyre prevailed over the girlish voices,
and the west wind and splashing waves that came from astern 910
carried the ship away. The Sirens' song became indistinct.
But even so, before he could be stopped, one of the crew (Butes,
the noble son of Teleon) leapt into the sea from his polished
rowing-bench, his soul melted by the Sirens' clear voices.
He swam through the surging swell to get to the shore, the poor 915
fool. They would have robbed him of his return there and then,
but divine Aphrodite, queen of Eryx, took pity on him and
kindly intervened. She saved him by snatching him up from
the swirling sea and gave him a home on Lilybaeum's heights.
In deep distress the heroes left the Sirens behind ... 920

The similarities to Apollonius' predecessor are obvious; the dissimilarities
are more interesting. Ringing the changes on Homer is very much part of
the game here, as the *Voyage of Argo* provides a different take on the
Sirens. The scholarly Apollonius fills in some of the details omitted in the

Odyssey (naming the Sirens' island and parents, describing their appearance, telling of their earlier career and so on); this makes for a sharper picture, although it does also mean that some of the mystery in Homer is lost. Apollonius' episode is more concise, and in the *Voyage of Argo* the encounter with the Sirens is not foretold, so that there is more immediate impact. One of the crew of experts employs his expertise to improvise unaided a different means of escape and a neater one (using music against music), and here aptly (as they are drowned out) we don't learn what the Sirens actually sang. This time all of the heroes get to hear the song (albeit briefly) and the divine intervention comes at the end, to save one of them who (so far from being bound to the mast) actually leaps overboard. Apollonius also brings out more the beauty of their island (892, 901) and uses stronger language to express the seductiveness of their song (904, 914), and this greater allure is combined uneasily with their monstrous form (specified in 899) and their ominous vigilance (900) and persistence (911).

In other Classical authors

There is great diversity in the information about Sirens in other Classical authors. In Homer there are two of them, but in later writers we find two, three, four and even eight. There is also variation in connection with their parentage and names. These singing monsters of the sea were most often said to be the daughters of one of the Muses (goddesses of poetry and music) and one of the water gods. So in Apollonius they are the offspring of Terpsichore and the river god Achelous (although elsewhere we are told that they sprang from the blood that dripped from Achelous' horn after it had been broken off by the great Greek hero Heracles). The various names attributed to them are suggestive – for example, Aglaophonos (= Glorious-voiced), Ligeia (= Clear-voiced), Molpe (= Music) and Thelxinoe (= Mind-enchanter). The Siren's form varies too – she is sometimes a woman above and a bird below the waist, sometimes a girl with wings, and at other times she has a bird's body with a woman's head. And we also find some Sirens playing the lyre and pipes as well as singing (forming a sinister sort of musical trio or quartet!).

Some Classical writers maintain that after Odysseus or the Argonauts escaped them the Sirens drowned themselves, either in pique or because it was fated for them to perish if anyone eluded them. Before long dead Sirens were washing up all over the place: the body of one (called Parthenope) came ashore in the bay of Naples (which was then named Parthenope after her and was said to contain her tomb), and the nearby island of Leucosia was supposed to be called after another Siren of that name buried there (many located the island on which the Sirens originally did their singing in the Naples area). There were different tales to explain their bird form: they prayed successfully for wings to help them look for

their abducted companion Persephone (the daughter of the goddess Demeter mentioned by Apollonius above), or they were turned into birds by
Demeter for not having prevented the abduction of Persephone, or that it
was a punishment inflicted by the goddess of love (Aphrodite) because they
chose virginity over love. There was also a story that the Sirens entered
into a singing contest with the Muses but the Muses won and plucked out
the Sirens' feathers to make themselves victory crowns (rather like Red
Indian head-dresses!). According to another tradition there were Sirens
who were not singers by the sea but daughters of Earth, divinities of the
Underworld connected with the grave and the dead.[1] And in the last book
of Plato's *Republic* they lose all their negative associations: there are eight
of them, each sings out a note and the notes together make up a single
scale, producing the music of the heavenly spheres.[2]

Rationalizing explanations of the Sirens began with Greek and Latin
writers and were common in late antiquity. They were said to be the
personification of flattery or the dangers of pleasure or knowledge or
poetry; they were said to be prostitutes who ensnared and reduced to
poverty passing strangers and thus 'shipwrecked' them, or prostitutes
with charming voices and musical talent who devoured not the hearers but
their money and after ruining them quickly departed (hence the birds' legs
for them in the story).[3]

Sirens were also used metaphorically, denoting for Classical authors
the allure of eloquence, persuasion, sloth, etc., and for the Church Fathers
worldly pleasures in general and lust in particular. Among the latter,
Clement of Alexandria, with no apparent sense of incongruity, likened the
song of the Sirens to the lure of pagan Greek wisdom and culture, and also
to the voice of God in the scriptures (which forces hearers to believe and
obey without proof), and also explained the Sirens as pleasure (a deadly
trap from which one must flee). Similarly Hippolytus compared the good
Christian sailing through the sea of heresy to Odysseus passing the
enticing songstresses. Early Christians came to view the mast (with its
cross-stay) as the cross on their ship (the church) and Odysseus tied tightly
to the mast as the Christian holding firmly to the cross while making the
port of salvation. Eventually, and bizarrely (given that Odysseus was
among other things a liar, philanderer and killer), Odysseus lashed to the
mast was identified with the crucified Christ.[4]

In medieval, Renaissance and later authors

Of the various mentions of Sirens in the medieval period two are particularly worthy of note. Early on in Geoffrey of Monmouth's *History of the
Kings of Britain* (written about 1136) we read that years after the fall of
Troy, Brutus (great-grandson of the Trojan hero Aeneas) sailed to Britain
with a large contingent of Trojan exiles, and on that voyage as they sailed
out to exit from the Mediterranean they had a strange encounter with

some Sirens (1.12): 'they sailed for the Pillars of Hercules, where those monsters of the sea called Sirens appeared to them. They surrounded the ships and almost sank them. However, the Trojans escaped somehow ....' This is a tantalizingly brief and indistinct reference, but the Sirens do seem to have changed quite remarkably here: as the Trojans' ships numbered over 300, it seems that a huge pack of Sirens or several whale-sized Sirens must have swum up to the fleet and attacked it, rather than trying to lure the sailors.

More full is the allusion in Dante (1265-1321), who fabricates for allegorical purposes an arresting and intriguing Siren of a dream-like strangeness, in a brand new location and with novel (and graphic) touches in connection with her physical appearance. Dante depicts his arduous journey towards god in a long poem entitled *The Divine Comedy*. In its first part (*Inferno*) Dante represents himself as being guided through Hell by the spirit of the wise Latin poet Virgil and being chastened by the sight of the punishments of the sinners there. In the second part (*Purgatorio*) Dante is guided by Virgil through Purgatory, a lofty mountain rising in circular terraces inhabited by various groups of souls of repentant sinners. At the top of this mountain is Paradise, which is described in part three of the poem (*Paradiso*). In canto XIX of *Purgatorio* Dante falls asleep on the mountain and dreams of a woman, a stammering, squint-eyed, club-footed woman with crippled hands and a pallid complexion. As he gazes at her, her cheeks acquire an attractive colour, she draws herself upright and she begins to sing enchantingly. She sings that she is the sweet Siren who leads sailors astray and turned aside Ulysses (the Latin name for Odysseus). In the dream suddenly a holy and alert lady summons Virgil, who rips the Siren's clothes and shows Dante her belly, which gives off such a foul stench that he wakes up. Virgil then takes Dante off further up the mountain and says that the Siren is: 'that ancient witch for whom alone the mount above us weeps' (referring to the three remaining terraces occupied by those who had been avaricious, gluttonous and lustful in life). Interpretation is disputed but it seems that the Siren represents tempting worldly pleasures, especially those that lead to avarice, gluttony and lust. As in the dream, at first sight the soul recoils from such pleasures, but when it contemplates them further the soul starts to invest them with beauty and charm, until their true horror is revealed by reason (the wise poet Virgil). In religious literature and art the world was often represented as a beautiful female with a body which when unveiled or viewed from behind is seen to be rotting. The alert and holy woman may stand for temperance, philosophy or some divine grace.

During the Renaissance John Milton (1608-74) presented a brief but brilliant picture of a Siren at *Comus* 880ff.: 'fair Ligea's golden comb,/ Wherewith she sits on diamond rocks/ Sleeking her soft alluring locks.' Samuel Daniel (1563-1619) devoted a whole poem to a series of exchanges between Ulysses (Odysseus) and an enticing Siren. In his *Ulisses and the*

Syren she tries to tempt the hero to come to her, offering him ease, safety, pleasure and peace, but he rejects her, preferring toil and danger, which bring fame, honour and enjoyment and make a better world. Here, rather surprisingly, Ulysses hears only a single Siren and does not merely listen but actually replies, and engages in a protracted debate, and wins it – for so far from enticing him, she actually goes over to him, saying:

> Well, well Ulisses then I see,
> I shall not have thee heere,
> And therefore I will come to thee,
> And take my fortunes there.

The poem is a moralistic meditation on the life of action and the life of inaction, with these two different courses represented by two opposing characters. Ulysses is manly, honourable, virtuous and steadfast, so these are the qualities of the life of action. The defects of its opposite are conveyed via the Siren, who is insidiously beautiful and alluring, but also soft and weak, lacking in worth and high moral purpose, and misleading (e.g. she claims of herself and her sisters: 'No widdowes waile for our delights,/ Our sportes are without bloud').

In more modern times William Morris in his long poem *The Life and Death of Jason* (first published in 1867) employed the Sirens to put across a similar message. Basing his romantic epic on Apollonius, Morris depicted Jason and the Argonauts winning the Golden Fleece and returning successfully with it by rejecting a series of actual or apparent earthly paradises, including that offered by the Sirens. In a singing-contest between the Sirens and Orpheus for the souls of the Argonauts, the females hold out a voluptuous existence of comfort, free from toil, change and fear, while Orpheus counters with the necessity of struggle in a just cause and the dutiful and joyous life of work. Although Orpheus won the contest, the Sirens described their wonderful paradise in some appealing and sensuous lines (14.269ff.):

> If ye be bold with us to go,
> Things such as happy dreams may show
> Shall your once heavy eyes behold
> About our palaces of gold;
> Where waters 'neath the waters run,
> And from o'erhead a harmless sun
> Gleams through the woods of chrysolite.
> There gardens fairer to the sight
> Than those of the Phaeacian king
> Shall ye behold; and, wondering,
> Gaze on the sea-born fruit and flowers,
> And thornless and unchanging bowers,
> Whereof the May-time knoweth nought.
> So to the pillared house being brought,

Poor souls, ye shall not be alone,
For o'er the floors of pale blue stone
All day such feet as ours shall pass,
And, 'twixt the glimmering walls of glass,
Such bodies garlanded with gold,
So faint, so fair, shall ye behold,
And clean forget the treachery
Of changing earth and tumbling sea...

Come to the land where none grows old,
And none is rash or over-bold,
Nor any noise there is or war,
Or rumour from wild lands afar,
Or plagues, or birth and death of kings;
No vain desire of unknown things
Shall vex you there, no hope or fear
Of that which never draweth near;
But in that lovely land and still
Ye may remember what ye will,
And what ye will, forget for aye.

As the Argonauts (also called Minyae) rowed away, the Sirens tried one last, haunting appeal, in vain (14.413ff.):

Ah, will ye go, and whither then
Will ye go from us, soon to die,
To fill your three-score years and ten,
With many an unnamed misery?
And this the wretchedest of all,
That when upon your lonely eyes
The last faint heaviness shall fall
Ye shall bethink you of our cries;
Come back, nor grown old, seek in vain,
To hear us sing across the sea.
Come back, come back, come back again,
Come back, O fearful Minyae!

In the twentieth century Norman Douglas' *Siren Land* (published in 1911) is an erudite and charmingly discursive travel book about the Bay of Naples area (associated with Sirens since ancient times). Douglas speculates wittily on how the old Sirens passed their time on days of wintry storm: 'Modern ones would call for cigarettes, Grand Marnier, and a pack of cards, and bid the gale howl itself out. But those ancient feathered fowls – did they peck at each other viciously, or content themselves with shivering in silence among their crags? So have I seen, during a blizzard, the bedraggled vultures perched among the bleak hills of Asia Minor.'[5] Among various snippets about the monsters he mentions records preserved in the Portuguese royal archives of actual litigation between the Crown and the Grand Master of the Order of Saint James as to who should possess the Sirens cast up by the sea on the Grand Master's shores (the king won the case); and Siren charm amulets to ward off the evil eye which Douglas had seen himself in the streets of Naples; and contemporary stories about a Siren who nobody had seen but who lived on the nearby Galli islands, where she 'called the weather' and about a local Siren whom 'the English caught and took away' (for some reason best known to themselves).

Similar but much older stories are to be found in Borges (see the Select Bibliography) under the entry for Sirens: 'In the sixth century, a Siren was caught and baptized in northern Wales, and in certain old calendars took her place as a saint under the name Murgen. Another, in 1403, slipped through a breach in a dike and lived in Haarlem until the day of her death. Nobody could make out her speech, but she was taught to weave and she worshipped the cross as if instinctively.'

So too Italo Calvino in his 1956 book *Italian Folktales* (translated by G. Martin in 1980) retells the tale of 'The Siren Wife'. The Sirens are in many respects like Classical ones, but there is some interesting modification and blending, and there are also some imaginative and comic touches. Typically for Italian folktale, there is love and wonder and a feeling for beauty. This is a bittersweet story, with its mixture of betrayal and love, loss and recovery, entrapment and rescue, cruelty and kindness.

A beautiful woman married to a sailor and lonely during his long absences has an affair. Although he loves her and she begs for forgiveness, he takes her out to sea and throws her overboard. She sinks to the bottom of the sea, where the Sirens take her in (because she is so lovely), making her one of them, naming her Froth, decking her out in finery and taking her to their brilliant underwater palace which is filled with dancing men and women. Later on, when a ship approaches, they sing and a man on it leaps into the sea. The Sirens want to turn him into coral or shell, but the wife recognizes him as the sailor (whom she still loves) and rescues him. Back on land, he feels guilty because his wife saved him and wanders sadly in a fairies' forest, where a mysterious voice offers to restore his wife if he can get a flower called 'the loveliest' that grows only in the Sirens' palace. He sails off, calls up his wife and asks her to get the flower. She explains that it is a flower that the Sirens stole from the fairies and when the fairies get it back the Sirens will die. She tells him to go off, sell all his possessions, buy the finest jewels and come back with them draped over his ship. When he does this, the Sirens (who love jewellery) all follow his ship, begging for the jewels, and in their absence the wife steals the flower. The Sirens are swept off under the sea and drowned, the wife flies off with an old fairy on an eagle and when the sailor gets home he finds his wife waiting for him.

Rather different and more intellectual is James Joyce's *Ulysses* (1922), which is concerned with the thoughts and actions of a certain Leopold Bloom as he wanders around Dublin one day in 1904, and which takes as its framework the plot of Homer's *Odyssey*. Packed with references to and echoes of the Greek epic (adapted as Joyce saw fit), *Ulysses* presents Bloom as a latter-day Odysseus among modern equivalents of places and characters from the *Odyssey*. It is a naturalistic novel of city life, exposing much of its shabbiness and shoddiness. The Homeric parallels give it a certain universality (making the Dubliners representatives of all men, with counterparts as far back as Homer); they also produce pointed and at times humorous contrasts between the glorious and extraordinary world of Odysseus and sordid, mundane, provincial Dublin.

So the two mysterious and otherworldly Sirens with their beautiful song in never-never land become in *Ulysses* two barmaids (called Miss Douce and Miss Kennedy) with coral lips singing snatches from popular songs as they go about their work in a Dublin pub. At the start of the episode they chat and giggle at passers-by and are cheeked by the boot-boy, who brings them their tea. Such are Irish Sirens, who threaten to 'wring his ear for him a yard long' (rather than killing him), then go on to gossip about remedies for sunburn and worry about getting a rash. The Irish Odysseus is similarly diminished: when they see Leopold Bloom go by, so far from enticing him, they burst out laughing at the idea of being married to such a man with his greasy eyes and nose and his bit of a beard, and one of them splutters her tea out of her mouth. These Sirens take holidays too: Miss Douce next talks to a customer about her vacation spent getting a tan at the seaside, and he calls her a temptress (for sunbathing). Miss Douce also flirts with customers by reaching right up for a flagon ('her bust, that all but burst, so high'), pulling her skirt above her knee and snapping her 'nipped elastic garter smackwarm against her smackable woman's warmhosed thigh'. Bloom actually enters Sirenland (the pub), where he eats liver and bacon and mashed potatoes. However, he doesn't go right up to the bar but orders his food and drink from a waiter, who cannot hear properly. With another neat twist the customers then sing, to a piano. During the singing Bloom gazes at Miss Douce in the mirror (and she knows that he is looking), but he doesn't take it any further. Instead he just leaves, feeling the gassy effect of the cider that he has drunk.

Different again is *The Ulysses Voyage* (1987) by Tim Severin, which concerns a modern real life adventure. In a replica of an early Greek galley Severin and his crew actually sailed from Troy to the island of Ithaca (Odysseus' homeland) off the west coast of Greece, following the route that he thought Odysseus would most obviously have taken. Severin tried to find sites along the way that matched descriptions of places encountered on the hero's voyage in the *Odyssey* and attempted to uncover explanations for the fabulous tales connected with it. In chapter 11 he speculates that the Sirens inhabited Cape Yrapetra, a low foreland on the island of Levkas (a little to the north of Ithaca), where there are remains of burial mounds (which remind him of the bones in the Sirens' meadow); he notes also that elsewhere on the island there is a tall cliff and the Sirens were said by some to have thrown themselves into the sea from such a cliff the first time that they failed to ensnare a traveller.

Derek Walcott, the West Indian poet and playwright, based his play *The Odyssey* (1993) on Homer's epic, but this is a very free and highly creative version that boldly blends episodes from Homer with modern Greek and especially Caribbean characters and themes, to produce an arresting new flavour. There is strangeness and sly humour in connection with the Sirens incident, and also a curious doubling, with them represented first by mermaids (= their sexual allure) and then by old hags (= the appeal of their singing).

At the start of Act 2 Odysseus, scorched by the sun, is drifting alone on a raft when two fish leap aboard. He puts them inside his shirt for later, and suddenly there are two lovely mermaids on his raft, tempting him to stroke their glittering wet breasts and offering to make his fantasies come true ('Never dreamt of two girls together in one bed?'). When Odysseus rejects them ('You're very beautiful. But you're talking fishes'), one of them claims that fish do mate with men ('Mum was a dolphin. Dad hailed from Nicosia'). However, the hero takes one of the fish from inside his shirt and throws it overboard, at which one of the mermaids screeches and dives overboard. As the second one thrashes around on the raft, he tosses her overboard too.

Next some drowned sailors from his crew (Stavros, Costa, Tasso and Stratis) board the raft, to help him steer past the Sirens – two old crones who crouch in a yellow field and collect sailors' skeletons for kindling ('their jaws hang like empty purses, but from them, songs … music comes, Captain, to break your heart with pleasure'). Odysseus gets them to tie him to the mast and cram their own ears with wax as they row by. When they are beyond the Sirens, Odysseus says of their song: 'I felt such joy, no soul could bear it … through the veils of their song I saw my beloved's eyes.' The crew respond: 'their song is smoke fluting from a mountain … everything you loved or fought for was in that bliss.'

Greg Doran, the director of the Royal Shakespeare Company's production of the play, faced great difficulties in representing on stage the irresistible song of the Sirens, something which would daunt any composer. He explained their ingenious solution: 'We … leave the sound entirely to the imagination. We have a tape of lapping surf running continuously throughout the scene. At the moment when the sailors have tied Odysseus to the mast and cram wax into their ears, we cut out all sound. The effect is just like what happens when the central heating suddenly cuts out; you notice the absence of the sound, the silence is audible. So here, the sea stops. And in that silence as you watch Odysseus writhe in the ecstasy of the song he alone hears, you can only imagine how beautiful it must be. Once they have rowed past the sirens, the sailors unplug their ears and the sound of the sea comes crashing back into the scene.'

Finally, and on a far less serious note, Sirens even figure in the sword and sorcery genre. Most notably, Piers Anthony's *The Source of Magic* (1979) contains a rather improbable addition to the tradition, as well as much else – for this highly sophisticated narrative is jam-packed with Classical monsters (sphinx, harpy, manticora etc.), non-Classical ones (such as trolls, rocs, zombies) and brand new ones (like ant-lions and cactus-cats), not to mention ghosts, shoe-trees, winged fruits, demons in bottles, wood nymphs and hephalumphs.

The novel's hero Bink sets out on a quest to find the source of magic in the land of Xanth along with a motley band of companions – a Centaur, a soldier (metamorphosed into a griffin), a magician and a golem. On their journey they are entertained at a village consisting entirely of females (elves, gnomes, fairies, trolls and so on). Their males have been lured away by a Siren in the nearby forest whom the females could not destroy because she is protected by that well-known species, a magic tangle tree, which lets only males through to the Siren and grabs any females who approach it.

That night the Siren begins to sing her eerie song ('a distillation of the sex appeal of all womankind'). The village females try to drown it out by singing themselves and attempt to restrain the companions by swarming over them, smothering them under their soft flesh and pneumatic limbs, but they frantically fling the women off and run towards the Siren. As they reach the tangle tree, its tentacles quiver with suppressed desire for them. One of them attacks the tree (for no reason whatsoever), which then grabs them and drags Bink towards its slavering maw, replete with flowing saliva sap and ingrown knots for teeth. The magician temporarily saves Bink by conjuring up and shoving into the tree's mouth a spiced cheese-cake. But the tree recovers and pushes Bink into its mouth, until it is set on fire by torches thrown by the village females (who strangely had never thought of such an obvious means of attacking wood until it was suggested to them by a male – the soldier-griffin).

As the tree is burned up, the Siren calls again and the companions follow the sound to a lake with two tiny islands. A path over the water leads to the island from which the sound is coming. In dealing with a 'battering ram' (a sort of trained attack sheep) by tricking it into butting a tree of exploding pineapples (which fall on it and knock it silly), the Centaur is rendered deaf by a pineapple that goes off right in front of him. Immune now to the Siren's allure, he fires an arrow at her, and her melodious song ends in a sudden squawk. However, it turns out that the Siren has been unfairly maligned all along, because before she dies she protests that she killed nobody but had only love for them. The magician promptly brings her back to life with a handy healing elixir, and she reveals that all the men who she attracted always went across to the other island to her sister, a Gorgon. The Siren (who is not too bright) didn't know that the Gorgon's gaze turns men to stone and never had worked out why not a single man came back to her. Now that she has some males at last, she offers them sex, but the Centaur pleads a headache and the others say that they just want food and rest.

In the morning the companions leave for the Gorgon (after thoughtfully breaking up some wood for the Siren's cooking fire). It turns out that the Gorgon is about as dim as her sister: she had not realized the power of her gaze either and thought that the stone statues all over the places were mementoes left behind by the men who had mysteriously and rather rudely just disappeared. The magician helpfully solves her problem by making her face invisible (thus removing her ability to turn people to stone at the sight of her eyes), and the companions then resume their quest. One can only hope that all this was actually meant to be comic.[6]

By way of an exercise, look at Margaret Atwood's poem 'Siren Song' in her 1974 collection *You Are Happy*. The poem consists entirely of the words of a Siren and puts the reader in the role of her prey. Examine how she initially intrigues and draws one in, and then ends with a darkly humorous twist, luring in a new way and playing with her victim. Consider also what this poem has to say about the power of words, their ability to distort, mislead and exploit altruism and obtuseness.

Other Winged Monsters

Sirens are by no means the only winged monsters. This chapter will touch on several more, highlighting two in particular. We have already met the *strix* (see pp. 9ff.), and we will be meeting Gorgons and Typhos (who was winged according to several authors) in Chapters 8 and 11 (pp. 105ff. and 146ff.), where they are more conveniently handled. There was also Pegasus, a marvellous winged horse which carried Zeus' thunder and lightning for him, and which also acted as the hero Bellerophon's mount, enabling him to attack from the air and kill the Chimaera (a fire-breathing combination of lion, goat and snake) in a combat that remarkably pitted a good monster against a bad one. The same horse also threw Bellerophon when he got above himself and tried to fly on it up to heaven to join the gods. Born from the blood that gushed from the neck of the snaky-haired Medusa, Pegasus itself created with a stamp of its foot various springs on earth, including Hippocrene (which means 'horse-fountain'), whose waters provided inspiration for poets. Eventually Pegasus was placed in the sky as a constellation by Zeus.[1]

The Stymphalian Birds

Then there are the terrible Stymphalian Birds. As his fifth Labour the great hero Heracles (Hercules) had to rid the area around Stymphalus, a town in southern Greece, of these monstrous creatures. After fleeing from some wolves, these birds had settled in thick woods on the shore of lake Stymphalus and plagued the surrounding territory. Brought up by Ares (god of war), they had claws, wings and beaks of bronze, and used their pointed feathers as arrows, dropping them on animals and humans, whom they then devoured. To get rid of them was both dangerous and difficult, as there were so many of them ensconced in dense woodland. Ingenuity was needed. Accounts vary, but Heracles used a bronze rattle or castanets (which he made himself or was given by the goddess Athena) to make an enormous din, terrifying the birds and making them fly up from cover; then he either drove them all off by keeping up the noise, or shot some with his bow and arrows and drove off the rest.

Some believe that the survivors should be identified with some very similar birds on the Isle of Ares, which were subsequently encountered by Jason and the Argonauts as they sailed in quest of the Golden Fleece. In

Apollonius of Rhodes' epic poem, *The Voyage of Argo* (written in the third century BC), when the Argonauts approached this island, a bird flew over their ship and dropped a feather which wounded Oileus in the shoulder. Then another one came swooping in to the attack, but Clytius shot it with an arrow and brought it spinning down. The Argonauts then organized themselves. Half of them rowed the ship to shore, while the other half locked their shields together over the rowers and themselves to form a roof. They roared and banged on their shields to make a huge racket, following Heracles' example. The birds flew up in their thousands, fluttered about in panic, discharged a heavy shower of feathers at the ship and then flew off. In Apollonius' poem Jason and the Argonauts generally come off second best to the mighty Heracles (who was with them for the earlier part of the voyage). So here they are just following in his footsteps, and it takes all of them (nearly fifty) to achieve what Heracles had managed on his own, and even then (unlike him) one of them is wounded and they need to protect themselves carefully against the birds.[2]

Griffins

Also relevant are griffins, those fierce and fabulous beasts so common in art, heraldry and literature throughout the ages.[3] In the ancient Classical world they were generally said to have the body of a lion and the head and wings of an eagle (according to Pausanias they also have spots like leopards) and to dwell in the far north, where they guard the gold of the land from the thieving Arimaspians (a race of humans with one eye in the centre of the forehead).[4] But a late writer, Aelian (born AD 170) spoke of griffins in India and filled out the picture with some colourful and intriguing information about them in *On Animals* 4.27:

> I hear that the Indian creature called the griffin is a quadruped like a lion and has extremely powerful claws like those of a lion. According to common report it has wings, and the feathers along its back are black, those on its front are red, while the actual wings themselves are white. Ctesias records that its neck is variegated with dark blue feathers and that it has the head and beak of an eagle, just as it is depicted by artists in paintings and sculptures; and he says that its eyes are fiery.
>
> It makes its nest in the mountains and although it is impossible to capture a full grown griffin, men do take its young. The people of Bactria (near India) say that griffins guard the gold there, digging it up and building their lairs from it, while the Indians carry off the gold that they drop. However, the Indians deny that the griffins guard this gold, as they have no need of it (which seems credible to me). They say that they themselves turn up to collect the gold and the griffins, fearing for their young, do battle with these invaders; and griffins fight with other animals too, and beat them easily, but will not stand up to a lion or an elephant. So the Indians are afraid of these

Bronze griffin head from the shoulder of a wine-bowl. Probably from
Rhodes, *c.* 650 BC. British Museum, London.

creatures' strength and do not set out in search of the gold by day but travel
at night, thinking themselves more likely to escape detection then.

The area where the griffins live and the gold is mined is a dread waste-
land. Those seeking this substance arrive, one or two thousand strong,
armed and carrying spades and sacks. They watch for a moonless night, and
dig then. If they elude the griffins, they not only escape with their lives but
also take their load home, and when the skilled smelters have refined it, they
possess immense wealth in return for the dangers I have described. But if
they are caught in the act, they are finished; and, I am told, it is three or four
years before they get back home again.

I myself am particularly intrigued by the final sentence there. Initially it looks as if the griffins kill the Indians. Then the men get home again, but only after three or four years. Have they been killed and somehow reanimated? If so, why the reanimation? Or were they not killed at all? Why the lengthy delay over their return? And what have the griffins been doing with them in the meanwhile – torturing them, using them as slaves, or what? It's all very mysterious and rather chilling.

The sphinx

Another enigma is the sphinx. This creature has been variously explained (as a symbol of kingship, a guardian spirit, an embodiment of different kinds of mystery etc.), was assigned various parents (including the monsters Orthus, Typhon and Echidna) and originated somewhere or other in the orient (it has been traced back to Mesopotamia and Egypt in the middle of the third millennium BC). It also took different forms, but in Greece and Rome was usually represented as a creature with the head of a woman, the body of a lion and the wings of a bird (although bearded male sphinxes are sometimes found in archaic Greek art). Etymologizing connected the name sphinx with the Greek verb *sphingein* (= 'to bind, hold fast'), and some believe it means 'strangler'.

In Classical literature the sphinx plays an important part in the famous myth of Oedipus and is associated with the best known Greek tragedy – *Oedipus the King* (also known as *Oedipus Tyrannus* and *Oedipus Rex*), written by Sophocles in the fifth century BC. There it appears as a remarkable type of monster – one with superior knowledge that sets a riddle to which it alone knows the answer, until Oedipus turns up.[5]

In the story Oedipus' father, Laius, was king of Thebes (a city in central Greece), and Jocasta was his wife and queen. An oracle told him not to have children because if he had a son the child would kill him. Laius went ahead and fathered a boy anyway (Oedipus), but tried to escape fate by killing the child. He gave it to one of his shepherds to expose on a mountain, but the man handed it on to a shepherd from the nearby town of Corinth. The Corinthian took the baby to his king and queen, who were childless and who brought up the boy as their own.

So Oedipus grew up in the palace at Corinth thinking that he was the son of the king, until one day a Corinthian in a quarrel taunted him with not being the king's son. Disturbed by this, Oedipus went off to consult Apollo's oracle at Delphi about his parentage. The oracle told him that he would kill his own father and marry his own mother. Oedipus decided never to return to Corinth, so that this could not happen, and took the road to Thebes. At a crossroads he was forced off the road by an old man in a chariot and his servants. In a rage he killed all of them except one of the servants (who, to save face, when he got back to Thebes claimed that they had been attacked by a band of robbers). The old man was Laius, and so the first part of the prophecy had come true.

The Naxian Sphinx, dedicated *c.* 560 BC at Delphi. Delphi Archaeological Museum.

The sphinx played a part in making the second part come true. It had taken up position on a rock near Thebes, asking passers-by a riddle and murdering those who could not answer it (everybody so far). The riddle was: what is it that has one voice and yet becomes four-footed, two-footed and three-footed, and is slowest when it goes on most feet? The answer is man, who as an adult goes on two feet, as an old man goes on three feet (a stick counting as the third foot), and as a baby goes on all fours. When Oedipus braved the terrible monster and solved its riddle, the sphinx hurled itself from the rock to its death. Oedipus describes this himself in some powerful lines in the Latin play *Oedipus* by Seneca:[6]

> I did not flee from the sphinx or the tangled words of her
> obscure verse. I braved that sinister singer's bloody, gaping
> mouth and the ground beneath her white with scattered bones.
> She loomed over me on her lofty crag, spreading her   95
> pinions to pounce on her prey, lashing her tail,
> menacing me like a savage lion. I asked her what
> her riddle was. She shrieked out horror on high, snapped her
> jaws together; her talons tore splinters from the rock,
> she couldn't wait to swoop down and get at my flesh.   100
> Her response was a knot of words, entwined
> trickery, a terrible riddle. But I solved it.

The grateful people of Thebes made Oedipus their king and gave him as his wife Jocasta (his own mother, if he only knew it!).

The prophecy had come to pass. It remained for the truth to be found out. Years later, after children had been born to Oedipus and Jocasta, a terrible plague descended on Thebes. This is the point at which Sophocles' play opens. The god's oracle at Delphi is consulted and says that the plague will not end until Laius' murderer is punished. Oedipus proclaims an investigation and curses the murderer (himself!) with exile. When he examines the Theban prophet Teiresias and is told the truth by him (that he is the murderer himself), he refuses to believe the prophet and decides that he must be in league with Jocasta's brother (Creon) in a plot to seize the throne. She defends her brother and, to show that the words of prophets are empty, tells Oedipus how an oracle had said that Laius would be killed by his own son but in fact he was murdered by robbers at a crossroads on the way to Corinth. Disturbed by the similarity to the murder at a crossroads that he had himself committed, Oedipus sends for the surviving servant.

Meanwhile a messenger arrives from Corinth and announces the death of the king there. When Oedipus rejoices that the prophecy that he would kill his own father was incorrect, the messenger reveals that he himself years ago had been a shepherd, had been given the baby Oedipus by one of Laius' shepherds and had passed him on to the king of Corinth (who was not his real father). Jocasta suspects the truth and tries to stop Oedipus from further investigation, but he will not be deflected. She exits just before the survivor from the murder at the crossroads turns up. He reluctantly admits that he had been the shepherd of Laius all those years ago and he had handed over Oedipus (the son of Laius and Jocasta) to the other shepherd. A horrified Oedipus leaves the stage, finds that Jocasta has hanged herself, takes the brooches from her dress and plunges them into his eyes repeatedly, producing great founts of blood. The play ends with the blind king about to go off into exile.

As well as being important for the plot, the sphinx has a bearing on the play's 'message' (Greek tragedies did not just present a story but also raised issues for contemplation and had things to say on a religious and moral level). One major lesson of *Oedipus the King* is that life is not random but ruled by a divine Order, whereas humans' attempts to control their lives fail. In the play Oedipus brags about and is praised for his cleverness in solving the riddle, and that success helps to make him rely on and over-rate his own intelligence (which, as we can see, is in fact flawed). So he is led to *hubris* (arrogance, especially towards the gods; thinking oneself above one's mortal station) – the assertion that human prophets and the gods' oracles are untrue, and that life is really governed by chance. Events show just how wrong Oedipus is over that, as his *hubris* is inevitably succeeded by *nemesis* (divine retribution).[7]

Harpies

Finally, there are the Harpies ('Snatchers'). In Homer they are personified stormwinds that carry people off. In Hesiod they appear as females with lovely hair and wings who fly as fast as the winds and birds. But later authors make them into disgusting, sombre and terrifying figures – birds with pale girls' faces and talons. Their main role in myth is to punish the blind prophet Phineus for offending heaven: they prevent him from eating by snatching away his food and polluting what they cannot carry off with their filthy touch and foul droppings, until Zetes and Calais, the winged sons of Boreas (the North Wind), drive them away.[8]

This story is first told at length by Apollonius of Rhodes in his *Voyage of Argo*, an epic that relates how Jason and his crew of heroes (the Argonauts) sailed off to distant Colchis on a quest for the marvellous Golden Fleece and had various adventures on the way there and back. On the outward journey at 2.178ff. they arrive at the home of the prophet and we are told of his appalling suffering (for revealing Zeus' will he was blinded and given a lingering old age, with the Harpies stealing almost all of his food and leaving him just a few stinking scraps to keep him barely alive). As soon as Phineus hears the Argonauts' footsteps and voices outside his house, he knows that they are the ones supposed to let him enjoy food again according to an oracle of Zeus. So he gets up and creeps to the door (terribly weak and trembling, just skin and bone, like a phantom in a dream), and then he faints. This makes us feel great sympathy for Phineus, so that we really want to see him rescued from the Harpies.

At 2.209ff. he revives and appeals to them in the name of various gods to help him, blind, miserable and tormented by the Harpies as he is. He tells them that there is an oracle that the sons of Boreas will deal with his problem, and he points out that he is the (once famous and wealthy) king who married their sister. He tries very hard to get the Argonauts to help him, flattering, imploring and attempting to make them feel sorry for him in his awful plight. All of this arouses in the reader still more sympathy for Phineus and makes one now expect immediate aid from the sons of Boreas. And they begin by expressing pity and weeping; but then Zetes asks Phineus why he is persecuted like this, wonders if he has sinned against the gods with his prophetic skill, and actually refuses to give assistance unless Phineus assures them on oath that they will not offend heaven in so doing. Only after he duly swears the oath do they help him. The suspicious questioning and refusal to assist are unexpected and so take the attention. Zetes is being careful and correct; but Phineus is a tormented relative, and he has said that there is a divine oracle that they will deal with the Harpies. The rather formal exchange here lowers the emotional pitch and works against perception of this encounter with the monsters as a romantic daring deed.

The Argonauts now prepare a meal for Phineus and stand by him on guard as he begins to eat. This is what happens next:

> The instant that the old man touched his food,
> the Harpies (like terrible stormwinds or lightning-flashes)
> suddenly leapt out from the clouds and swooped down,
> screaming in their craving for food. The heroes spotted them
> in mid-flight and shouted, but as they cried out the Harpies   270
> had gulped down everything and were flying over the sea,
> far off and away, having left behind an intolerable stench.
> The two sons of Boreas raced off in pursuit of them
> with drawn swords. Zeus granted them indefatigable
> strength. Without Zeus they could not have followed   275
> the Harpies, who always outstripped westerly
> stormwinds on their way to or from Phineus.
> Just as on a mountainside trained hunting-dogs
> run on the track of horned goats or deer
> at full stretch just behind their quarry   280
> and snap at it with their front teeth in vain,
> so Zetes and Calais sped along very close to the Harpies
> and just touched them with their fingertips, but in vain.
> They caught up with them far out at the Floating Islands
> and despite heaven's will would have torn them to pieces,   285
> if the swift goddess Iris hadn't seen them, leapt down
> from heaven and restrained them with these persuasive words:
> 'Sons of Boreas, you're not allowed to take your swords to the
> Harpies, those hounds of mighty Zeus. But I will personally
> swear that they'll never come into contact with Phineus again.'   290
> So saying, she took an oath by the waters of the Styx (which for
> all the gods is the most dread and holy of oaths) that they
> would not subsequently approach the home of Phineus,

the son of Agenor; for so it was in fact fated.
The heroes, yielding to the oath, turned to speed back   295
to the Argo. That is why the Floating Islands
are now called the Strophades ('Turning Islands').
The Harpies and Iris parted. They entered
a cavern on king Minos' Crete, while she darted up
to Olympus, soaring on her swift wings.   300

After this passage Phineus gives the Argonauts lots of useful information about the rest of their voyage to Colchis, and it is only at 2.426ff. that the sons of Boreas finally get back to their companions and report what has happened, to general rejoicing.

Especially as the end to such a lengthy incident, this seems to me somewhat low-key, even anticlimactic. The Harpies' attack is not caught vividly or in much detail (although the brevity does suggest the speed of it). The sons of Boreas do succeed in dealing with the problem, but there is no combat with and killing of the monsters (as some readers will have expected, and as did occur in some versions of the story). There is also undercutting in the sly humour of Iris' oath (just the thing for the punctilious Zetes!). The erudite material at 296ff. seems rather dry too. And the actual return of the sons of Boreas is long delayed (with the attention diverted from them by Phineus' prophecy) and is not especially triumphant when it does take place. This incident is a feat, but it is definitely downplayed. All of this is typical of Apollonius' intelligent, questioning and gently deflating approach to myth and epic poetry.

Also typically the Latin poet Valerius Flaccus in his *Voyage of Argo* (written much later, in the first century AD) bases his account of this episode on Apollonius and follows his Greek model's general outline, but also shows independence, making substantial variations on Apollonius and trying to outdo him at several points. In particular Valerius makes this a more impressive deed for the sons of Boreas, and he produces a version of it that is more moving and exciting.

As in Apollonius, so in Valerius (at 4.423ff.) the Argonauts approach the home of Phineus (whose tribulations are described for us). But this Phineus knows that it is them before they even land, goes down to the shore and greets them. As well as being a more perceptive prophet, he is, tragically, more desperate for their help (he does not wait for them to come to him). So too again Phineus appeals to them, but here his appeal is stronger, as his depiction of the Harpies' persecution is more detailed and affecting. This time the compassionate Zetes immediately offers to help his poor relative, only tacking on a brief proviso at the end (if this isn't divine punishment, or if the gods' anger can be appeased). In this much warmer exchange there is no cross-questioning of Phineus, no refusal to assist and no extraction of an oath. Whereas in Apollonius Phineus now formally gives his solemn word, in Valerius he aims at the sons of Boreas an

emotional speech in which he explains that he has been punished for
revealing the will of Jupiter (Zeus) out of pity for humans (a touching
detail not found in the Greek model). The Argonauts are all deeply
moved and are eager to help. Before long the Harpies appear. This time
we learn a bit more about them, including the name of one of them
(Celaeno) and their parentage (their father is the terrible monster
Typhos, who is imprisoned for all time in the dark land of the dead
beneath our world).

> They set up the couches with their coverlets, welcome him into
> their midst and recline around him, keeping watch on the
> sea and sky, telling him to eat and not to worry.
> Suddenly the poor old man trembles and pales, and his fingers   490
> fall from his lips: the birds that plague him, without any
> warning, are visible in among the food. There's a
> horrendous, reeking stench – the smell of their father's
> Hell. All against one, they go for Phineus, attacking with
> beating wings. There's a hellish cloud of them,   495
> gaping, running riot, a repulsive sight. They spoil
> the feast and foul the ground and coverlets with their
> moist droppings. Amid whirring wings dread Celaeno
> keeps the food in her grip from Phineus and from
> her wretched sisters too, maddening them all with hunger.   500
> Now with a shout the sons of Boreas suddenly streak
> up into the air, sped on by their father. The monsters
> are startled by these unfamiliar enemies and drop the filched
> food from their jaws. First they flutter around Phineus' home,
> then they make for the deep sea. The Argonauts stand on the   505
> shore transfixed and follow the roaming fiends with their eyes.
> When the peak of Vesuvius erupts thunderously, bringing
> destruction to Italy, the fiery storm has scarcely convulsed the
> mountain and already ash is covering towns in the orient –
> just as quickly as that the Harpies whirl past distant   510
> peoples and seas, not allowed to land anywhere.
> They approach the coast of the great Ionian Sea and the rocky
> islands in its middle (now called the Strophades by the locals),
> become exhausted and pant with fear of imminent death.
> Trembling with terror, and flying low and sluggishly,   515
> with dreadful shrieks they beg their father Typhos to help.
> He rises up, bringing nether night into our upper world,
> and from the midst of the darkness are heard these words:
> 'It's enough to have driven the goddesses this far. Why try to
> rage on against Jupiter's agents, the chosen instruments of   520
> his great wrath (on top of his thunderbolt and aegis)?
> Now the same deity bids them leave Phineus' home.
> They acknowledge his command and withdraw as ordered.
> But soon you too will flee like this, pressed by a deadly
> bow. The Harpies will never lack new sustenance so long   525

as mortals bring divine anger deservedly on themselves.'
The sons of Boreas hover uncertainly, calming down; then
they depart, returning in triumph to their comrades' ranks.

Unlike his predecessor, Valerius dwells on the attack by the Harpies (so that we can picture it clearly), making it more colourful and sensational. He gains pathos at 490f. by showing us the effect of these monsters on poor old Phineus; and there is the sinister touch of them suddenly somehow being in there among the food, not having been seen beforehand as in Apollonius. Valerius highlights the stench, which is worse than in his model. It is hellish, and (with a bold and suggestive expression) the Harpies too are described as a hellish cloud. They are also more malicious this time (attacking Phineus as well as stealing his food) and more repulsive (the moist droppings befouling everything). And at 498ff. there is the horrific detail of Celaeno scaring off her own sisters too from the food with a show of real greed and savagery.

The response to the monsters and the pursuit at 501ff. are also lively and effective. Valerius is working within the tradition in which there is no actual fight and the Harpies escape with their lives, but he does his best to turn this into a great exploit for Zetes and Calais despite that. His sons of Boreas react more swiftly and dramatically than they do in Apollonius (where they only move after the fiends have sped off). He also builds up the Harpies as opponents. So his sombre and impressive simile likens them to whirling volcanic dust, thereby attaching to them speed, and also terror, destructiveness, darkness etc. (whereas the Greek epic's simile had simply compared them to goats and deer fleeing from hunting-dogs). But these great adversaries at 514ff. are severely distressed (not in Apollonius) and are far more clearly beaten than in the Greek poem, and there is also the novel and pointed inversion whereby the monsters themselves (rather than their victim) are afraid and appeal for aid. Similarly with Typhos at 517ff. it takes a more awesome intervention than that of Iris to get Valerius' Zetes and Calais to let their prey survive. There is the extraordinary picture of Typhos actually rising up from Hell, weirdly bringing darkness with him and from the midst of it solemnly uttering words which are more imperious than Iris' in ordering the sons of Boreas to desist, and which also reinforce their opponents' status. Finally at 527f. this time Zetes and Calais are not immediately cowed (even by Typhos) and they are explicitly said to return in triumph (so that we end on a high note).

Before Valerius, in the first century BC, Virgil in his epic *Aeneid* had taken a rather different approach to Apollonius, not engaging with him as closely. In the third book of the *Aeneid* he clearly had the Greek poem in mind (so, for instance, there is allusion to Phineus and the Strophades), but he presented an attack by and repulse of the Harpies which involved not Phineus and the Argonauts but a later group of heroic travellers on another quest. These were Aeneas and the rest of the Trojans who had survived the fall of Troy and gone off with him, sailing around the Mediterranean in search of the promised land in which heaven allowed them to settle – the area of Italy called Latium. Virgil presented a much briefer and more concentrated narrative than Apollonius, using the monsters to add the uncanny, the sinister and the mysterious to Aeneas' voyage. He also tied in this passage with the rest of the *Aeneid* by means of Celaeno's prophecy (at 3.251ff. below) about the Trojans having to eat their own tables before they can build their city in Italy: later, in book 7, after landing in Latium the Trojans make a meal of fruit served on thin platters of bread, which they also eat; and when Aeneas' son remarks that they are even eating their tables Aeneas recalls the prophecy and announces that they have reached their new home. Here is Virgil's account, spoken by Aeneas himself (and representing the Harpies as hellish monsters sent up from the river Styx in the Underworld). As you read it, see if you can spot the variations on the Greek source.

Saved from the stormwaves, I first found shelter on the shore	
of one of the Stophades. These islands (called by their Greek	210
name) are set in the great Ionian Sea. Dread Celaeno and the	
other Harpies lived there since being shut out from Phineus'	
home and frightened from his table where they used to feed.	
They are the grimmest of all monsters, the most savage scourge	
ever sent up from the river Styx by angry gods.	215
These birds with girls' faces discharge utterly	
disgusting droppings, and they have hands	
with talons and faces permanently pale from hunger.	
On sailing into the harbour there, we suddenly	
saw scattered across the grass herds of sleek cattle	220
and flocks of goats with no herdsman. We rushed on them	
with drawn swords, promising their share of the spoil to	
Jupiter himself and the other gods. Then we heaped up turf	
for couches on the curving shore and feasted on the fine food.	
Suddenly with a nightmare swoop down from the mountains	225
the Harpies were there, flapping their wings with clamorous	
clangs. They savaged our food, polluting whatever they touched	
with their filth; amid the foul stench a hideous screeching.	
In a secluded spot deep within a cleft in the cliff,	
enclosed by trees and their shifting shadows, we set up	230
the tables again and lit a fire on a new altar. Again from their	
hidden lair, flying in from a different part of the sky, the noisy	
flock hovered around their prey with their taloned feet	
and befouled the food with their mouths. At that I told my men	
to arm themselves: we would wage war on that awful brood.	235
They did as they were bid: they hid their swords here and	
there in the grass and concealed their shields out of sight.	
So when they swooped down noisily along the winding shore,	
Misenus our lookout on high sounded the alarm on his trumpet.	

My men attacked and in a strange new form of combat tried to 240
savage with their swords these sinister, filthy sea-birds. Their
plumage was impervious to our violent blows and their backs
were unwounded. They quickly flew off, soaring to the stars,
leaving behind half-eaten food and foul traces of themselves.
One of them (Celaeno) perched on a lofty crag and prophesied 245
evil. These were the words that burst from her breast:
'Is it war, Trojans? Are you actually prepared to wage war
to repay us for the killing of our cattle and heifers
and to drive us harmless Harpies from our ancestral kingdom?
Well then, take my words to heart and never forget them. 250
I, the greatest of the Furies, hereby reveal to you what the
Almighty Father prophesied to Apollo and He passed on to me.
You seek Italy, invoking the winds for your voyage. You
shall go to Italy, you shall be permitted to enter her harbours.
But you won't gird with walls the city granted to you 255
until terrible hunger and the sin of trying to kill us
compel you to gnaw at your tables and devour them.'
With that she flew off, fleeing back to the forest for refuge.

There are many clever and grim twists to Apollonius. Here the heroes are
defending their own meal, and the Harpies (rather than stealing food and
punishing one who offended Zeus) are protecting their cattle from thieves,
who are trying to sacrifice them to Jupiter and eat them. Here there is
actual combat, although these Harpies cannot be wounded (like the Stymphalian Birds). The Trojans surpass the Argonauts: they endure a full
three attacks; they are better organized (Misenus as lookout); and although they don't have the winged sons of Boreas among them, they still
drive off their assailants. Virgil also makes his Harpies more formidable:
unlike Apollonius, he describes them (in a graphic and forbidding sketch
at 214ff.); he gives Celaeno (rather than Phineus) prophetic powers; and,
while actually letting her speak, he attributes to her an aptly imposing and
menacing speech, which really builds her status and character (she is
angry, indignant, proud etc.). Her words also mean that although the
monsters are seen off, there is a much gloomier close than in the Greek
epic, as her prediction is very enigmatic and unsettling (so the Trojans are
terrified by it and pray to the gods not to let it come true).

One final point. Valerius wrote after Virgil and obviously had an eye to
Virgil's account of the Harpies too. Re-read Valerius and see how ingen-
iously and dexterously he utilizes, varies and tops Virgil's passage at the
same time that he is engaging critically and creatively with Apollonius.

6

A Monster-Slayer

For a change, this chapter will focus not so much on monsters themselves as on a slayer of them, looking at the major events in his career and paying close attention to his encounters with monstrous opponents (especially the famous Minotaur). The slayer is Theseus, the most renowned Athenian hero and a very common subject in ancient literature[1] and art.[2] There is an intriguingly mixed tradition in connection with Theseus. Of the numerous stories attached to him some show him in a good light (as a great Athenian and king[3]), while others show him in not such a good one (as an abductor and rapist). And, as we will see, he is treated quite differently by three poets in particular – Bacchylides (who puts him across as a glorious warrior); Catullus (who presents him as dubious and flawed, more of an antihero than a hero); and Ovid (who depicts him as a somewhat negligible character and a figure of fun).

A definition of 'hero' will help sharpen our perception of Theseus. This word comes from the Greek *heros*, which denoted somebody of aristocratic birth (often with a god or goddess as one of the parents) who lived in the mythical period (until shortly after the Trojan War); often the hero was a king or chief, or related to one; and generally heroes exceeded ordinary mortals in certain qualities – handsomeness, prowess of various kinds, and especially strength and courage (for most heroes were warriors). There are standard aspects to the career of a typical hero. His birth and childhood often contain extraordinary elements. He generally faces obstacles and challenges of some sort from an enemy/enemies, and frequently must undergo great labours or depart on a quest. A journey to the Underworld and the fulfilment of a task involving a monster are common. Normally he receives aid from at least one helper, human or divine. There are also rewards for overcoming the obstacles and challenges (like the hand of a beautiful woman, glory, booty or a kingdom).[4]

While fitting into this general pattern, Theseus is rather an interesting kind of hero. Originally he seems to have been not very well known and not particularly important, receiving only short and isolated references in poetry and not appearing all that frequently in art either. But then in the sixth and fifth centuries BC it appears that the people of Athens in general and some of their politicians in particular built him up into their own great Athenian hero, to rival other major names like Odysseus, Perseus and Jason. They did this by adding exploits to his story, by making him into a wise and kindly king, and by associating him closely with Heracles (Hercules), the most famous and respected of all Greek heroes (so Theseus was said to have modelled himself on Heracles, performed six Labours which are reminiscent of the twelve Labours of Heracles, and like him fought against monsters and Amazons). At the end of the process Theseus emerged as someone not without faults certainly but also a splendid warrior and statesman, a memorable representative of Athenian greatness, and the embodiment of their ideals (bravery, justice, altruism, patriotism etc.).[5] Subsequent (non-Athenian) writers did not always agree with this idealized version of Theseus, as we will see shortly.

Theseus' early life and conquests

According to some Theseus' father was Poseidon (the god of the sea himself) and his mother was Aethra, the daughter of the king of Troezen (a Greek town not too far from Athens). According to others Aethra was his mother but his father was Aegeus, king of Athens. Some colourful details are attached to this latter tradition. Aegeus was initially childless, went to Delphi and consulted the oracle of the god Apollo there about children. The oracle gave a typically oracular response (i.e. ambiguous and vague).[6] It told him not to open the projecting foot of the wineskin until he reached Athens again. Aegeus was completely baffled, but the oracle in fact had a twofold reference. First, it meant: don't drink wine. Also (because the wineskin was formed from the skin of a goat with one leg hanging down to form a spout) the projecting foot was a phallic symbol and wine coursing through it when it was opened denoted the emission of semen. So the second meaning of the oracle was: don't have sexual intercourse before getting home (because the son so fathered would eventually be responsible for Aegeus' death, as we will see). Aegeus just did not understand, which is why he disobeyed on both counts. On his way home he stopped at the town of Troezen just across the bay from Athens, where he was entertained by the king. Aegeus got drunk and ended up in bed with the king's daughter. The next day, when he realized what he had done, he told her to bring up any boy who was born without saying who the father was. He also placed a sword and sandals under a great rock and said that when the boy could move the rock he should bring the sword and sandals to Athens as a sign that he was the son of Aegeus.

A son was born (Theseus) and when he was sixteen he moved the rock with ease (rather like Arthur pulling Excalibur from the stone). When Theseus was seven, Heracles had visited and greatly impressed the young boy. When Heracles removed the large lionskin that he wore and put it on the table, all the children in the palace thought it was a real lion; the others ran off in fear, while Theseus seized an axe and attacked it. Theseus admired Heracles above all other heroes and wanted to emulate him, so when it came to going to Athens Theseus refused to take the easy way (going by sea) and opted instead to go overland, even though the road was very dangerous. It was on this journey that he performed his own six 'Labours' and cleared the route of six terrors for travellers (including a monster) very much in the way that Heracles made the world a safer place by destroying similar brigands and monstrous beasts.

First Theseus encountered Periphates (who beat travellers to death with a bronze club) and killed him, taking the club for himself (so that he was armed with a club just like Heracles). Then he came upon another outlaw, a son of Poseidon called Sinis, or the Pine-bender (because he used to pull down and lash to the ground two pines, tie his victim to them and then cut the trees free, so that the victim was torn in half). Theseus tied the Pine-bender to his own pines to dispose of him. Next he killed an enormous and very ferocious sow (the monstrous offspring of the monsters Echidna and Typhos), which had been ravaging the crops and slaughtering men at Cremmyon (near the Isthmus of Corinth). After that came Sciron, who lived on top of a cliff and forced travellers to wash his feet; while they did so he kicked them off the cliff into the sea, where they were devoured by an enormous turtle. When he tried this with Theseus, the hero seized him by the feet and threw *him* to the turtle. His next exploit was to defeat by superior technique Cercyon, a great ox of a man who forced people to wrestle with him and put them to death when he beat them. Finally there was Procrustes, who invited weary travellers to stay in his house and gave them a bed for the night. But they had to fit the bed exactly. If they were too long, he chopped their legs off. If they were too short, he used a hammer (inherited from a certain Polypemon) to hammer out their legs to the right length. Theseus applied his own treatment to Procrustes and destroyed him by making him fit his own bed. So he made the road safe henceforth and then arrived in Athens.

This journey is memorably caught by a Greek author, Bacchylides (who wrote in the fifth century BC), in his poem 18, which describes how an alarm was sounded at Athens on the approach of this great (but unknown and potentially dangerous) warrior, and how Aegeus related to his citizens the report of a herald without realizing that it was in fact his own son's deeds that had been reported to him. The piece glorifies Theseus and his native city, and so was probably composed for performance at an Athenian festival. Bacchylides seizes on one (exciting) moment and employs (vivid and immediate) direct speech, quoting the words of the king and his subjects. By breaking off short of Theseus' actual arrival and recognition he gives the myth an unusual focus (events are viewed rather differently, through the eyes of people ignorant of the hero's identity). There is a lighter aspect too: the reader is initially kept unaware of the real subject (and so should be stirred by emotions similar to those of the speakers), but then at 20ff. realizes that it is Theseus of all people who so affects Aegeus and the other Athenians.

6. A Monster-Slayer

ATHENIANS
'Sovereignlord of sacred Athens,
ruler of refined Athenians,
why was a warlike alarm blared out
by a brazen-belled trumpet just now?
Is some enemy at the   5
head of an army ringing our
country's borders?
Are bloody-minded brigands
forcibly driving off flocks of
sheep and flouting our   10
shepherds? Or does something else rend
your heart? Speak. For I feel that if any
person has valiant young
men to back him up, it
is you, son of Pandion and Creusa.'   15

AEGEUS
'Just now a herald came who had
covered the long Isthmus-road on foot.
He says a mighty man's done in-
describable deeds. He slew brutal
Sinis, that supremely strong   20
mortal, son of earth-shaking
Poseidon (whose sire
is Cronus); he killed the man-
killing sow in Cremmyon's dells
and savage Sciron;   25
he closed Cercyon's wrestling-school
also, and Procrustes dropped the mighty
hammer of Polypemon
when he encountered his
better. I'm afraid of where all this will end.'   30

ATHENIANS
'But who does he say this man is,
where's he from, and how is he equipped?
Does he lead a great army in
warlike array, or journey just with
attendants, like a traveller   35
roaming to a foreignland,
this one who's so
strong, valiant and bold, who quelled
the powerful might of so many?
Surely a god speeds   40
him, that he may bring the unjust
to justice. For it's not easy for one
who's always in action not

73

to encounter trouble.
All things find their end in the long course of time.'   45

AEGEUS
'He says that just two persons are with
him and he has, slung from his shining
shoulders a sword ...
and two polished javelins in his hands,
a well-crafted Laconian   50
helmet on his flamehaired head, a
purple tunic
around his chest, and a woolly
Thessalian cloak as well; from
his eyes a crimson   55
Lemnian fire flashes forth; a
lad in the prime of youth, he's intent on
Ares' amusements – war
and bronze-clanging battle;
and he is seeking splendour-loving Athens.'   60

The glorification of Theseus here is extensive. It begins openly in line 18, but before that at 1ff. all the consternation caused by just one person enhances his standing too. At 18-19 a short, snappy sentence is dominated by praise of Theseus, and then at 19ff. comes the roll-call of his achievements in a long sentence which has real cumulative impact (as deed after deed is tacked on) and builds up his opponents (and consequently his triumph over them) by means of various details. The awe and fear at 31ff. (especially 37ff. and 40ff.) further increase his status. Lines 46ff. represent a striking and colourful climax which draws still more attention to Theseus, representing him as a warrior with the blond hair of gods and heroes and with the purple of gods and royalty, as a suitably splendid character for splendour-loving Athens, and as a dazzling figure of brightness and fire (the light of salvation, and also the imposing, powerful and deadly flames of the volcano on the island of Lemnos near Troy).

When this as yet unknown hero entered Athens, he gave further proof of his might. Wearing a long tunic, and with neatly plaited hair, he was looking around a temple whose roof was still being completed, when the workmen up above mockingly asked what a virgin was doing wandering round by herself. His answer was to unyoke the oxen from a nearby cart and throw them up higher than the temple roof. But Aegeus was still unaware that this was his son. However, Aegeus' wife Medea (a powerful witch from the east) knew who he was, saw him as a threat and tried to eliminate him. She persuaded Aegeus that the stranger was an enemy and got him to put on a banquet for the young man and give him in a drink a poison that had a monster connection (it derived from the foam dripped by the three-headed dog Cerberus when it was carried off from the Under-

Heracles and Cerberus, from a black-figure hydria from Caere, 530 BC.
On the left the king Eurystheus has taken refuge from the monster
in a large jar. Louvre, Paris.

world by Heracles as one of his Labours). The Latin poet Ovid (writing
round about the time of the birth of Christ) provides the following account
of this very close call for Theseus at *Metamorphoses* 7.406ff.

> Medea prepared a deadly drink containing aconite,
> which she had brought with her long ago from Scythia.
> They say that this poison came from the fangs of Echidna's
> Cerberus. There is a dark cavern with a gloomy, gaping
> mouth and a down-sloping path, along which Hercules   410
> dragged off Cerberus in chains of adamant.
> It struggled and twisted its head away from the
> daylight and bright sunbeams, and, mad with rage,
> it filled the air with simultaneous triple howls
> and spattered the green fields with white foam.   415
> Men think those flecks congealed, drew nourishment from
> the fertile, rich soil and acquired the power to harm.
> Because they grow and thrive on hard rock people in
> the country call them aconite. Tricked by Medea,
> Aegeus offered this poison to his own son as if to an enemy.   420
> Theseus had accepted the drink given to him unwittingly
> when Aegeus recognized the family crest on his son's
> sword-hilt and struck the goblet from his lips.

Wisely Medea made herself scarce at once, concealed in dark clouds
summoned by her spells. It was at about this time that Theseus had

another encounter with a monster – a huge, fire-breathing bull which was ravaging the plain of Marathon (near Athens), and which was identified by some with the wild bull of Crete brought to mainland Greece by Heracles as one of his Labours. In his combat with this beast Theseus literally took the bull by the horns. Showing supreme strength, he seized a horn in one hand, gripped its nostrils in the other hand and forced it down to the ground. Having mastered the creature in this way, he put it on a rope and led it to Athens, where Aegeus sacrificed it to Apollo. All of this was preparation for an even more monstrous bull and Theseus' most famous exploit.

The Minotaur

Theseus now resolved to save his city from a terrible tribute which it had to pay to Minos, king of Crete. To atone for the death of Minos' son (Androgeos) at Athens, every ninth year the Athenians had to send seven young men and seven young girls to the island of Crete. There they were put inside the Labyrinth, an inextricable maze inhabited by the Minotaur, a savage monster which was half man and half bull, and which devoured them.[7] To put an end to all this, Theseus decided to kill the Minotaur, and so he now volunteered to form part of the tribute and sailed off from the Piraeus (Athens' harbour) to Crete with the rest of the young Athenians. When he arrived there, king Minos' beautiful young daughter (Ariadne) fell deeply in love with him. She helped him, giving him a ball of thread to let out behind him, so that he could find his way back out of the Labyrinth, and in some versions also giving him a sword to use on the Minotaur. Theseus entered the maze, encountered the creature and killed it. He then retraced his steps, using the thread, and sailed off, taking Ariadne with him. According to the Latin poet Catullus (first century BC) Theseus was not so impressive on the way home. During that journey the hero and the princess spent the night together on an island (Dia), where Theseus callously abandoned her and she subsequently cursed him for leaving her (before the god Bacchus turned up and claimed her as his bride). As punishment for forgetting Ariadne Jupiter made Theseus forget to change the sail on his ship. Aegeus had been deeply despondent and fearful about Theseus' journey and so had sent him off on a ship with a sombre black sail, which was to be changed to a joyful white one if Theseus was victorious. The change was not made, and when Aegeus, anxiously scanning the sea from a high point at Athens, caught sight of the ship in the distance returning with a black sail, he imagined that his son had been killed and in great grief flung himself to his death. So Theseus arrived back at Athens to find his father dead.

Bacchylides takes a very positive attitude to Theseus in connection with this episode. In his poem 17 he tells how on the voyage out to Crete Minos laid lustful hands on one of the Athenian girls and, when she complained

to him, Theseus boldly warned the king off, pointing out that Minos might
be a son of Zeus but he himself was a son of Poseidon. Minos angrily asked
Zeus for a sign of his connection to him and challenged the hero to prove
his descent from Poseidon by fetching a gold ring which he then threw into
the sea (Poseidon's domain). Zeus thundered in support of Minos' claim
that he was his father, and the king repeated his challenge to Theseus to
prove his parentage. When the young man bravely dived in, joining the
daughters of Nereus (sea-nymphs) beneath the waves, Minos tried to sail
on and leave him to his death. But something extraordinary happened.

<pre>
          Theseus' spirit
    did not flinch. He stood on the well-built
    stern and leapt; and the
    sacred precinct of the sea
    gave him a kindly welcome.   85
    Minos, son of Zeus, was amazed,
    and ordered the helmsman to keep
    the ornate ship before the wind.
    But Fate provided a different course.
    The swift-scudding ship raced along, sped   90
    on by a northerly wind blowing astern.
    All the young Athenians were
    frightened when the hero
    sprang into the waves, and they
    shed tears from their bright   95
    eyes in expectation of a dreadful doom.
    But dolphins of the sea quickly
    carried mighty Theseus to
    the home of his father (the god of
    horses), and he arrived at the   100
    divine palace. There he looked with
    awe on blessed Nereus'
    glorious daughters, for their splendid
    bodies glittered with a radiance
    like fire, and gold-braided ribbons   105
    were twirling about their
    hair, as they danced
    delightedly on flowing feet.
    In that lovely house he saw
    his father's dear wife –   110
    august, ox-eyed Amphitrite.
    She threw a purple cloak around him
    and put on his thick hair
    the exquisite, rose-dark garland
    which artful Aphrodite had   115
    given her at her wedding.
    Nothing that the gods wish is
    past belief for sane men.
</pre>

Theseus appeared beside the slim-sterned ship.
Ha, he put an end to Minos'   120
confident assumptions, when he
came from the sea unwetted,
a marvel to them all, with the
gods' gifts glittering on him.

This incident (mentioned first by Bacchylides) represents a substantial addition to the Cretan expedition and invests Theseus with splendour and marvel. Complementing the depiction of him earlier in the poem as a defender of the Athenian girl's chastity and a proud and confident champion of law and order (rather than a lawless abductor of females), the lines above showcase his courage and adventurousness, highlight his contact with various divinities, and put real stress on the colourful, the brilliant and the miraculous. Theseus never does bring back the gold ring, but contemptuously ignores that and returns instead with two, much more impressive, items to top Minos' ring. There is also clever foreshadowing here, presaging the glorious achievement on Crete. Minos loses his ring here, as he will later lose the Minotaur and Ariadne. Theseus escapes death and wins a victory at sea, as he will do subsequently on land. The helpers and kindly welcome by females at 97ff. prefigure the assistance he will receive from Ariadne, and the garland given by Aphrodite (goddess of love) at 114ff. looks forward to Ariadne's love for the hero.

Catullus had a rather different attitude to Theseus. The Latin poet's depiction of him is more complex and critical. He concentrates on the female (Ariadne) rather than the male, and he puts the stress on pathos rather than glory, undercutting and souring Theseus' triumph over the Minotaur.

Catullus' poem 64 is a short epic which contains two stories. The outer one (at the beginning and end of the poem) relates the love and marriage of the Greek hero Peleus and the sea-nymph Thetis, parents of Achilles (the best of the Greek warriors who fought at Troy). Early in the piece Catullus tells how Peleus and Thetis originally met and fell in love, and goes on to describe the human wedding guests arriving at Peleus' palace, next the magnificent palace itself, and then the marriage-bed. On this bed is a coverlet, and on the coverlet is depicted Ariadne being abandoned by Theseus and elsewhere the god Bacchus and his followers (about to take her as his bride). This gives Catullus his chance to present the inner story (that of Ariadne and Theseus), which occupies about half the poem and is broken up into separate episodes, with flashback (to events before the abandonment) and flashforward (to Aegeus later killing himself when he sees the ship returning with the black sail). Finally Catullus says that such were the figures embroidered on the coverlet of the marriage-bed of Peleus and Thetis, and then he moves back to the outer story, describing the departure of the human guests and the arrival of the divine guests and a wedding song performed by the Fates on that day.

6. A Monster-Slayer

Poem 64 is a bold and stimulating variant on epic, and in it Catullus does something novel and interesting with the by then old tale of Theseus and the Minotaur. He combines it with another story rather intricately, achieving various correspondences (e.g. in each case there is a male and female protagonist linked by love) and contrasts (e.g. the happy love and marriage of Peleus and Thetis is opposed to the unhappy love and affair of Theseus and Ariadne). He effectively alters the chronological order of events in his narrative. He adds new details and new twists. There is much vivid description. He plays up very much the emotional aspects of the myth and, to heighten the impact, lets his own feelings come through (in the form of exclamations, addresses to characters in the story, etc.). His focus is not on the hero and fighting (as it would be in standard epic) but on the heroine and love. And he shows no uncritical acceptance of the code and conduct of the ancient heroes, but is questioning and presents a more realistic and thoughtful picture (e.g. underscoring Theseus' shabby treatment of Ariadne and her consequent anguish and lamentations).

There were various explanations of what actually happened on the island of Dia.[8] Catullus opts for one that shows the hero in a very poor light. He opens his inner story as Ariadne awakes to see Theseus leaving, and quickly creates contempt for him and great sympathy for the young princess.

> This coverlet, embroidered with the figures of mortals of old,   50
> with wonderful skill depicted the brave deeds of heroes.
> For there, looking out from the wave-sounding shore of Dia,
> Ariadne with the wild frenzy of love in her heart,
> gazes at Theseus sailing away on his swift ship;
> and even now she does not believe what is before her eyes,   55
> naturally, as she has only just woken from treacherous sleep
> and sees herself abandoned, miserable, on the lonely shore.
> With no thought for her Theseus flees, oars beating the waves,
> leaving behind his empty promises for the gale to dissipate.
> From afar, from the seaweed-line, the princess, like a marble   60
> statue of a bacchante, stares at him, ah, stares at him with
> sad eyes and is tossed on great waves of anguished emotions.
> She has lost the delicate headband from her blonde hair
> and the light dress that covered her chest
> and the smooth band that bound her milk-white breasts –   65
> all these garments have fallen from her and the
> waves are playing with them at her feet.
> But at that moment she did not care about her floating
> dress and headband, but, ruined, she was hanging on you,
> Theseus, with all her mind, all her heart, all her soul.   70
> Ah, the poor girl, driven mad with constant grief by Venus,
> who sowed thorny cares in her breast,
> from the time when fierce Theseus,
> after leaving the winding shores of the Piraeus,
> reached the Cretan palace of unjust Minos.   75

This is a powerful piece of writing, the most moving passage in the whole poem. As Catullus makes the transition to the inner story at 50f., he shows his critical stance at once: there is irony and mock-solemnity in 'brave deeds', since what immediately follows (Theseus' desertion of his helper) is far from brave. At 52 he chooses to begin his narrative at a late stage, at what is in fact the most moving point in the whole tale (which also allows him to employ the lively device of the flashback). The vivid adjective 'wave-sounding' in 52 brings out the menace of the sea and the vulnerability of the heroine (on a tiny island in the midst of the vast expanse of water). In 53 Catullus stresses her great passion for her man to contrast her genuine (and rejected) love with his callousness. The poet also stirs sympathy for her at 55-7, where she has just woken up (and so is confused and helpless) and can't believe her lover would do such a thing to her, and there is great emphasis in the close grouping of 'abandoned', 'miserable' and 'lonely' (like a series of hammer blows).

The focus so far has been very much on Ariadne. Theseus figured briefly in 54 and does so again at 58-9. The brevity is deliberate. It is a contemptuous brevity – somebody like that does not deserve more than the curtest mention, just enough to make the situation and his cruelty clear (note how quickly he flees, and how he has broken his word to his great benefactress).

At 60-2 we are back with the princess and pathos. The word 'stares' is repeated for emphasis (a futile action, but all she can do now). The poet himself intrudes with that exclamation 'ah' (showing his own pity for her and encouraging thereby a similar response in his readers). The seaweed-line is a small but considered detail, implying that she has wandered down there (from the point higher up the beach where she will have slept) in a daze, trying to see the ship better and/or get closer to Theseus. The dense simile suggests that like a statue she is silent, unmoving, impervious to the gale and has a fixed stare. She is likened to a statue of a bacchante in particular (one of the female followers of Bacchus who were renowned for their wild emotions and disordered clothing during their ecstatic worship of the god). Ariadne fits with those aspects clearly enough; and, more subtly, Bacchus will eventually come on the scene here, and like a bacchante Ariadne will be devoted to and protected by this divinity (as his wife). The force of the simile is reinforced by a metaphor in 62 (whose watery nature is very apt for this context), intimating that she was in a turmoil, tossed helplessly to and fro by wave after wave of powerful emotion.

An involuntary strip follows at 62ff. This is realistic enough: she will have loosened her clothing for sleep and for sex; the garments are flimsy, and there is a gale blowing. The effect is to make her appear pitifully vulnerable. We are reminded of her royalty (the expensive fine clothes) and beauty (blonde hair and white skin were regarded as attractive) to make us feel still more for her. And we can easily deduce that this modest young girl does nothing to cover her nakedness because she is stunned and totally focused on the ship leaving with her beloved Theseus.

That deduction is confirmed at 68-70. There 'ruined' economically conveys that she is deeply affected by love, and broken by misfortune, and as good as dead. Then the graphic 'hanging' implies that she is dependent on Theseus, and gazing intently at him, and leaning forward, almost joined to him by a rope (or thread). Again Catullus shows his own involvement by means of that reproachful address to Theseus. And there is tremendous stress in the threefold 'all her mind, all her heart, all her soul'.

At 71ff. the poignancy continues initially, with the exclamation ('Ah, the poor girl') and the stress on Ariadne's suffering (especially in the very painful image of the goddess of love digging and planting thorny cares in 72). But then the emotional pitch is wound down (by means of the rather dry and factual tone, and the distancing erudition at 74f.), providing a diminuendo close to this passage. This allows readers to relax a little before the poet goes on to screw up their emotions all over again later on in the poem (the temporary relief ensures that the sentimental appeal is not overdone so as to lose its effectiveness).

The lines that immediately follow the passage we have just been looking at present a flashback, clarifying the background to Ariadne on the beach. Initially Catullus explains how the tribute came to be imposed on Athens (Minos held the citizens responsible for his son Androgeos' death there and besieged Athens, and the Athenians had to surrender when plague broke out in their city). Then comes Theseus' trip to Crete, Ariadne's infatuation, and his combat with the Minotaur. Ask yourself how and why her love is played up and his fight is played down.

> They say that once, forced by a savage plague
> to pay for the death of Androgeos,
> Athens used to send as food for the Minotaur
> selected young men and the flower of the girls.
> The small city was really hurt by this terrible punishment,   80
> so Theseus decided to risk his own person for his
> beloved Athens rather than watch such living dead
> be carried across the sea from Athens to Crete.
> And so, sped on his swift ship by gentle winds,
> he came to the proud palace of great-hearted Minos.   85
> Ariadne was being brought up in her mother's soft embrace,
> still a virgin, her chaste bed perfumed by a lovely fragrance,
> like that of the myrtles that grow by the river Eurotas
> or the many-coloured flowers drawn out by the spring breeze,
> but from the moment that her gaze rested on Theseus   90
> she could not turn her longing, burning eyes away
> from him, the flame spread through her whole body and
> she blazed up with love, absolutely on fire, deep down.
> Ah Cupid, who cruelly stirs up madness in mortals,
> recklessly mixing pleasure with pain,   95
> and you, Venus, queen of Golgi and leafy Idalium,
> on what waves did you toss that girl, inflamed with love

Theseus and the Minotaur, from an Attic red-figure cup by the Dokimasia
Painter, 480 BC. Archaeological Museum, Florence.

and sighing again and again for the gold-haired stranger!
What fear she felt in her fainting heart, how often
did she grow paler than the gleam of gold, when   100
Theseus, eager to fight the savage, monstrous Minotaur,
made his way to death or glory as his reward!
But the gifts she promised the gods found favour with them
and her silent vows to them were not made in vain.
For just as a wild storm with its branch-shaking,   105
trunk-wrenching winds tears up an oak or a cone-bearing
pine with sweating bark on the top of mount Taurus,
and ripped up by its roots the tree falls flat its full length,
smashing everything in its path far and wide as it topples,
so Theseus overcame the massive monster and laid it low,   110
as it uselessly gored the air with its horns.

Then he retraced his steps, unharmed and covered in glory,
finding his winding way by means of a fine thread,
so that as he came out from the meandering labyrinth
its inextricable maze did not baffle him.   115

There is initially a favourable picture of Theseus' patriotism and bravery,
but that is soon undercut at 86ff., as the focus shifts from him to the
princess and the love that he exploited and then rejected. Touchingly she
is depicted as totally vulnerable (an inexperienced young girl) and the
helpless victim of two mighty deities, while her passion is instantaneous
and extremely powerful (brought out by a great accumulation of details
and images). She faces a pair of opponents greater than Theseus' lone
adversary, and Catullus here has much more to say about her anxiety and
fear, so that it seems that she suffers more than the man. The help that
she gave in the prayers at 103f. is clearly very important (note 'For' in 105),
as is the assistance mentioned at 112-15; and by means of this sandwich-
ing technique her aid appears on either side of the combat (105-11),
playing it down and so diminishing Theseus. Catullus does not directly
describe the fight and he passes over it quite quickly, devoting only a small
part of the inner story to it, and not allowing the hero to take centre-stage
even in this climactic encounter. Although the simile at 105ff. does imply
a lot (about the Minotaur's massiveness, Theseus' violence, etc.), it does
merely imply, so that we cannot form a precise picture of the struggle itself
and the hero's actions in his moment of triumph. So too lines 105-9 put the
emphasis on the tree (Minotaur) rather than the wind (Theseus), and the
monster also dominates 110f.

On top of this, Catullus goes straight on at 116ff. to bring out all that
the girl sacrificed and the pain that she caused her family by leaving Crete.
He then moves on to her very lengthy complaints on Dia (about how
treacherous and callous Theseus is in deserting her, how dangerous her
own situation now is, and so on). And later he describes Theseus' punishment – the suicide of Aegeus (because of his great grief over the supposed
loss of his dearly beloved son), so that this whole Cretan expedition ends
for Theseus with retribution, death and grief rather than rejoicing. In all
of these ways the Latin poet presents a darker version of our hero and
problematizes and undermines his celebrated defeat of the monster.

The chronology of Theseus' other adventures is confused, and there are
simply too many of them for them all to be covered here. He took over from
Aegeus as king and was depicted as an excellent ruler who engaged in very
important political activities. He is said to have united the scattered local
villages into one state with Athens as its capital, and to have set up
essential government bodies and institutions, laying the foundations for
democracy (and according to some actually abdicating so that democracy
could be established). He is also reputed to have introduced several
religious festivals, to have ensured equal rights for all (rich and poor

alike), and to have been a champion of justice and a friend and defender of various people in distress.

But again there is a negative tradition of less admirable actions, especially in connection with females. Theseus had a close encounter with the women warriors known as Amazons. When they welcomed him to their land, sending one of their number (Antiope) with presents, he invited her on board his ship and then promptly sailed off with her. An army of Amazons attacked Athens to get her back and was victorious at first, before being finally defeated. (Theseus fathered a son on Antiope called Hippolytus and was later misled into cursing his son and causing his death, when Poseidon in answer to Theseus' prayer sent from the sea a monstrous bull to terrify Hippolytus' team of horses, which threw him from his chariot so that he was horribly mangled, as is related in Euripides' tragedy *Hippolytus*.)

Then there was Helen of Troy, the most beautiful woman in the world. Before she reached marriageable age, when she was twelve, she was abducted by Theseus and his friend Pirithous. In some versions Theseus was fifty years old at the time, and raped Helen, who gave birth to a daughter. He was forced to return her to her big brothers when they invaded Athenian territory.

Theseus was also involved with Pirithous in an even more misguided kidnapping scheme. The pair wanted to carry off the goddess Persephone (queen of the Underworld). When they arrived in the land of the dead, they were welcomed by her wily husband, Hades, who invited them to join him in a banquet. But when they sat down, they became fixed to their thrones and could not escape by their own efforts. Heracles later freed Theseus by tearing him from his chair, but as he pulled him away part of his buttocks remained stuck to the seat. One account claimed that this was why the Athenians (as Theseus' descendants) had small bottoms, which they inherited from their ancient king.

Whether because of this negative tradition or because he had a natural tendency to subvert anything and anyone with some sort of name or elevated status, the Latin poet Ovid did not have much time for Theseus. Catullus in particular may have influenced his attitude, but Ovid goes in for a rather different treatment and quite dissimilar techniques. We will turn now to Ovid's poem *Metamorphoses* for two final adventures involving monsters.

The Calydonian boar

In his version of the Calydonian boar hunt at *Metamorphoses* 8.267ff. Ovid mocks Theseus rather than criticizing him and aims at humour rather than pathos. He tells how the Greek city of Calydon turned for help to the renowned fighter Theseus when its king failed to make offerings to the goddess Diana and by way of punishment she sent a dreadful boar to ravage Calydon's crops and cattle. Ovid's dramatic description of the boar at 8.281ff. makes it into a truly epic opponent: it is as big as a bull; its eyes glow with blood and fire; its tusks are as long as an elephant's; lightning flashes from its mouth, and its breath sets foliage on fire. Next we are told of the havoc that it wreaked and the terror it inspired. Then we are informed of all the heroes (including Theseus) and the great huntress Atalanta who gathered to destroy it under the leadership of Meleager, with a long roll call of famous names, and adjectives and short phrases added to bring out their fighting qualities. At 8.329ff. anticipation is raised as the hunters come to the wood where the boar has its lair, keen to close with it, and the creature charges out, scattering their dogs. In this way we are led to expect a major contest. But in fact what follows is a parody of a combat with a monster and a mock-heroic comedy of errors, which gets funnier and funnier the longer it goes on.

Echion throws his javelin first and manages to hit a tree instead of the boar. Then Jason throws, but Diana pulls the spear's head off in mid-flight, so that only the wooden shaft hits the beast. This just enrages it further, making it charge and kill several men. It nearly gets Nestor, but he uses his javelin to pole-vault up a tree to safety! The conspicuous demigods Castor and Pollux come riding up and both of them hurl their weapons, and would have hit the boar, but it takes refuge in dense woods where hunting-spear and horse cannot follow. Telamon does follow, on foot, but he is so careless and eager that he trips on a projecting root and falls flat on his face. At 8.380ff. at last the monster is hit, by an arrow which grazes its back and lodges under its ear. But the archer is a woman (Atalanta), and the men are ashamed at her success and Meleager's promise to her of a reward for her manly deed. So the heroes spur each other on and hurl their javelins, but throw so many at once that they get in each other's way and clash together harmlessly. Then Ancaeus boasts that he will show them how a man's weapons surpass a girl's and he will kill the creature even if Diana herself shields it. He goes to give it a powerful downward blow with his two-edged axe, but as he lifts the axe on high the boar gets in first and gores him in the groin. Ancaeus' entrails come pouring out amid streams of blood.

At this point (8.403ff.) Theseus' friend Pirithous advances on the beast, and Theseus puts in his appearance.

> Ixion's son, Pirithous, was advancing to face the enemy,
> brandishing a hunting-spear in his strong right hand.
> Theseus said: 'Stop, keep away from it, my friend, dearer to me   405
> than myself, my soul's other half! We can be brave from
> a distance. Ancaeus' rash courage did him no good.'
> So saying, he hurled his heavy javelin with its bronze point.
> It was well aimed and on its way to hit its target,
> but a leafy branch of an oak tree got in the way.   410

Initially Pirithous is being courageous, advancing to close quarters, but the mighty warrior Theseus holds him back! Our hero seems rather maternal towards his friend (his words are quite flowery too) and decidedly cautious, rather than dashing. He is protecting Pirithous, and also himself. Obviously he has been daunted by the disembowelling of Ancaeus. He tries to put a good face on this at 406f., but we see there a quaint concept of bravery, and Theseus looks wimpy next to Ancaeus and Pirithous and (in the following lines) Meleager, who all appear next to him in the immediate vicinity. Comically all his caution achieves nothing and he bungles his shot (surely it is a basic and obvious point of technique to avoid obstacles like branches when aiming at such a target).

Next Jason tries again, but his aim is even worse, and instead of the boar he hits a hunting-dog in the flank, pinning it to the ground. Finally Meleager (after missing with his first spear) gets the monster in the back with a second missile, provokes it to charge him and, when it does, drives a javelin into its advancing shoulder. Everybody is delighted, until Meleager gives his beloved Atalanta the spoils (for hitting it first). All the rest begrudge this and grumble; and in fact two uncles of Meleager seize the spoils from Atalanta, so Meleager kills them (only to be murdered himself later by his own mother in revenge for the death of her two brothers). Theseus is to be included among the begrudging grumblers, and he looks even more feeble beside the triumphant Meleager and the (to him) mere woman Atalanta. His role in this episode is late, minor and inglorious (as just one of a bunch of incompetents).

Theseus and the Centaurs

Ovid again depicts Theseus as rather negligible and again works in some humour in his account of another mass combat at *Metamorphoses* 12.210-535. There he tells of the wedding of Pirithous and Hippodame, to which Pirithous invited Theseus and other heroes and also the Centaurs (wild creatures which were half man and half horse). One of the Centaurs (Eurytus), inflamed by wine and lust, seized the bride, and the rest of the monsters grabbed other women. An enormous fight broke out between the Centaurs and the other guests. In Ovid's version this is not any sort of heroic battle but a drunken brawl (with wine-cups, trees and so on plied in place of real weapons). It is also a sensational and appalling bloodbath, darkly comic because the poet deliberately goes over the top and piles on awful detail after detail, demonstrating macabre ingenuity in ringing the changes on deaths (especially grotesque deaths) in the course of such a lengthy narrative.

This time Theseus figures quite early on, reacting to the seizure of the bride, according to the narrator (the hero Nestor, who was a guest there).

86

We all jumped up quickly,
and Theseus was the first to speak: 'Eurytus, what
madness drives you, while I'm still alive, to attack
Pirithous, ignorantly injuring two men in one?'
Eurytus didn't reply (he couldn't defend such actions
with words), but went for the bride's champion,
pounding his face and noble chest with his fists.
There happened to be a big, antique mixing-bowl nearby,   235
encrusted with figures in relief. Theseus was bigger;
he picked it up and threw it right in his face.
Spouting out brains, wine and gouts of blood from the
wound and his mouth, Eurytus fell on his back and drummed
his heels on the sodden ground.   240

Theseus does take the lead and make the initial response, but (apart from the fact that he seems to be rather usurping Pirithous' role!) amusingly all he actually achieves is to start the brawl, setting the precedent for hurling things at hand and sparking off vengeful violence in the Centaurs.[9] It might also strike some as rather unsporting of this big, noble hero (see lines 234 and 236) to respond to blows with fists not by punching back but by resorting to a huge bowl as a missile. As the fight for which he was responsible starts up in line 240, Theseus promptly drops out of the narrative, for over a hundred lines, not playing the major part that one has here (teasingly) been led to expect him to play. He does kill his opponent, but much more horrific and memorable violence immediately ensues, diminishing this brief victory of our hero. So, with similar assaults on the face that clearly undercut that of Theseus, at 245ff. Amycus hits Celadon in the face with a chandelier, crushing his features beyond recognition, making the eyes leap from their sockets, and driving his nose into the middle of his throat; and Exadius shoves a stag's antlers into the face of Gryneus, gouging out his eyeballs (one of which sticks to an antler, while the other rolls down on to his beard and hangs there in a mass of clotted blood); and Rhoetus smashes Charaxus in the face with a blazing torch, setting his hair on fire and making the blood in his wound sizzle, and then plunges the torch through the open mouth of Euagrus down into his chest.

Eventually, at 341ff., Theseus reappears, as Aphareus tries to avenge a friend who, while fleeing an enemy, has just fallen headlong down a precipice and impaled himself on an ash tree. How well does Theseus come out of the fighting this time?

Aphareus is there for revenge and tries to hurl a rock ripped
from the mountainside. But, even as he tries, Theseus
catches him first with his club of oak and shatters the
great bones in his elbow. He doesn't care or have the time to
finish off that useless body, but leaps on to tall Bienor's   345

back (which had never before carried another person).
He presses his knees into Bienor's ribs, grips his hair with
his left hand, and with his knotty club smashes his face,
his hard temples and his mouth as it shouts out threats.
With his club he also fells Nedymnus and the spearman   350
Lycopes and Hippasos, whose chest is covered by his long
beard, and Rhipheus, who is taller than the tree-tops,
and Thereus, who used to catch bears on the Thessalian
mountains and carry them home alive and struggling.
Demoleon can't stand Theseus' success in the fighting   355
any longer. With a massive effort he tries to rip up
an old pine with a sturdy trunk. He can't manage it,
so breaks off part of the tree and throws that at his enemy.
Theseus withdraws, well out of the way of the incoming
weapon, at Pallas' prompting (or so he would have us believe). 360

Theseus does win a series of victories here. But he catches Aphareus off guard (while focused on another adversary) and jumps Bienor from behind; and the handling of the successes at 350ff. seems somewhat perfunctory, while Nedymnus, Lycopes and Hippasus are not built up at all as opponents. When Demoleon throws the piece of tree at him, Theseus withdraws, getting well out of the way; and that is our last picture of him in this fight – retreating. And doubt is cast on his claim in 360 that this was done at the prompting of Pallas. There seems to be a playful twist as well: Theseus being missed by the spear-like tree may well look back to the Calydonian boar hunt, where his own spear missed the animal but hit the branch of a tree. So too, right after the above passage, at 361ff. when the missile meant for Theseus seriously wounds a companion instead, it is Peleus (not the intended victim) who responds, bravely grappling with the fierce Centaur and finally killing him. In subsequent lines there is more remarkable fighting, to lessen the impact of Theseus' efforts here (e.g. one Centaur raises his right hand to protect his face from a spear only for the hand to be pinned to his forehead, while another one is struck in the belly and leaps forward, trailing his entrails on the ground, tripping over them and bursting them underfoot). By the time we reach the end of the account we see that Theseus, despite being a celebrated warrior and Pirithous' great friend, appears only twice and only occupies 30 lines (less than a tenth of the whole narrative). In fact he drops out entirely for almost 200 lines at the end, and the character who gets the textual prominence (at 459-533) is Caeneus, who suffers an extraordinary death (smothered under a huge mass of trees thrown at him, unlike the wary and evasive Theseus), which so enrages the heroes that they make a final concerted effort and finish off the Centaurs.

6. A Monster-Slayer

Theseus' end

It remains to finish off Theseus. Late in his life political infighting broke out at Athens, he was outnumbered by his enemies and went into exile. He went to the island of Scyros, where he fell to his death or was pushed by the king from high cliffs. But that is not quite the end of the story. Theseus also figures in the historical period. In 490 BC at the battle of Marathon the Athenians (led by Miltiades) won a surprising victory against a much larger Persian army, and many of them maintained that they had seen an apparition of Theseus, clad in full armour and charging ahead of them against the enemy. Years later the oracle of Apollo told the Athenians to bring home the bones of Theseus and give them honourable burial in Athens. Cimon (the son of Miltiades) claimed that he carried out the oracle's command, much to his own credit. He conquered Scyros, and said that there he saw an eagle perched on a mound of earth, pecking it with its beak and tearing at it with its talons, which made him think that he should dig there. When he did, he found a coffin containing the skeleton of a huge man, and beside it a bronze spear and sword. He concluded that these were the bones of Theseus and took them back to Athens (in 473 BC), where they were received with great rejoicing and buried in the heart of the city. The tomb became a sanctuary for runaway slaves and all those who were poor, downtrodden and intimidated by those stronger than them, because throughout his life Theseus had always championed such people.[10]

There is one final passage from Ovid (*Art of Love* 1.527ff.) that is worth looking at. In it he depicts Ariadne (from Cnossos, on Crete) on the beach at Dia as Theseus sails away, and the arrival of Bacchus and his retinue of worshippers and lesser gods, and his superb wedding gift (placing Ariadne wearing her crown in the sky as a splendid constellation). Examine how Ovid (mindful of the happy ending) initially teases readers about his attitude to Ariadne, using reminiscences of Catullus 64.52ff. (quoted above) to reinforce the idea that he is sad and sympathetic; then drops some hints that he may not be so serious after all (at 533-5); and finally allows the levity to surface fully at 537f., and gaiety and humour to dominate the rest of his account, all the way down to his picture at the end of the god Bacchus as a fast worker and smooth operator.

> The girl from Cnossos was wandering, distraught, on unknown
>   sands where tiny Dia is pounded by the sea's waves.
> Just as she was, straight from sleep, dressed in a loosened
>   tunic, barefoot, her yellow hair unbound, 530
> she kept on shouting 'Cruel Theseus!' to the deaf waves, as an
>   undeserved downpour of tears drenched her tender cheeks.
> She kept on shouting and weeping, but both suited her;
>   she was not made less attractive by her tears.

Beating her breasts (which were extremely soft), she said: 535
  'That traitor has gone away – what will happen to me?'
As she said, 'What will happen to me?' cymbals sounded along
  the whole shore and tambourines struck by frenzied hands.
She fainted from fear, breaking off what she had just been
  saying; the blood drained from her swooning body.   540
Look – bacchantes, their hair tossed on to their necks;
  look – lively Satyrs, the band that precedes the god;
look – drunken old Silenus only just keeps his seat on a sagging
  ass and skilfully grips and holds on to its mane.
While he pursued the bacchantes (running away and towards   545
  him), while the poor rider urged on his mount with a stick,
he slipped from the long-eared ass and fell on his head;
  the Satyrs shouted, 'Come on, dad, get up, get up!'
Now in his chariot canopied with grape-clusters the god
  loosely held the golden reins over his team of tigers.   550
Ariadne went pale, forgot Theseus and lost her voice;
  three times she tried to flee and was restrained by fear.
She trembled, like barren corn-ears stirred by the wind,
  as a light reed shivers in a watery marsh.
To her the god said, 'Here I am – a more faithful lover.   555
  Don't be afraid. You'll be Mrs Bacchus from Cnossos.
Have the sky for your gift: there you'll be gazed at as a star;
  you will often guide ships in doubt, as the Cretan Crown.'
So saying, in case she was scared of the tigers, he jumped down
  from the chariot (the sand gave way under his foot).   560
Enfolded in his arms (not strong enough to fight), she was
  carried off – gods can manage all kinds of things.
Some sing the wedding song, some shout Bacchic cries,
  as the god and bride come together in the sacred bed.

A Good Monster:
Chiron

The vast majority of monsters are depicted as being bad, and the bad ones tend to be the most memorable and to have the most impact. But not all monsters were bad, and some of the good ones are also of interest. For example, there was the winged horse Pegasus, which we met in the last chapter, and the Hecatoncheires, three giants who had one hundred hands and fifty heads each and who helped Zeus defeat the powerful ancient gods called Titans by hurling three hundred rocks at a time at them. And not all of the Cyclopes were as savage as Polyphemus and his fellows (on whom see Chapter12). Another group of Cyclopes were famous wall-builders and assisted heroes in fortifying Greek cities such as Tiryns and Argos, while yet others made thunderbolts for Zeus and weapons for the other gods (one of these, named Brontes, sat the infant goddess Artemis on his knee when she visited, and she pulled out some hair from his chest with impunity, and boldly asked these Cyclopes to make her a bow, arrows and a quiver, which they did at once[1]). This chapter will look at another good monster (Chiron) and the different ways in which he was utilized by poets in four major appearances. It should change some preconceived notions and prejudices in connection with monsters.

Chiron was one of the Centaurs. Part human and part horse in form, they belonged originally to the mountains and forests of northern Greece (the fringes of civilization). In most of them the brutal element outweighed the human and they were filled with unbridled animal passions, ate raw flesh and were wild, lustful, violent and very partial to wine. These barbaric beings sometimes challenged civilization and were defeated by its heroes (such as Hercules and Theseus). In the most famous story about them they were invited to a wedding feast by Pirithous, king of the Lapiths (a people of Thessaly, in northern Greece), got drunk and tried to carry off the bride and other Lapith woman, thereby causing a great brawl, which the Lapiths eventually won. This battle between the Lapiths and Centaurs was often depicted in art[2] and was described at length and with gusto by the Latin poet Ovid.[3] The duality of these half-man, half-horse creatures of nature is also evident in the fact that two of them are not savages but civilized (this perhaps reflects the way in which the natural world can be wild and hostile or gentle and benign[4]). The two (who were of different parentage[5]) are the hospitable, benevolent and non-violent Pholus and our own Chiron.

Chiron was the son of the nymph Philyra and the god Cronos (in the form of a horse, taken on by him to elude his wife). Chiron was a healer, prophet and teacher (of music, medicine, hunting, morals etc.) and also a model son, husband and father. Kindly and courteous, he was a real friend to men and he was renowned for his great wisdom and justice. As in the tale of Beauty and the Beast, such a gentle monster is rather unexpected and appealing. He appealed in particular to three famous Classical poets (doubtless because of his connection with culture, wisdom and music) – the Greek Pindar (approximately 518-438 BC) and the Romans Horace (65-8 BC) and Ovid (43 BC – AD 17). They thought so highly of Chiron that they actually used this monster for glorification and moralizing, and showed and aroused sympathy for it.

Pindar wrote (for public performance, accompanied by music and dancing) elaborate and lofty poems celebrating athletic triumphs in the various games in Greece, and in those poems he normally recounted a myth that was in some way connected with the victor and/or his victory. His *Pythian Ode* 9 honours Telesicrates, who won the race in armour at the Pythian Games (at Delphi, in central Greece) in 474 BC. Telesicrates came from Cyrene, a Greek city in Libya (North Africa), and so for this winner at Delphi Pindar tells the story of how a god who was particularly associated with Delphi (the wise Apollo, god of prophecy) carried off to North Africa and married a nymph called Cyrene (who later became the queen of the city there that bore her name after it was founded by Greek colonists from the island of Thera).

In *Pythian Ode* 9, after naming and praising Telesicrates and his home town, Pindar describes how this nymph (who was the daughter of the mighty Hypseus, and who preferred hunting and killing animals to women's tasks) was wrestling with a lion in Thessaly near the cave of Chiron when Apollo saw her. The omniscient god called the Centaur out to look at the nymph and asked him about her origins and if it would be right for him (Apollo) to have sex with her, mischievously feigning ignorance to test and tease Chiron (to see how much he knew and put him on the spot). Chiron saw the joke and smiled. He was aware that it was right and that the god would marry her, but as part of the humorous banter he said (in rather obscure words, as was typical of prophets) that Apollo should persuade her first and allow her privacy (not just rape her there in the open). The Centaur explained that he said this because the god's desire had led him to try to mislead Chiron with his speech (and so it might lead him to go as far as rape).[6] Chiron will say nothing about her parentage (as the god knows all about that, and much else), but he does predict that Apollo will take her off to the fertile land of Libya (where she will be welcomed by the nymph there, who is also called Libya), and that he will make her queen of the future city of Cyrene and will wed her and father on her a glorious son (Aristaeus), who will be a god of the countryside. The Centaur's words came true on that very day.

Here is what Pindar says at 26ff.:

> Far-shooting Apollo with the spacious quiver
> once came on her when, alone and unarmed,
> she was grappling with a powerful lion. Immediately he
> called Chiron from his home, saying: 'Son of Philyra, leave
> your sacred cave and marvel at this woman's courage and great   30
> strength, at what an unflinching fighter she is, this girl with an
> unwearied heart shaken by no storms of fear.
> What mortal is her father? From what family was she torn to
> live in the glens of these shadowy mountains,
> testing out her boundless bravery?   35
> Is it right for me to put my glorious hands on her,
> to bed her and reap a honey-sweet harvest?'
> With a gentle expression the mighty Centaur smiled warmly
> and gave his advice at once: 'It is wise Persuasion who unlocks
> love's sanctuary, with secret keys, Apollo; and gods and mortals   40
> alike refrain from entering on sweet love in public. I say this
> because it was desire that led you (who may not lie) to make
> that misleading speech. Lord, do you ask about the girl's
> family? Yet you know the appointed outcome
> of all things, and all paths to it;   45
> and you perceive clearly how many leaves the earth produces
> in spring, and how many grains of sand in the sea and rivers
> are churned up by the waves and rushing winds, and what
> will happen, and how it will come about.
> But if I must match wits with a wise god,   50
> I will speak. You came to this glade to marry her,
> and you are going to take her across the sea
> to Zeus' finest garden and make her queen of the city
> that colonists from Thera will found on the hill in the plain
> there. For now Libya, the nymph of spacious meadows, will   55
> graciously welcome your glorious bride in her golden palace
> and immediately give her as her lawful possession a portion of
> the land there that yields all kinds of fruit and has animals
> too. There Cyrene will bear a son, and glorious Hermes
> will take him from his loving mother and carry him to Earth   60
> and the Hours enthroned in splendour. Those goddesses,
> gazing with wonder at the child on their knees, will drip
> nectar and ambrosia on his lips, making him immortal, a Zeus
> or a holy Apollo, a delight to his followers, a close guardian of
> flocks, called Hunter and Shepherd by some, Aristaeus by   65
> others.' So Chiron urged on him the joys of marriage.

Pindar here focuses on one particular (striking) scene, with one female involved in dangerous and dramatic action, while two males engage in relaxed contemplation and amusing conversation (tempting us to eaves-drop). There is humour not only in their joshing exchange but also in the notion of Chiron prophesying to the god of prophecy himself and in the whole picture of those two nonchalantly chatting away, while Cyrene wrestles with a powerful lion, and not helping her or encouraging her at all (they know she will not be harmed, but still ...). This light-hearted tinge enlivens the story, making it palatable and memorable, and it also fits with the exuberant mood of victory.[7] But there is also serious celebration here. The myth glorifies Telesicrates in that the original queen of his city was splendid enough to attract Apollo, making even that great god marvel at her and praise her (note the strong language employed to bring out her qualities at 27ff.); and, as well as being the daughter of an illustrious father, she was brave and strong, a tough fighter and the mother of a mighty god and great benefactor of man-kind. So, by means of the nymph Cyrene, Apollo and Aristaeus, Telesi-crates' city (which was founded only 150 years earlier) is given a rich mythological background.

Chiron also plays a part in all this. After his initial levity he speaks with dignity and authority, bringing out the divine majesty of Apollo (Cyrene's husband), acclaiming the nymph herself and the site of her future city, and magnifying her son Aristaeus in a climax of solemnity and marvel at 59ff. He thereby reinforces the praise by Apollo and by Pindar himself. So a monster is here used to flatter and extol the victor (which shows how loved and respected Chiron was). We also see here a playful monster, teased by a god and teasing him back, and enjoying a friendly relationship with Apollo (which makes Chiron a warm and sympathetic character). And a Centaur, so far from raping, urges Apollo against such an action and shows himself in general to be gentle, wise and civilized. Clearly Chiron is monstrous only in form.

The sage and prophetic Chiron also appears in Horace *Epode* 13, but there he is employed for moralizing rather than glorification. That poem takes the form of an address by Horace to some worried friends during a severe storm. Such bad weather would doubtless be rather depressing but would hardly cause the frowns, gloom and appalling anxieties referred to in lines 5 and 9; and storms do end definitely (whereas at 7f. Horace talks of a god *perhaps* changing things round). So it seems likely that they have some greater worry, quite possibly in connection with the Civil Wars which plagued Rome during this period (and which may have suggested the example of the warrior Achilles at 11ff.). The tempest comes on top of their existing troubles and is turned into an opportunity by Horace, who recommends that in view of the weather outdoors they should party indoors, cheering themselves up with wine, the lyre (a musical instrument invented by the god Mercury) and sumptuous perfume (commonly put on for parties in the ancient world). He backs up his suggestion with an allusion to similar advice given by Chiron to one of his pupils, Achilles (son

The Centaur Chiron Teaches the Young Achilles Archery by Giuseppe Maria Crespi (1665-1747). Kunsthistorisches Museum, Vienna.

of the sea-goddess Thetis), shortly before he went to the city of Troy. Achilles was the best fighter in the great Greek army that attacked Troy to recover Helen (with whom the Trojan prince Paris had eloped), but he was killed in the land of Troy (as Chiron predicts at 13ff., referring to an early king of Troy and to two Trojan rivers).

Here is *Epode* 13:

A dreadful storm has saddened the sky, and rain and snow
  are bringing down the heavens; now sea, now woods are
roaring with the north wind from Thrace. Friends, let's seize
  the opportunity today presents; while we're still vigorous and
it's not unseemly, let's put an end to frowns and gloom.   5
  Bring wine from grapes trodden when Torquatus was consul.
Don't talk of other things: perhaps a kind god will change things
  round and put them back the way they were. Now is the time
for easing our hearts from the burden of appalling anxieties
  by means of Mercury's lyre and Persian perfume,   10
just as the illustrious Centaur sang to his mighty pupil:
  'Invincible boy, mortal son of divine Thetis,
Assaracus' land, bisected by tiny Scamander's chill waters
  and by gliding Simois, lies in wait for you.
The spinning Fates have definitely cut off your return from   15
  there, and your sea-blue mother will not take you home.
While there, ease all your troubles with wine and song,
  sweet relief from unlovely melancholy.'

This is a poem that seizes and keeps the attention, to ensure that Horace's message comes across strongly. There is an arresting start, thanks to the gloomy picture presented (of heaven, mid-air, land and sea in turmoil), and also thanks to the vigorous expression. So, for example, Horace's opening words (*horrida tempestas caelum contraxit*) contain vehement alliteration (repetition of the initial letter c), stress by putting first *horrida* (which economically combines various senses – 'dreadful', 'harsh' and 'shivering with cold') and include the very suggestive verb *contraxit* (which also blends several meanings – 'has saddened', 'has narrowed', 'has made frown' and 'has caused to shrink with pain'[8]). Then suddenly at 3ff. comes the positive spin of making the weather an excuse for a party. Even more lively and surprising is the introduction of Chiron and Achilles at 11, abruptly switching back to remote mythical times and providing an unprecedented speech by the Centaur.

He not only supports Horace's advice but actually adds depth and reverberations to it. There is lots to explore in Chiron's speech, and it is fascinating to probe its subtle implications. Getting the illustrious Centaur (a sympathetic figure famed for wisdom) to reinforce exactly Horace's recommendation about easing one's troubles with song and wine gives it real weight and makes it more acceptable, and Chiron's speech (which takes up nearly half of the poem) is left until the end, so that we go away with it uppermost in our thoughts. The repetition of Horace's exhortation in the mouth of the Centaur also gives it a wider application: it is relevant not only to Horace's friends but also to Achilles, and to mortals in general. Achilles had bad experiences (the fighting at Troy, the loss of his beloved slave-girl Briseis, the death of his great friend Patroclus, and knowledge of his own early demise), but the astute and caring Chiron told him to use wine and song as a way of dealing with such major problems. We are reminded that even that mighty son of a goddess experienced deep sorrow and died young, and so we can easily infer that suffering and death are part of our human lot and we should enjoy ourselves (partying) while we can. In fact it's even more grim than that for mortals and for one of their supreme heroes when you examine Chiron's words closely. 'Invincible' in 12 has a tragic irony, as Achilles *was* finally defeated (and killed). In 13 the chill waters of the Trojan river Scamander conjure up a bleak final resting-place for the hero (who was buried near there). And 'tiny' is a surprising adjective to apply to the river (which in the revered Homer[9] was described as large) and deflates one of Achilles' greatest feats (his battle in Homer *Iliad* 20 with that river, which summons the neighbouring river Simois to its aid and very nearly overwhelms him). At 15f. we see that (just like us) even the son of a deity is powerless before fate. Finally 17f. conjure up a picture of the warrior at a very low ebb, at Homer *Iliad* 9.186ff., where Achilles sings to relieve his distress and drinks with friends after he has withdrawn from the fighting, angry and brooding because Agamemnon (the commander of the Greeks) had dishonoured him by taking Briseis away from him. So all in all it is a quite thoughtful and rather melancholy monster that we see here.

In Ovid we find a monster with a wife and daughter, and we feel quite sorry for the monster, which is itself upset and weeps. Ovid wrote a long poem called the *Metamorphoses* which contains a series of myths connected in some way with metamorphosis (change). At 2.633ff. he tells the story of Ocyrhoe. Her father (Chiron) had taken on Apollo's baby son Asclepius and was bringing him up when Ocyrhoe appeared and foretold that Asclepius would be a great healer but for bringing a man (Hippolytus) back to life would be killed by Jupiter's thunderbolt; but then Asclepius would be restored to life himself, as a god once more. She also foresaw the death of Chiron, who when visited by Hercules would drop one of the hero's arrows (smeared with the poisonous blood of the monstrous Hydra) on to his foot and die (allowed by heaven to escape the eternal agony that he would have faced if he had remained immortal). These predictions angered the gods and Ocyrhoe was punished by being changed into a mare (and acquired a new name – Hippe, which means 'mare'). Here are Ovid's lines:

> Meanwhile the Centaur enjoyed bringing up the god's
> son and was delighted at this onerous honour.
> Suddenly his daughter appeared, her red-gold hair streaming   635
> over her shoulders. The nymph Chariclo had given birth
> to her on the banks of a racing river and called her
> Ocyrhoe. She was not satisfied with learning her
> father's arts: she foretold the secrets of fate.
> So, when prophetic frenzy possessed her mind and she was   640
> inflamed by the god of prophecy hidden in her breast,
> she looked at the child and said: 'Grow, boy, health-bringer

to the whole world. Mortal bodies will often owe their life
to you, and you'll be allowed to bring back departed souls.
By daring to do this for one man you'll offend heaven and   645
be stopped by Jupiter's thunderbolt from giving that gift again.
From a god you'll become a pale corpse, and then a god again
(shortly after being a corpse), twice renewing your destiny.
Dear father, you're immortal now and it was ordained at
your birth that you would live on through all time, but   650
you'll long to be able to die when the dread Hydra's blood
enters your body through a wound and brings agony.
The gods will make you capable of dying, instead of being
immortal, and the three Fates will cut your thread.'
There was more to foretell, but she sighed from the depths   655
of her heart, welling tears flowed down her cheeks
and she said: 'The Fates prevent me, I'm forbidden
to say more, and my power of speech is stifled.
The art which has brought the wrath of heaven upon me
was not worth this. I wish I'd not known the future. Now, it   660
seems, my human appearance is being stolen from me, now
grass appeals as food, now I want to run on the broad plains:
I'm being turned into a mare (to which I'm kin), but why
entirely so (my father is only half-horse, for sure)?'
Even as she spoke, the last part of her complaint   665
was unintelligible and her words were indistinct.
Soon they seemed not words but the sound not of a mare
but of someone imitating a mare; shortly afterwards she
definitely neighed and thrust her arms into the grass.
Then her fingers coalesced, and a light hoof of solid horn   670
bound five finger-nails together; her mouth and neck
extended; the greater part of her long cloak became a
tail; the straggling hair that lay along her neck fell as a
mane on to her right shoulder; her voice and appearance were
changed together, and from this miracle she got a new name   675
too. The son of Philyra wept and asked for your aid
in vain, Apollo.

There is a melancholy tone here too, but it is rather more developed than in Horace. For example, after foreseeing her own father's death Ocyrhoe is chastised (by the gods for being filled with the god of prophecy!), and, to her great distress, she actually realizes what is happening to her, but is powerless to stop it; and the poet dwells on the pitiful metamorphosis, catching it vividly and drawing it out, as she gradually loses the power of speech (for misusing it) and on top of that her human (and beautiful) form too. As well as being skilled at manipulating his readers' emotions, Ovid was also adept at producing poetry that was different and fresh. So this is the only place in surviving literature where Ocyrhoe is connected with Asclepius, and this is the first extant account of her metamorphosis. And here, unusually, she overshadows her illustrious father, and she is the one who predicts while the famous prophet Chiron is the subject of prophecy himself.

Ovid is renowned for the subtlety, ingenuity and complexity of his writing too, and all that is particularly evident in the above passage. With a neat parallelism both Asclepius and Chiron will forfeit their immortality and die; while Asclepius, who will restore lives that men lose, will lose his own life and have it restored. There is an element of tit for tat in Ocyrhoe's metamorphosis: for speaking too much she is deprived of the ability to speak, and for predicting modification for others she is herself subject to modification. There is a dark irony as well. She can see the future for others but not for herself. In the very act of prophesying change for Asclepius as a punishment for offending heaven, she personally offends heaven and incurs a punishment consisting of change. And just after foretelling an altered state for Chiron she in turn enters on an altered state. Note also the black humour at 657ff., where even as she is being penalized for saying too much and prevented from saying more, the verbose Ocyrhoe still runs on for several lines.

But it's all even more intricate than that, as a look at the wider picture will show. Ovid's account of the mutation of Ocyrhoe is just one in a series of three tales (at 2.531ff.) which are concerned with the dangers of talking to excess and which have supplementary stories embedded inside them. Our passage comes just after the tale of the raven (which was originally a white bird) being chastised by Apollo with the loss of its whiteness for telling the god about his pregnant girlfriend Coronis being unfaithful to him (Apollo in a fit of anger killed Coronis, but rescued from her womb their son Asclepius and handed him over to Chiron). While the raven is flying to Apollo, a crow comes up, asks the reason for the raven's journey and tries (unsuccessfully) to dissuade the raven from informing. It does this (a black bird speaking, in mid-flight, to a white bird, which will soon become a black bird!) by coming out with the first embedded story – how it was demoted from being Minerva's favourite for informing (on a heroine who had disobeyed the goddess's orders by opening a box she had been ordered not to open). The crow then tells a second story, about how it had once been the daughter of a king (called Coroneus, rather confusingly) and had been saved from rape at the hands of Neptune by being changed into a crow by Minerva. The crow finally adds a third story when it complains that it is now rated below the owl and relates briefly that the owl was originally a heroine, who for committing incest with her father was made into a bird of the night. After the tale of the raven comes that of Ocyrhoe's metamorphosis (which contains two inset stories – on the deaths of Asclepius and Chiron). The third main tale concerns an old man called Battus. He saw Mercury steal and hide some cattle belonging to Apollo but in return for the gift of a cow swore to Mercury that he would keep quiet about the theft. Mercury subsequently returned in disguise and offered Battus a cow and a bull as a reward for information about the missing cattle. Battus immediately revealed where they were (ratting on Mercury to Mercury himself), and for that betrayal the god turned the old man into a touchstone. This tale has embedded in it another story (about Apollo at this time working as a herdsman).

So Ovid presents three main tales (those of the raven, Ocyrhoe and Battus) which all contain further stories (the first has three inset stories, the second has two, and the third has just one). As part of the patterning those three major tales also occupy successively fewer lines (the raven is covered at 536-632, Ocyrhoe at 633-75, and Battus at 676-707), so that they form what is known as a tricolon diminuendo (a group of three members in which the second is shorter than the first and the third is shorter than the second). And the three main tales and the embedded stories are carefully bound together by various linking themes (e.g. the danger of talking too much, mutation, punishment, death, heroines and Apollo). Taken together all this amounts to a typically dazzling and elaborate tour-de-force in story-telling.

Ovid also mentions Chiron at *Fasti* 5.381ff., where he describes his demise, and, although one cannot be sure that this passage was written after *Metamorphoses* 2.633ff., it certainly looks as if Ocyrhoe's prophecy there comes true here. Again we find Chiron in his cave and tutoring Achilles (the son of Peleus), who would later cause Troy much trouble in the Trojan War and kill Hector, the Trojans' best warrior. Upon the arrival of another enemy of Troy (Hercules, who was the son of Jupiter and who had earlier led an army against the city and killed its king) Chiron has the accident with the arrow and ends his existence on earth, becoming a constellation (a group of fourteen stars that formed the outline of a Centaur and were named The Centaur). Here is Ovid's account:

> Pelion is a Thessalian mountain that faces south;
>   its top is green with pine, the rest is covered by oaks.
> Philyra's son lived on it. There stands a cave of ancient rock
>   which they say the righteous old man inhabited.
> He is believed to have occupied with playing tunes on the lyre   385
>   the hands that would one day send Hector to his death.
> Hercules arrived, with his Labours partly completed and little
>   but the final tasks remaining for him to do.
> You'd have seen two scourges of Troy together by chance –
>   here the boy Achilles, there the son of Jupiter.   390
> Philyra's heroic son warmly welcomed the young man;
>   he asked, and was told, why Hercules had come.
> Meanwhile he gazed at Hercules' club and lionskin and said:
>   'This man deserves such arms, and the arms deserve him.'
> Achilles' hands couldn't keep themselves from daring   395
>   to touch the shaggy, bristly pelt.
> While old Chiron was handling the arrows coated with poison,
>   one of them slipped and stuck in his left foot.

Chiron groaned and pulled the metal point from his flesh;
    Hercules and the boy Achilles groaned as well.   400
But the Centaur blended together herbs picked on Thessalian
    hills and tried to ease the wound with various treatments.
The voracious venom was beyond treatment, the deadly
    poison permeated his body and bones.
The blood of the Hydra from Lerna mingled with the   405
    Centaur's blood, forestalling any antidote.
Achilles stood drenched with tears, as if before his father:
    he would have wept like that for Peleus if he was dying.
He often caressed the ailing hands with his loving hands,
    and his teacher was rewarded for so moulding his character.   410
Achilles often kissed him, and often said to him as he lay there:
    'Live, please; don't leave me, dear father.'
The ninth day had come, Chiron, you paragon of justice,
    when your body was outlined by fourteen stars.

Although the poet here reverts to the story of Chiron, he is inventive as ever and does do different things with it. In his writing Ovid sometimes gives characters an unusual or brand new prominence. As well as providing a surprising twist and a different focus for old stories, this process is often very functional, as here. So, to attract the reader's attention, uniquely in extant versions of Chiron's death his pupil is present and prominent, and intriguingly Achilles and Hercules are brought together, two of the greatest Greek heroes. And the pathos in this account (and the sympathy for the monster) is even greater than it was in the *Metamorphoses*. A tale that is sad in itself is made still sadder by the presence of the Centaur's pupil, who reinforces Hercules' groan at 400 and then takes the mourning much further at 407ff. It is tragic for a child to witness someone's death, even more so when that person is a beloved teacher and father-figure and dies slowly and irrevocably. And Ovid catches Achilles' misery in detail and at length, highlighting his tears, his great closeness to Chiron, his need to touch him and his desperation (hence the repeated 'often' at 409ff. and his animated but futile appeal in 412).

Such novel or uncommon prominence often involves cleverness and complexity too. So here there is adroit foreshadowing (looking forward to and hinting at things that will happen later). The allusions at 386 and 389 to Achilles slaughtering Trojans clearly point the way to the coming end of Chiron. Achilles' great misery here anticipates his deep sorrow at Troy over the loss of his dear Briseis and the death of his friend Patroclus. And Chiron's demise prefigures the eventual passing on of both Achilles (shot by an arrow) and Hercules (because of contact with the devouring blood of a monster). There is extensive irony and inversion as well. Achilles' hands (famously described by Homer as 'man-slaying'[10]) here touch the Centaur with tender affection, and this hero who will cause so much grief to mothers, wives etc. by inflicting death is here himself grieving over death.

Achilles begs his tutor not to die, the same Achilles who will later kill so many men without pity. In particular (especially after the reference to the slaughter of Hector in 386), when Achilles stands over the loved but fatally wounded Chiron where he lies and tells him to live, we may well be meant to think of him at Troy (after he has fatally wounded his hated enemy in their duel) standing over Hector where he lies and telling him to die at Homer *Iliad* 22.365.

There is a further important and interesting aspect. At several points this passage has the feel of a film. Cinema is, of course, just another form of narrative, and various literary procedures are classified by critics as 'cinematic' techniques, a term which usefully encourages awareness of their visual impact (something particularly important in the case of Ovid, who was very fond of optical effects). The poet opens the above passage with something resembling the camera's 'establishing shot' (a long shot at the beginning of a scene to provide the viewer with context) and then 'zooms in' on the important cave (where Chiron meets his end). Like many movie directors, Ovid was sensitive to lighting and here there is a tone-conscious start: the heavily wooded mountain is aptly dark, and Chiron's cave on it would be still darker, making for a sombre start to a sombre tale. Next, at 385f., together with the poetic equivalent of a 'flashforward' (the process whereby brief anticipatory glimpses of future events are shown on screen), there is a 'close-up' on Achilles' hands. Ovid also zooms in on those hands at 395f. (where they stand out via contrast with the colour and texture of the lionskin) and at 409 (a vivid optical representation of the closeness between tutor and pupil). The hands at this point in Achilles' career are engaged in activities quite different from killing, and the close-ups draw attention to the unusual slant which Ovid here gives them; but they still represent a gloomy 'motif' because they are linked overtly or covertly with death in each case. Line 409 in particular contains a striking image: the repeated touching there catches this very sad moment with something akin to the 'freeze frame' (a shot composed of a single frame repeated on a filmstrip so that it gives the illusion of a still photograph). There is also powerful close-up at 397f. (on Hercules' arrows, and on one of them fixed in Chiron's foot), and that is followed at 399f. by the Centaur groaning and pulling out the arrow and by Hercules and Achilles groaning in literary 'reaction shots' (which cut to a character's reaction) to build foreboding. At the very end with a sort of 'low angle shot' (which photographs from below) we look up to the constellation in the sky; this accentuates the Centaur's ultimate eminence and provides a bright climax (in contrast to the dark opening). All in all this would have made a moving and visually arresting short film, and it could easily have featured the first monster as a movie star.

Compare Chiron with the monster in Mary Shelley's novel *Frankenstein* (published first in 1818, then in a revised edition in 1831) or in a film version of the story. Examine in particular how Frankenstein's creation is

102

put across as basically a good monster, is invested with pathos, and is employed to convey various messages (about society's irrational prejudice against anything different; the dangers of science; the damaging effects of the refusal of affection, and so on).

Metamorphosed Monsters

This chapter will examine the handling of two monsters (Medusa and Scylla) by the Latin poet Ovid (43 BC – AD 17) in a lengthy epic written about two thousand years ago, called the *Metamorphoses*. That poem consists of a series of mythical and legendary tales that all involve change (metamorphosis) of some kind. It has long occupied a central position in the western literary tradition, and in it Ovid, a highly accomplished story-teller, gave many myths and legends their most memorable and enduring form to date.

Lively, versatile and unpredictable, Ovid loved to stand things on their head and provide a new slant or focus or mood (this too was a form of metamorphosis). Lots of his accounts are amusing – frivolous, witty and ironical – as when the god Apollo, deeply in love with the nymph Daphne (who can't stand him), literally pursues her and chats her up on the run, trying futilely to impress her with his divine parentage and attributes, and, when the ground becomes rough, begging her to slow down in case she hurts herself, and claiming that he will sportingly slow down as he runs after her. There are also many tales of cruelty: for example, Marsyas as the loser in a musical contest with Apollo has all the skin stripped from his body and becomes just one big bloody wound, with his throbbing veins and palpitating entrails uncovered. Several of the stories seem to have been invented by Ovid himself (e.g., as far as we can tell, nobody earlier had told of Narcissus, the handsome boy who fell in love with his reflection in a pool and pined away because his love was unattainable), and ingenuity is often in evidence (as when he depicts the soul of the dead Narcissus being ferried across the river Styx in the Underworld and gazing even then in the water at its own reflection). Ovid was also very much aware of earlier literary treatments and constantly gave them dexterous twists. So Virgil had depicted the marvellous musician Orpheus charming Hell with his music, so that even the rotating wheel on which the sinner Ixion was bound and doomed to whirl forever, suddenly came to a stop. When Ovid later produced his version, he too had Ixion's wheel stop, but he went one better by dragging in other mythical sinners, especially Sisyphus. He was punished by having to spend all eternity trying to roll to the top of a hill a huge boulder, which always overpowered him just as he neared the crest and rolled back down again. In Ovid that task is halted by Orpheus' song, so Sisyphus takes a break, hopping up on the boulder and having a seat there.[1]

Perseus, Gorgon and Hermes, from a black-figure olpe by the Amasis Painter, 550-530 BC. British Museum, London.

Medusa

Of our two monsters we will first examine Medusa, who according to the standard tradition was one of the most terrible creatures of Classical myth. She was one of three sisters called the Gorgons, dread enemies of mankind who lived in Libya, a remote area of northern Africa. They had scaly, hissing snakes growing among their hair; they also had great tusks like those of pigs, hands of bronze and wings of gold. The eyes of either just Medusa or in some accounts all of the sisters turned to stone anyone who looked at them. Medusa alone of the three was mortal, and she was eventually killed by the Greek hero Perseus. He flew to her distant lair on winged sandals given to him by the god Mercury (Hermes) and beheaded her while she slept, averting his eyes and looking at her reflection in a bronze shield, to avoid being petrified. According to some, his divine patroness Minerva (Athena) guided the sword in his hand. Weirdly, from the monster's severed neck were born Chrysaor and the winged horse Pegasus. Minerva took blood from the veins on the left (a deadly poison) and from the veins on the right (whose blood could restore the dead to life) and also cut off a lock of Medusa's hair (which when brandished three times could turn an attacking army to flight). Perseus flew off with the head, and drops of blood fell on to the Libyan desert below engendering the deadliest of serpents. The head was later set in the aegis, a breastplate which belonged to Jupiter (Zeus) and was often used by Minerva, and there it terrified and turned to stone the enemies of the gods.[2]

Although he wrote about sixty years after Ovid's *Metamorphoses*, in *The Civil War* 9.624ff. the Latin poet Lucan (to explain the origin of Libya's highly noxious snakes) produced a lively account of the awful Medusa and Perseus' courageous exploit that gives a good idea of the tradition against which Ovid seems to have reacted:

> On the furthest borders of Libya, where the Ocean that
> is heated by the setting sun laps the burning earth, 625
> lay the broad and arid domain of Phorcys' daughter Medusa,
> not shaded by forests' foliage, not softened by ploughing,
> but rugged with rocks created by her gaze.
> It was from her body that nature first produced these
> killers: from her severed neck came serpents with 630
> flickering tongues that gave sibilant hisses.
> She loved to feel her snakes lashing her neck;
> and they hung down loose over her back, but in front they
> reared straight up over her forehead, just like a woman's hair.
> When she used her comb, viper's venom flowed freely. 635
> They were the only part of baleful Medusa that all could gaze
> on safely. For who had time to fear the monster's gaping mouth
> and face? Whoever looked directly at her, had already been
> killed by Medusa. Before he could experience terror, she
> hurried along hesitant death; while the breath remained, his 640
> limbs were destroyed, and his spirit was petrified before it left
> the body. The Furies' snaky hair only drove men mad,
> Cerberus' serpents lost their ferocity when Orpheus sang,
> and Hercules actually looked at the Hydra as he conquered it;
> but monstrous Medusa was dreaded by her own father Phorcys 645
> (a sea-god second only to Neptune), her mother Ceto and even
> her sister Gorgons. She had the power to threaten sea and sky

with a strange paralysis and to cover the world with a coating
of stone. Birds suddenly grew heavy and fell from the sky,
wild animals became motionless as rocks and entire tribes   650
of the neighbouring Ethiopians were stiffened into stone.
No creature could bear to look at her, and even her
own snakes reared back to avoid her face.
Her head turned into stone Atlas, the Titan who stands at
the Pillars of the West; and once it put an end to an awful   655
battle with the gods at Phlegra: set in the centre of Minerva's
aegis, it transformed into towering mountains
the snake-legged Giants who were terrorizing heaven.
Perseus (the son of Danae and the shower of gold) went to her
lair, borne by the winged sandals that he had been given by   660
Arcadian Mercury (inventor of the lyre and gliding wrestling).
As he flew, he raised another gift from Mercury – a scimitar
already red with the blood of a different monster (used to
slay Argus, the guard set over Jupiter's beloved Io).
Virginal Minerva helped her brother Perseus in return   665
for the monster's head, telling him to turn towards
the rising sun when he reached the frontier of Libya
and to fly backwards through the Gorgon's realm;
and she put in his left hand a shining shield of yellow bronze
and told him to use it as a mirror to look at petrifying Medusa.   670
Medusa was enveloped by the sleep that would bring her the
eternal rest of death, but not totally: much of her hair was
awake, some of her serpents rose up from it to protect her
head, while others lay right across her face, covering her
closed eyes and doubling the darkness of sleep.   675
He was afraid, and his hand trembled as he held the
scimitar with eyes averted, so Minerva herself guided it,
hacking through the juncture of body and great snaky neck.
What an expression the Gorgon had as her head was severed
by the curved sword! How much poison did her mouth breathe   680
forth, how deadly was the discharge from her eyes!
Even Minerva couldn't look at her, and her gaze would have
frozen his face although it was averted, if Minerva hadn't
spread out Medusa's hair and veiled her face with the snakes.
So he seized the head and soared off into the sky.

When Ovid told of Perseus and Medusa in the *Metamorphoses*, he
provided a very different take on both of them. He presents a most unusual
picture of Medusa before she became a monster and actually arouses
sympathy for her. He turns her from a creature of horror into a beautiful
heroine (her original form) and then back into a monster (when metamorphosed) with a story that is unknown before his poem. Either he got hold
of an existing tale that was extremely rare or he made it up himself,
expanding on brief references in earlier authors to the god Poseidon
(Neptune) having intercourse with Medusa and to her being a beauty who

vied with Athena and was punished by being beheaded.[3] As for the great hero Perseus, Ovid consistently debunks him. He begins his account of Perseus' adventures with his flight home *after* the beheading of Medusa, and shows us first a hero who is nervous about night-flying and who appeals to Atlas for permission to stop in his realm and, when that is refused, overcomes his opposition by some rather unheroic guile (he turns Atlas into a mountain by showing him the severed head of Medusa). Next comes his comic encounter with the sea-monster threatening the heroine Andromeda (discussed in detail on pp. 154ff. below). Thanks to his victory over that creature Perseus wins Andromeda as his bride, speedily marries her and at the wedding feast is asked by one of the noble guests about his fight with Medusa. That combat is then finally described, briefly, in retrospect and in reported speech, so that it is minimized. Directly after that the feat is further undercut by the following lines on the rape of Medusa by Neptune and the revenge taken by Minerva, daughter of Jupiter, at *Metamorphoses* 4.787ff. (where we also find the very uncommon detail of Medusa alone of the sisters having snaky hair):

> Perseus also told of the genuine dangers of his long flight,
> the seas and lands he had seen beneath him from on high
> and the stars he had brushed with his beating wings,
> but he fell silent before they expected him to. One of the   790
> nobles seized on his words and asked why Medusa
> was the only sister who had snakes among her hair.
> Perseus replied: 'You're asking about something worth
> telling, so listen and I'll explain the cause. She used to be
> renowned for her beauty and had many hopeful and jealous   795
> suitors. Of all her charms her hair was her most conspicuous
> feature (I met someone who told me that he'd seen it).
> The Lord of the Sea, they say, deflowered her in Minerva's
> temple. The daughter of Jupiter turned away and covered her
> virginal face with the aegis. As punishment for what happened   800
> she transformed the Gorgon's hair into hideous snakes.'
> To this day, to terrify her enemies and stun them with fear,
> she bears on her breastplate the serpents that she created.

Perseus told the guests readily enough about his victory over Medusa and about his subsequent journey (with bragging exaggeration in 789), but initially he withheld this information about Medusa's origins, quite possibly because he was aware that it might well arouse pity for his opponent and detract somewhat from his victory over her. As it is, Ovid depicts him as making little of the incident and careful not to express criticism of the gods involved or sympathy for his enemy. However, at the same time Ovid also subtly enables his readers to make extrapolations from this rather cool and concise passage and to be affected by the gist of it.

Line allocation is one of the ways in which Ovid achieves this with his readers. For three-and-a-half lines (the longest segment of this short account, and early on in it) there is dwelling on how attractive Medusa originally was, which helps us grasp how extensive and poignant the transformation was. Then she is raped in just over one line, which suggests a shocking suddenness and speed (with apparently no overtures, declarations of love etc.) and also intimates her powerlessness to resist this mighty deity. Next in almost three lines Ovid lingers on Minerva's ominous aversion of her eyes and the terrible punishment that she inflicted. There is a certain symmetry in (roughly) three lines on Medusa before the rape, one on the rape, and three on Minerva's reactions to the rape, but then at 801f. comes a somewhat unexpected and distinctly unpleasant addition, with further debasement as the once beautiful Medusa is mutilated, reduced to an adornment for a breastplate and employed to terrify.

When one thinks about this incident and really reflects on Ovid's lines, one can perceive even greater poignancy. Medusa was not just raped but deflowered. Presumably she was in Minerva's temple to pray or worship, but that reverence is ignored by Neptune, and by Minerva (and to be raped in such circumstances and by a god must have been particularly traumatic for Medusa, but that too is ignored). As the heroine was taken against her will, the punishment of her is unfair; it is also cruelly aimed at her most attractive feature. And this was done by a female to a female, by a virgin to one who had been forced to lose her virginity. The helpless mortal suffers under a succession of blows from these two powerful immortals. They come out of all this badly, and so to a lesser extent does the unfeeling Perseus, while the one who emerges with the most sympathy is in fact Medusa. These gods rather than Medusa seem monstrous; she is loved and the innocent victim of cruelty who is transformed (instead of being a hateful and vicious creature who transforms others with her gaze); and repulsion and sadness attach to what is done to her rather than to what she does. That is quite a metamorphosis.[4]

Scylla

Ovid does something rather similar with our second subject, Scylla, but this time there is wit and humour in connection with the monster as well as pathos and horror; and there is also a more complex literary aspect, as Ovid is simultaneously adopting and adapting two particular passages in earlier poetry. Scylla was a fierce creature who lurked in a cave on a crag high above the sea and attacked passing ships. Opposite her was another crag, with at its base another dreadful monster, Charybdis, which three times a day sucked down the sea, creating an inescapable whirlpool. To surivive, ships had to steer between these two hazards, and those that escaped Charybdis became Scylla's victims (in Homer their exact position is unclear, but later writers place Scylla and Charybdis in the Straits of

Messina between Italy and Sicily). Once more in his version Ovid changes things round by picking up an unusual tale and giving us the background to the monster Scylla (she too was originally a beautiful girl who was metamorphosed into a creature of savagery). Ovid also rings the changes specifically on the accounts of Scylla found in Virgil's *Aeneid* and Homer's *Odyssey.*[5]

In the *Odyssey* Homer tells of the long and eventful voyage home by the hero Odysseus after he and his fellow Greeks had captured and destroyed the city of Troy. In book 12 of the poem Odysseus relates his prior adventures to the Phaeacians, who helped him on the final stage of his journey. There he explains how earlier the divine witch Circe (who loved him and had entertained him for a year) had given him some valuable advice about the dangers that faced him in his onward voyage after he left her island. First, she said, he would reach the Sirens (see Chapter 4 above), who would try with their lovely song to entice him to come to them, so that they could kill him; then, if he escaped them, he would have to choose between two courses – to the Planctae (sheer cliffs which had destroyed all ships bar one that had sailed up to them) or to Scylla and Charybdis. Odysseus quotes what she said about the latter pair (in the earliest and most celebrated description of them) at 12.73ff.:

'There are two crags. One reaches the broad heaven
with its sharp peak and is covered by a dark cloud
which never leaves it. There is never clear sky   75
around that peak, not in summer and not at harvest-time.
No mortal man could scale it or get a foothold on it,
not even if he had twenty hands and feet.
For the rock is smooth, as if polished.
Halfway up the crag and facing westwards, towards   80
the Realm of Darkness, is a murky cave. You will probably
steer your hollow ship past this, glorious Odysseus.
Even a strong man could not reach that vaulted cave
with an arrow shot from a hollow ship beneath it.
Inside lives Scylla, that barking horror.   85
True, her voice is no louder than that of a young puppy,
but she herself is an evil monster, a sight
to appal anyone encountering her, even a god.
She has twelve feet, really, all of them misshapen,
and six long, long necks, each of them   90
ending in a hideous head with three crowded rows of
teeth, masses of teeth, full of black death.
Her lower half is hidden in the vaulted cave,
but her heads protrude from that awful yawning cavern.
She greedily scans the water around the crag and fishes   95
there for dolphins, seals and whatever she can catch of the
thousands of larger creatures that live in the loud-groaning sea.
No sailors can boast that they have sped past her

110

without loss: she carries off a man with each of her heads,
snatching them up from their dark-prowed ship.   100
The other crag is lower, as you will see, Odysseus
(the two crags are near to each other, a bow-shot apart),
and on it there is a large and leafy fig-tree.
Beneath it awesome Charybdis sucks down the water.
Every day she spews it up thrice and sucks it down again   105
thrice, horribly. I hope you aren't there when she sucks down,
for not even Poseidon could save you from destruction then.
No, steer close to Scylla's crag and get
your ship past it quickly, as it is much better
to lose six of your crew than all of them together.'   110
So she spoke, and in answer to her I said:
'Come now, goddess, tell me truly –
is there some way of getting by deadly Charybdis
and fighting off Scylla when she seizes my men?'
The awesome goddess immediately replied: 115
'You never give up, you're set on battling away
again. Won't you give in even to immortal gods?
Scylla is not mortal, she's an immortal monster –
terrible, hideous, ferocious and impossible to fight.
There is no defence against her. It's best to flee her.   120
If you linger near her rock while arming yourself,
I fear she will lunge out and pounce for a second time,
snatching away another six men with her six heads.
No, row past with all your strength and call on Crataiis,
Scylla's mother, who bore her to wreak havoc among mortals.   125
She will stop her from lunging out again.'

First of all Homer carefully elucidates the setting for Scylla and gives it a
sense of looming, brooding menace. Ominously and aptly her cave itself is
murky, it faces the Realm of Darkness (through which the souls of the
dead pass on their way to Hades) and it is constantly covered by a black
cloud (a strange, supernatural touch). All the darkness is perfect for
lurking, and in addition to that the cave is high up, on a dwarfing crag,
and unassailable by any means. A strong sense of human helplessness is
thereby created.

Then, even more unsettlingly, we are taken inside the cave and are
shown Scylla herself, in a vivid sketch. Arrestingly the description of her
begins with her unnatural barking and the weirdly anomalous detail of
her voice being no louder than that of a (tiny, harmless, appealing) puppy.
Also unnatural is the multiplicity of (misshapen) feet and, especially
disturbing, of the (very long) necks and (rending, devouring, deadly) teeth
so hard to combat or elude. When Homer goes on to add to all that the fact
that she is a greedy predator and is inevitably successful in her onslaughts
on passing sailors, a feeling of inevitable doom is built up.

The following lines on Charybdis only reinforce that feeling, because to escape certain death from her whirlpool ships have to make themselves vulnerable to Scylla. And then that feeling is reinforced yet again, by Circe's response to Odysseus' fighting words (especially the densely emphatic 119).

Picture it – a place like that, with a ghastly monster lurking high above you and ready to lunge out, and you have to sail under it, unable to get far away because of Charybdis! There is a great build up to the actual encounter as a result of all this and real foreboding (it seems certain that Odysseus will lose six men, horribly, and it may even be worse than that if he does decide to fight Scylla). In what follows Homer keeps us in suspense for over a hundred lines before Odysseus and his men finally reach Scylla and Charybdis. First (after further advice from Circe) they sail off from her island. Then they approach the Sirens, which they escape by following Circe's recommendation to put wax in the ears of the crew, so that they can't hear their beguiling song, and to lash Odysseus to the mast, so that he can hear but cannot get to them. Once past the Sirens they approach Charybdis. The tension is increased when Odysseus warns his frightened crew to steer clear of Charybdis but does not mention Scylla to them, in case they just huddle together in the hold in terror, and then actually arms himself, seemingly ready to fight in spite of Circe's command. He goes to the prow to keep an eye out for Scylla, but cannot see a trace of her anywhere. What happened next (as told by Odysseus to the Phaeacians) is described at 12.234ff.:

'We sailed up the strait, groaning.
On one side was Scylla, and on the other awesome   235
Charybdis sucked down the salty sea-water horribly.
When she spewed it out, she was completely convulsed and
boiled up like a cauldron on a large fire, and high overhead
the spray fell on the tops of the two crags.
But when she gulped down the salty sea-water, her interior   240
was exposed, completely convulsed, while all around her
the rock roared horribly, and the dark and sandy sea-bed
was exposed. Pale fear seized my men. While we
looked at Charybdis with the fear of death upon us,
Scylla seized from our hollow ship six   245
of my comrades, the strongest and sturdiest that I had.
I turned to check my swift ship, looking for my comrades,
and I saw their feet and hands already above me, as they
were heaved high into the air. They called out to me
despairingly, screaming out my name, for the last time.   250
Like an angler with a long rod on a jutting rock,
who casts bait for the little fish into the sea,
his line protected by an ox-horn tube,
and tosses his writhing catch ashore,
so Scylla heaved my writhing men up to her crag.   255
There, at the entrance to her cave, she devoured them, as they

shrieked and stretched out their hands to me in that dreadful
death-struggle. Of all my ordeals while exploring the sea's
routes that was the most pitiful sight that met my eyes.'

The fact that Homer makes Odysseus himself the narrator here means
that we go through this harrowing episode with him and identify with the
hero. Like him we are on the prow looking up at 247ff., and before that
with the dramatic 235ff. like him we have our attention focused on
Charybdis, so that Scylla's attack is sudden for us too and has real impact.
As well as all the drama there is poignancy and revulsion here: Odysseus'
vigilance and arming is all in vain; Scylla gets his best men; they are
already beyond his help before he even sees her or realizes what has
happened; they scream, and make a directly personal appeal (calling on
him by name) to which he is powerless to respond; she devours them before
his eyes (her lair is *inside* the cave, so there may well be malevolent
intelligence here, with the monster trying to distress Odysseus and/or get
him to stay and fight); and the rare personal aside by Odysseus at 258f.
stresses the pathos. Even this great warrior and famously resourceful hero
can do nothing against Scylla but silently and prudently follows Circe's
advice, fleeing without a fight from his truly formidable opponent.

The Latin poet Virgil also wrote about a renowned voyage after the end
of the Trojan War, but one made by Trojans instead of Greeks. The hero
Aeneas and other survivors from Troy sailed off to found a new city and
eventually settled in a part of Italy called Latium, but before that they
spent several years travelling over the Mediterranean Sea in search of
that promised land, encountering various dangers and setbacks (as Odysseus and his men did on their journey). At one point the Trojans stopped
off with a seer called Helenus, and he (rather like Circe) gave Aeneas a
prophecy and advice about the rest of his trip. He warned him of Scylla
and Charybdis, in the straits between Sicily and Italy, and told him to get
to Italy by going around the far side of Sicily rather than passing between
the island and Italy. At *Aeneid* 3.420ff. he says of the straits:

'The right side is besieged by Scylla, the left by insatiable   420
Charybdis, who thrice a day with her deep whirlpool sucks
giant waves into her sheer abyss and each time throws them
up again into the heavens, lashing the stars with the spray.
Scylla lurks inside a dark cavern, from which her
mouths come darting out and she drags ships on to her rocks.   425
Her upper part is human, down to the groin she's a girl with
beautiful breasts, but below she's a monstrously misshapen
sea-beast, with wolves around her belly and dolphins' tails
attached. It is better to lose time by going all the way round
Cape Pachynus on Sicily in a long detour than to set eyes   430
even once on Scylla down in her vast cave and on
the rocks that her bluegreen hounds make resound.'

Subsequently at 3.682ff., when the wind takes the Trojans towards these two creatures, the men decide that they must turn back, remembering Helenus' words, but then the wind suddenly changes and bears them safely away from Scylla and Charybdis down the east coast of Sicily.

Virgil wrote his *Aeneid* with Homer very much in mind, including reminiscences but also making variants, and constantly inviting his readers to compare and contrast Aeneas and Odysseus. So at 3.420ff., like Homer, Virgil is all very serious and has concerned advice for temporarily halted travellers about the coming danger of these two menacing predators. But Virgil's account is much shorter, Aeneas has no actual encounter with the monsters (so that this is something of a non-adventure) and this Scylla has a different form. Virgil's description of her still has impact (a more economical impact): she drags whole ships on to her rocks; she is a disturbing combination of girl and beast, of the erotic and the horrific; and there is an intriguing and unsettling mysteriousness about her – to what are the dolphins' tails attached, does she have wolves and dogs around her belly or just wolfish dogs, how many mouths does she have, how do they dart out, and are they human mouths (which means that her upper body has multiple heads) or the mouths of her wolves/dogs? Often it is more effective not to let readers know everything about something as uncanny as a monster and to leave aspects for them to explore in their own imaginations.

At *Metamorphoses* 13.730ff. Ovid in turn metamorphoses that metamorphosis of Homer (and the Homeric original too), breathing new life into an old monster and making it human. In the course of his own (miniature and much emended) version of the *Aeneid*[6] in books 13 and 14 of the *Metamorphoses*, Ovid here greatly expands Virgil's reference to Scylla, changes the tone and emphasis, and (typically) works in other tales and a lighter amatory element. He begins with a clear reminiscence of *Aeneid* 3.420ff., so that an account similar to Virgil's seems imminent, but before long abruptly sheers off into a prequel. When Ovid's Trojans (on the same voyage after the destruction of Troy) arrive at the Straits of Messina, we are told that the right side is infested by Scylla and the left by Charybdis, and that the latter devours ships, while the former has wild dogs around her belly but has a virgin's face. In fact, Ovid continues, she was once a virgin with many suitors, and also a friend of the sea-nymphs. One of them (Galatea) told Scylla about one of her own suitors (the one-eyed giant Polyphemus), and when Galatea had finished her long story, Scylla went for a walk along the shore. There she was spotted by Glaucus, who had been mortal but had recently been changed by herbs into a sea-god. He immediately fell in love with her, and when she rejected his advances he went to Circe, asking her to use her magic to make Scylla love him. Circe herself promptly fell in love with Glaucus and made advances to him. When he spurned her, saying that he would never stop loving Scylla, Circe decided to harm her rival. She bewitched a pool in which Scylla used to bathe, and when the poor girl next waded into it, dogs suddenly grew from her loins. Glaucus would have nothing to do with the cruel Circe, but Scylla stayed where she was, and when she got the opportunity to vent her hatred of Circe she did so by attacking her beloved Odysseus' ship. She would have sunk Aeneas' ships too, but before they arrived she was transformed into a rock, which the Trojans passed by safely, and which sailors avoided even in Ovid's day.

In contrast to Virgil Ovid does not mention any ominous warning in advance by Helenus, and for Ovid's Trojans this episode is even more of a non-adventure. But at the same time Ovid makes Scylla figure in a much longer passage, at first actually making her a minor character (as a listener to Galatea's story), and then giving her (in her own story) a lot more prominence than she has in the *Aeneid*. Ovid goes both backward and forward in time (to the original Scylla, and to the rock avoided in his own day). So too the tone in Ovid (see further below) is initially flippant, and subsequently sad (in place of Virgil's mystery and menace). In fact, Ovid's Scylla is no real threat to the Trojans (finally she is seen to be just a rock!) and actually arouses love in her suitors and sympathy in the reader. Of course, many of these changes to Virgil's Scylla also represent changes to Homer's Scylla. In addition, Ovid virtually eliminates Charybdis (in contrast to the important role that she played in Homer) and transfers the suspense, horror and pathos from Scylla's attack on Odysseus' ship to her transformation into a monster (see further below). Ovid's explanation of the reason behind Scylla's attack on Odysseus is an additional (and ingenious) twist to Homer. This is all typically Ovidian.

Also part of the entertainment is all the clever inversion, wit and irony in connection with Scylla in book 13. So, for example, when we first meet her, Scylla actually has suitors, and men actually seek her out, and she rejects them (rather than grabbing and devouring them). Then at 738ff. in a cosy girls' chat Galatea complains to Scylla of all people about being courted by a repulsive and terrifying monster who lives in a cave, loves slaughter and fiercely attacks ships; who was warned by a prophet of a coming encounter with Odysseus; who loved but was repulsed (by Galatea); and who killed (Galatea's boyfriend; and he was promptly changed into a river god and stood out from the water waist-deep). At 898ff., when Galatea has finished her story, she swims off, but Scylla is afraid of the deep sea and walks along the beach, refreshing herself in pools. The recently metamorphosed Glaucus is another one attracted to Scylla and even propositions her, but *she* flees from *him*, wondering if he is a monster and marvelling at the lower part of his body that ends in the form of a fish. Then there is again fun with Scylla as the recipient of a speech, when Glaucus assures her that he is no monster or savage beast, that he has great power over the waves, and that he had been a human but was transformed into a denizen of the sea.

All of that is primarily humorous, but there is also a subtle underlying pathos (e.g. in such a beautiful, girlish and timid young woman who enjoys intimate contact with Galatea, soon to become a fearsome and shunned monster, and in her rejection of Glaucus' love, soon to lead to her mutation into an object of loathing). In book 14 the pathos begins to predominate, and there is a strong emotional impact (all the stronger for the contrast with the preceding frivolity). Now the narrative turns into a tragic story of love (Glaucus') going horribly wrong and love (Circe's) being horribly perverted, all shot through with a dark irony. So, after Glaucus' journey to Circe (1ff.), ironically at 12ff. he asks her of all people to help him and show pity; he also claims that nobody knows better than he does the power of herbs because of his own transformation (but Scylla and he will soon know even better thanks to her more extensive and terrible transformation), and he actually requests the witch to use a spell and herbs on Scylla (to make her fall in love with him). There is also a sense of foreboding in that claim and that request, which foreshadow what will follow; so too, when Circe responds by propositioning Glaucus, we see an anticipatory glimpse of an aggressive and predatory female; and then at 40ff. (after Circe has been turned down by Glaucus) we see a callous and destructive female:

> The indignant goddess couldn't harm the god himself   40
> (and didn't want to, since she loved him), so grew angry with
> the one he preferred. Offended at the rejection of her love,
> she immediately ground together noxious herbs whose juices
> had horrific powers and then added the spells of hellish Hecate.
> She put on her bluegreen cloak and set out from the heart of   45
> her palace through a throng of fawning wild animals.
> As she made for Rhegium that lies opposite rocky Zancle,
> she stepped on the surging, seething waves,
> treading on the sea as though on solid ground,
> speeding along its surface with dry feet.   50
> There was a small pool curved in a crescent, a peaceful place
> that Scylla liked. She would go there to escape the heat of the
> sea and sky, when the sun at its strongest, halfway through
> its course, produced from its zenith the shortest shadows.
> Before Scylla's arrival, Circe polluted the pool, contaminating it 55
> with poisons of monstrosity. She sprinkled it with a brew
> distilled from a deadly root and with her witch's lips muttered
> thrice nine times a dark spell, a tangle of weird words.
> Scylla arrives and wades in water halfway up her stomach,
> when she sees her loins disfigured by barking monsters.   60
> At first, not imagining that they are part of her own body,
> she leaps back in fear and pushes away the dogs with their
> vicious mouths, but in trying to escape them drags them along
> with her. When she looks for her thighs and legs and feet,
> she finds in their place gaping jaws like those of Cerberus.   65
> She stands amid rabid dogs, holding fast the beasts below

by means of her mutilated loins and projecting belly.
Her lover Glaucus wept and shrank from a relationship with
Circe, who had used her potent herbs too maliciously.
Scylla stayed there and, as soon as she got the opportunity,   70
gave vent to her hatred of Circe by carrying off Odysseus' men.
She would also have sunk the Trojan ships shortly after that,
if she hadn't been transformed into a stony rock,
which juts out even today. Sailors avoid the rock as well.

The suspense increases at 40-4, as the awesome witch and goddess reacts
so violently to her repulse, turns against Scylla and immediately has
recourse to (highly potent) magic. At 45-50 there is a heavy sense of
inevitability, as Circe sets off (obviously to harm her rival), in an ominously dark cloak, through humans whom she has changed into animals,[7]
and miraculously walks on the (surging) waves, and does so with dry feet.
That graphic picture of Circe's supernatural power arouses sympathy for
Scylla, and more is aroused at 51ff., where Circe somehow just knows
about Scylla's favourite retreat and uses that beautiful and tranquil place
of escape as the site of an attack on her, when she is at her most
vulnerable. At 55-8 a full four lines on a very significant act, packed with
magic details and strong language, build up apprehension and revulsion.
Then in 59 with shocking suddenness poor, unsuspecting Scylla within a
single line is already in the tainted water. Also shockingly sudden is the
mutation, for within another single line (60) the dogs are instantaneously
there, fully formed and barking. But Ovid devotes more than just one verse
to this climactic metamorphosis. He lingers on it at 60-7, to bring out fully
the pathos and the horror, especially by means of the realistic 61-2, the
nightmarish 63-4, the stress through repetition (in 60 and 67) on maiming,
and maiming of the loins in particular (maliciously closing off the sexual
organs to Glaucus), and the frequency throughout of words denoting the
ferocity and menace of the dogs (including allusion in 65 to the watchdog
of the Underworld, which has highly appropriate connotations of terror,
darkness and death).

When the passage ends at 68ff. none of the three protagonists comes out
of this grim tale unscathed – obviously not Scylla, but also not Glaucus
(who loses the girl he loves and is in fact partly responsible for her terrible
mutation), and not Circe either (who does not get Glaucus, and whose
beloved Odysseus is pounced on by Scylla). The account also concludes
with a couple of extra twists. At 70f. there is the novel and clever touch to
explain the particular motivation behind Scylla's assault on Odysseus
(and in retrospect this episode gives a whole new flavour to Circe's advice
to the hero in the *Odyssey*). And at 72f. there is the unexpected petrifica-
tion of Scylla. This is particularly unexpected after the start of this whole
narrative – 13.730ff. – where we were told, in lines reminiscent of Virgil,
that the right side of the straits was infested by Scylla with the face of a

virgin and with wild dogs around her belly, and where we naturally assumed that Ovid was referring to the standard predatory monster. Now we realize with a start that in fact Ovid meant Scylla and her dogs in stone form making the place unsafe as a rocky hazard on which ships might be wrecked. In this way at the very end Ovid slyly works in yet another metamorphosis of Virgil as well as a second metamorphosis of Scylla.

Something similar to what we have seen in this chapter also happens in connection with Grendel, the famous monster in the old English poem *Beowulf*. Read the first 900 lines of *Beowulf*, and then look at John Gardner's book *Grendel* (published by Vintage Books, New York, 1985), and see how he provides a whole new take on the monster, injecting poignancy, humour and so on.

9

Jason and the Argonauts

At my university I teach a course on the ancient world and cinema, and one of the most popular films with classes is always *Jason and the Argonauts* (released by Columbia in 1963).[1] This is an enjoyable (and at times unintentionally amusing) version of the quest for the Golden Fleece, clearly based on the account of the myth by the third-century BC Greek poet Apollonius of Rhodes in his epic *Voyage of Argo*. For the cinema there is a deliberate re-writing of the poem with a 1960s mass audience in mind, and analysis of that process of revision usefully sharpens perception of important aspects of the literary treatment of the story. This chapter will compare and contrast the handling of three episodes involving monsters in the film and in the epic poem.

In the myth Jason's father was the rightful king of a region in northern Greece, but was deprived of his throne by his half-brother Pelias. When Jason grew to manhood, he went to claim the kingdom, and Pelias agreed to give it back, if Jason would go and fetch for him the Golden Fleece. This was the fleece of a flying golden ram, which was in the possession of a fierce oriental king (Aeetes) in remote Colchis (modern Georgia), and which was hung up in a massive grove and guarded by a monstrous serpent. Pelias' intention was for Jason to lose his life on this hazardous quest. A ship was built (called the *Argo*), and many great heroes, known as the Argonauts (= sailors of the *Argo*), came flocking to accompany Jason on his mission. After many adventures on their outward journey they arrived at Colchis. There two goddesses helped Jason by getting the love god Eros to shoot the king's daughter (the beautiful and skilful witch Medea) and make her fall deeply in love with Jason. When asked for the Fleece, Aeetes agreed to hand it over, if Jason could pass an arduous test. He had to yoke two fire-breathing bulls, plough a field with them, sow a dragon's teeth there and kill the armed men who would grow from them and spring up out of the ground. He too thought that the task enjoined on Jason would kill him, but the hero managed it, thanks to the cunning advice and awesome magic of Medea. When the enraged king then refused to give up the Fleece, Jason stole it from the terrible serpent with the help of Medea. He then sailed off with her and the Fleece, and after many more adventures (including escape from the pursuing Colchians thanks to the murder of Medea's brother) they got back safely to Greece.

This is a strange and provoking myth, with elements of beauty, mystery

119

and cruelty. Apollonius in his version brings out the romance and marvel of this journey to the ends of the known world. He includes impressive sights (such as the golden-haired god Apollo striding by the Argo, making the ground quake and the sea run high). He constantly adds learned asides on the exotic nature of the places visited (like the territory of the Tibareni, where when a woman is in childbirth it is the husband who goes to bed, and the land of the Mossynoeci, who do in the open things others do in private, such as having sexual intercourse). But this scholarly and intelligent poet also takes a critical and subtly deflating approach to the myth. He represents Jason as a rather ordinary person thrust into a quite extraordinary expedition, a man possessing some qualities but also many faults (indecisiveness, inertia, despondency etc.), one who definitely needs Medea's magic to succeed. Apollonius' Jason is an enigmatic figure who elicits a variety of responses, a character who differs interestingly from the standard epic hero and really makes you think about the nature of heroism.

The cinematic treatment is very different, not at all intellectual or questioning (naturally enough, given the target audience). *Jason and the Argonauts* does have its good points: for example, it is lively and easy to follow, slimming down a long and involved story to five episodes (Talos; the Harpies; the Clashing Rocks; the Hydra; the Earthborn Men); it contains humour in connection with the gods and an entertaining rivalry between the king and queen of heaven; and some spectacular scenery adds visual appeal. But there is also a tinkering with the plot that is neither necessary nor effective. And there is typical Hollywood commercialization and simplification, trivializing the myth, reducing it to action and adventure alone, and reverting to the clichéd and one-dimensional type of hero. Jason here appears in a totally favourable light (brave, cheerful, polite, good-looking etc.). Hand in hand with that (so that the male is not upstaged) we find in place of the powerful and rather chilling Medea of the epic a colourless little helper with a much reduced role in events.

Talos

The film transfers to the outward journey an incident which occurs on the return leg in the poem. At *Voyage of Argo* 4.1638ff. the Argonauts reach Crete (the island in the Mediterranean Sea), which was guarded by the bronze giant Talos.[2] It is only thanks to Medea that he is overcome, when due to her magic he grazes his vulnerable ankle, so that the ichor (supernatural blood) comes gushing out.

> When they reached the sheltered harbour of Dicte,
> bronze Talos broke off boulders from the massive cliff
> and prevented them from mooring there.   1640
> A descendant of the bronze race sprung from oak trees,
> he had survived into the age of heroes,

and Zeus had given him to Europa to guard Crete, striding
around the island three times a day on his bronze feet.
Most of his body was made of bronze and was   1645
invulnerable; but under the tendon on his ankle
there was a blood-red vein covered by a thin skin,
and his life and death depended on that.
Though suffering from exhaustion, the Argonauts
quickly backed off from the shore in horror.   1650
Then they would have been carried far from Crete,
afflicted by thirst and by weariness, if Medea hadn't
spoken to them as they were in the act of withdrawing:
'Listen to me. For I think that only I can conquer that man
for you (whoever he is), even if his whole body   1655
is made of bronze – unless he is immortal.
Just agree to keep the ship over there beyond
the boulders he hurls until I manage to kill him.'
So she spoke; and they took the ship out of range
and rested on their oars, waiting to see what wonderful   1660
stratagem she would employ. Holding a fold
of her purple robe in front of both her
cheeks, she went up on deck, and Jason took
her hand in his and led her along the thwarts. Then
with incantations she propitiated and invoked the   1665
Death-spirits, those swift hounds of Hades that devour souls,
circling in the sky everywhere and pouncing on the living.
In supplication she summoned them thrice with incantations
and thrice with prayers. Setting her mind to destroy, with a
gaze of hatred she bewitched the eyes of bronze Talos.   1670
Her teeth ground out bitter rage at him, in a frenzy
of anger she sent images of death against him.
Father Zeus, my heart is really surging with amazement:
it is not only diseases and wounds that cause dismal
death, but also people can crush us from far off.   1675
So Talos, bronze though he was, submitted to destruction
by the mighty sorceress Medea. While he was heaving up
heavy boulders to keep them from anchoring,
he grazed his ankle on a jagged rock, and the
ichor gushed out of him like molten lead. He did not   1680
stand there up on the jutting cliff for long after that.
He was like some gigantic pine high up in the mountains
which woodmen have left half-felled by their sharp axes
on returning from the forest; in the night it is
shaken by blasts of wind and then snaps off at the base   1685
and falls down. In the same way he stood
on his tireless feet for a while, swaying, but then
weakened and collapsed with an enormous crash.

Comparison with the film makes Medea's pre-eminence in this passage
especially clear. This predominance of the female (especially in the epic

genre with all its mighty heroes) would have been quite provocative for ancient Greek readers, who belonged to a society in which males prevailed.[3] The Argonauts do not come out of this all that well: despite being weary and thirsty they would have just left, if it had not been for Medea; they carry out her bidding and simply sit there, totally dependent on her; and the most that their leader does is help her to make her way along the ship. Medea is the one who acts (and is victorious) here. The passage begins by depicting Talos as a dread opponent, and then moves on to the crew's horror and readiness to flee, so that Medea's brisk and confident speech and her subsequent success appear particularly impressive. She dominates the narrative, receiving many more lines than the Argonauts and being the only one to speak. The poet dwells on her act of bewitching and also builds it up by means of authorial intervention (expressing his great amazement at her powers). In addition, her sorcery is imposingly mysterious, and for such an adversary she does need various modes of attack but defeats him without too much difficulty. There is also a typically scholarly aspect and a darker tinge here. This is Medea's final appearance in the poem, and it is an ominous one, as a raging witch who can destroy enemies at a distance. This clearly foreshadows the murders that she will later commit back in Greece (in a rage, by means of magic and at a distance), when she kills Pelias, the new bride that Jason takes there and his new father-in-law, and also her own children.

Of course, in a 1963 Hollywood epic film you just couldn't have the hero worsted by a woman or any kind of intellectual or gloomy content. In *Jason and the Argonauts* on the trip out to Colchis (before they meet Medea) the crew stops at an island for supplies. Two of the Argonauts (Hercules and Hylas) come across a treasure-house with a huge bronze statue of Talos on top of it. Despite being warned by Jason not to take anything but food and water, from the oversized jewellery (belonging to the gods, but down on earth for some unexplained reason) Hercules takes a brooch-pin for use as a javelin (even though Hylas already has a javelin and Hercules has his characteristic club). The door closes, shutting them in, but Hercules forces it open again. As they leave Talos turns his head, sees them and slowly gets down from the plinth, creaking loudly (rather like the plot). He pursues them, ineptly, losing them entirely and ending up at the beach where the *Argo* is. The men promptly row off and Talos goes after the ship, even though the two thieves are not on it. He walks off to the harbour mouth and stands there, straddling the exit, and the Argonauts (slow on the uptake) helpfully row right up to him, deciding to back water only when it is too late. The statue grabs the ship, shakes the men out of it and then drops it into the water, badly damaging it. Jason (while floating around in a bit of improbably blue water) asks for advice from the *Argo*'s broken-off figurehead (a carving of the goddess Hera which can speak and open its eyes, rather fetchingly). He is told to look to Talos' ankle. Jason and the others from the ship swim ashore. Hercules and Hylas finally make it back to the beach, and Jason reprimands Hercules for disobeying his orders. Jason then hides in the rocks as Talos approaches and the rest of the Argonauts lead him on by shouting and throwing things at him. While Talos is distracted by them, Jason notices a sort of man-hole cover on the statue's ankle, runs out and with a great effort opens it up. Hot liquid comes pouring out of it. Talos roars, grabs his throat and starts to totter. The Argonauts hastily run off, except for Hylas who goes back for the brooch-pin, which Hercules dropped in flight (even though Hylas was the one who told him not to take it in the first place). Talos cracks up, keels over on top of Hylas and smashes him to hash. Subsequently the crew mend the boat but have no idea where Hylas might be (despite the huge statue lying on top of the sand where he was last seen), so Hercules stays behind to look for him.[4]

In addition to the obvious flaws in logic and motivation here, the special effects (though good for their day) now seem crude, so that the overthrow of Talos is comical rather than awesome. This occurs before the Argonauts encounter Medea, so she cannot figure, still less steal the show.[5] The only female element is provided by Hera (a goddess), in the form of a carving, and she just offers rather vague advice which the bright and brave leader has to interpret and put into effect. This is very much a male adventure, with Jason as the great hero of it. The Argonauts come over well this time, rowing hard, quickly recovering from the shipwreck, and boldly taunting Talos to get his attention. Jason in particular is totally rehabilitated: he is perfectly right about the need to take only food and drink; he censures the mighty Hercules for disobeying; and he plays the major role in the defeat of Talos, courageously taking him on at close quarters (not at a distance like Medea), and having to employ a lot of strength too.

The hydra

The next episode to be considered involves the monster that guards the Golden Fleece. In the film the Argonauts proceed to Colchis (saving Medea from a shipwreck on the way), but there Aeetes is enraged by Jason's request for his treasure and locks the Argonauts up (except for Acastus, who has turned traitor and gone over to Aeetes). That night Medea (who has fallen for Jason) frees them from jail, takes Jason overland to the grove where the Fleece is and tells the rest how to sail near to it on the Argo. Acastus had arrived ahead of them, only to be seized by the monster, a huge snake with seven heads, a sort of cut-price hydra (which normally had nine heads). Jason turns up and, as Medea stands back as a mere spectator, goes to get the Fleece from the tree where it hangs. At that the hydra comes out of its cave, gripping Acastus with its tail, and sees the armed intruder. It promptly loses interest in Acastus, drops him and goes for Jason. While its heads dart to and fro (actually achieving nothing) and its tail flicks (like an irritated cat's), Jason slashes away at it with his

123

sword, missing, missing, missing. He obviously has problems with depth perception, as I count 27 slashes that are too short to make contact with the hydra. After throwing his shield at the snake (why?) and climbing up on to a rock (to make himself a better target?), he suddenly forgets all about the fight and decides that now would be an excellent time to get the Fleece. While he is trying to lift it down, the hydra's tail grabs him round the waist, to his great surprise. It does not kill him but holds him there for a while, not even squeezing very tightly, and its heads don't attack the helpless hero but just writhe politely in the background. Jason inflicts a few feeble blows with his sword on the tail, and the monster lets him go (no doubt in astonishment at actually being hit by him). He rolls over and over under the heads, which strike at him and miss (the hydra also needs glasses, several pairs). Finally it 'rushes' him (in slow motion) and he stabs it in the chest twice. The snake now goes into fast motion, with its heads thrashing round and making a high-pitched whistling sound ('kettle's boiling!'), and finally dies. At this point Acastus decides to die finally too. When the rest of the Argonauts turn up and warn of Aeetes' approach, Jason tells them to get the Fleece and goes to recover his sword from the creature's chest.

There is a slight problem with all this, and that is that it is absolute rubbish. The bungling of three elements in particular seriously reduces the effectiveness of this episode: the monster itself is laughable; the fight is totally unconvincing; and it takes place in what is clearly a fake studio set, complete with plastic boulders, rubber trees and strangely but help-fully bright lighting for this pre-dawn combat. Note also that this time Medea is allowed to figure, but only for 'reaction shots', as the camera switches briefly to her every now and then, to show her horror, anxiety, fear and finally relief, purely as a way (supposedly) of heightening the impact on us of the male's courageous exploit.

This is actually meant to be an improvement on Apollonius, to whom we will now turn. In his poem, after Jason has successfully performed Aeetes' task (yoking the bulls etc.) thanks to Medea, the king retires to his palace in a rage, with no intention at all of handing over the Golden Fleece and suspecting Medea's complicity. She slips out to join the Argonauts, guides them on the *Argo* to a landing-place near the grove where the Fleece hangs, and then (at 4.123ff.) takes Jason to it early in the morning before dawn. As you read the lines, look to see how effective the depiction of the snake is here and the defeat of it and the setting.

> They went along the path to the sacred grove,
> looking for the massive oak tree on which was hung
> the fleece, like a cloud that is turned red   125
> by the fiery rays of the rising sun.
> But right in front the serpent with its keen, unsleeping
> eyes saw them coming, stretched out its immense

9. Jason and the Argonauts

Jason is regurgitated by the Colchian dragon as Athena looks on and the golden fleece hangs on a tree in the background, from an Attic red-figure kylix by Douris and Python, *c.* 480-470 BC. Vatican Museums, Rome.

neck and emitted a monstrous hiss. All around the river's
long banks and the enormous grove echoed with the sound.   130
It was even heard by those Colchians who lived far away
from Titanian Aea, by the mouth of the Lycus
(which parts from the roaring river Araxes
and blends its sacred water with that of Phasis,
flowing on together with it into the Caucasian Sea).   135
Mothers awoke in terror and anxiously
hugged tight their new-born babies,
asleep in their arms and trembling at the hiss.
Then that monster's countless coils, encased
in dry scales, began to undulate,   140
just like the endless eddies of sooty smoke
that curl above a smouldering forest,
one quickly succeeding another and constantly
rising up in continuous convolutions.
As the snake writhed, before its eyes came the girl,   145
and her sweet voice called on Sleep, the highest of the gods,
to help her and charm the monster. She also asked the
night-wandering queen of Hell for her gracious support.
Jason was behind her, terrified. But the snake, already

bewitched by her song, was relaxing the long spine   150
of its great, sinuous mass; its myriad coils spread out,
like a dark swell rolling across a sluggish sea
in absolute silence. Yet despite that it
raised its terrible head high above them,
longing to close its deadly jaws about them both.   155
But Medea chanted a spell, dipped a newly cut
sprig of juniper into her potent brew and sprinkled
the serpent's eyes. The pervasive magic scent smothered it
and sent it to sleep. It let its jaws sink to the ground,
and its innumerable coils stretched out   160
far behind it, back through the dense wood.
At that, when the girl told him to, Jason snatched
the golden fleece from the oak. She stayed there and
smeared the creature's head with the magic salve
until Jason himself urged her to go back   165
to the ship. Then she left the shadowy grove of Ares.

In contrast to the film, the setting here is imposing. It is both numinous and ominous. The grove is a holy place, and one devoted to the terrible, murderous god of war (Ares) at that, while oak trees were sacred to Zeus himself, the king of the gods. There is a stress on massiveness, which is intimidating and also complements the huge monster that resides there. The wood is dense and shadowy too, i.e. sombre and menacing, the kind of place where the snake can lurk and strike unexpectedly. And there is the effective chiaroscuro of the Fleece's unearthly effulgence amid the darkness of night. That highlights and focuses attention on the prize, which is like a cloud (i.e. glowing, fluffy, high up, beautiful and ethereal). Presumably the Fleece provides just enough light for Medea to see what she is doing with the snake, so that the overall effect of the eerily lit blackness is decidedly atmospheric.

Apollonius' monster is genuinely unnerving. Aptly it bulks large, dominating the passage. There are telling touches, like its tremendously loud hiss (that scares poor mothers and babies, making it look really bad), the countless coils (bringing out its immensity), the minatory movement of them at 139ff., and the (repellent) dry scales encasing them. The poet does not provide the lengthy and very detailed description of the serpent that would be the literary equivalent of the cinematic showing of the hydra. Instead he gives his readers a few bold strokes and leaves us to fill in the rest in our imagination. The simile at 141ff. also draws one in like this. The endless eddies of sooty smoke from a whole forest smouldering conjure up coil after coil of a dark mass rising up, with the snake towering above the grove containing the glowing Fleece. And, suggestively, the forest in the simile would seem to be quite capable of suddenly blazing up and inflicting pain and death.

The depiction of the subduing of the serpent is also effective. Supernatural methods (rather than a sword) are needed to deal with this supernatural creature, and it takes a lot to beat such a mighty adversary. At 145ff. Medea calls on two divine helpers, and it seems at first as if she has been successful. The simile at 152f. conveys intense quiet and unthreatening relaxation, which greatly increases the impact of the sudden rearing up at 153ff. Medea now has to resort to two magical devices of her own, and the monster only succumbs finally to this second onslaught. Even then she smears its head (because after all the foregoing it could still wake up and pursue them). So the engagement with the serpent in the poem is a tense and uncanny business, a real accomplishment for Medea (who in Apollonius is again the one who acts and is prominent, in contrast to Jason's brief and rather ignominious appearances).

The earthborn men

The third episode involves Jason's fight with the earthborn men. In *Jason and the Argonauts* this comes at the very end, after the seizure of the Fleece, as part of the action-packed climax, and these monsters represent a final danger for the hero to face and overcome. In the *Voyage of Argo*, more correctly, they form the last part of Aeetes' test for Jason (after the yoking, ploughing and sowing) prior to getting the Fleece. In the third book of the poem after this test has been outlined for him, Jason has to turn to Medea for help, flattering her and promising her rewards. She loves him deeply, and so tells him to sacrifice and pray to the goddess Hecate, and to anoint himself and his weapons with a magic charm of hers which will give him supreme strength and confidence and make him and his equipment impervious to the bulls' fire and the earthborn men's spears. She also tells him to throw a boulder in among the monsters as they rise from the ground, since they will fight over it and he can attack them while they are diverted like this. The hero duly sacrifices and prays to Hecate, then anoints his body and his gear with the charm. He duly acquires miraculous, indomitable might and a great eagerness for battle, and when he tests his spear and sword they cannot be broken by any blows. After that he yokes the bulls, ploughs and sows without any problem. He then goes to the river for a drink and lashes himself into a fury ready to deal with the monstrous products of the dragon's teeth, which start to grow up from the ground at this point.

> By now the earthborn men were shooting up all over
> the field. That precinct sacred to murderous Ares   1355
> bristled with sturdy shields, two-pointed spears
> and gleaming helmets. The glitter flashed up
> through the air all the way to Olympus.
> The warriors sprang from the earth, shining
> like the host of stars that glint through   1360

127

the darkness of black night after a
heavy snowfall, when the winds have blown
away the wintry clouds. But Jason
kept cunning Medea's advice in mind and
picked up from the ground a huge round boulder,   1365
a formidable mass which Ares might have thrown, and
which four strong men could not have budged a bit.
Rushing forward with it in his hands, he hurled it from afar
into the warriors' midst, then sank down out of sight behind
his shield, confident. The Colchians gave a great shout   1370
like the roar of the sea crashing on sharp rocks,
while Aeetes was speechless when he saw him hurl the great
boulder. But the warriors, like nimble dogs, leapt on
one another, yelling and slaying. With their spears they
stretched each other out on their mother earth,   1375
as pines or oaks are beaten down by gales.
Like a fiery star that speeds from heaven,
leaving a shining trail, a portent for those
who see it flashing through the sky,
so Jason rushed on the earthborn men   1380
with his sword unsheathed and mowed them down
indiscriminately, wounding many who had half emerged
with their bellies and flanks exposed, others who had
only their shoulders clear, some just standing upright,
and others already charging into the fight.   1385
Just as a farmer during a battle over boundaries,
afraid that the enemy might reap his fields first,
snatches up a newly-sharpened curving sickle and
hastily cuts down the unripe crop, not waiting
till harvest-time for the sun's rays to ripen it,   1390
so Jason cut down his crop of earthborn men. Blood
filled the furrows as water fills a spring's channel.
Down they fell, some on their faces, biting the field's
rough clods, some on their backs, and others on
their hands and sides, looking like sea-monsters.   1395
Many were struck before they got their feet clear
and lay there, with their heads and whatever else
of them had emerged bowed down to the ground.

Jason is victorious and does achieve something, but this is not simply a glorious deed by him. Apollonius complicates the issue and undercuts the feat. For a start it is clear that Jason could not have managed this without Medea. And there is something of an anticlimax here. Before this he had done what she told him to do and everything had turned out as she predicted it would. He had acquired the great powers and performed the earlier parts of the task with ease. So, as we strongly suspected would be the case, there are no problems now, and this last part is a foregone conclusion, as he duly follows the cunning witch's advice[6] about throwing in the boulder (a ruse which works at once) and attacks the warriors, using an indestructible sword (with speedy and total success). In fact this is just slaughter, as he catches most of them before they can properly defend themselves against blows or fight back. They are not built up as particularly terrifying opponents, and 1386ff. liken them to (inert, unresisting, non-threatening) corn being just mowed down. There are also lots of similes in the above passage, which slow down the pace and distract, and there is lots of detail at 1382-5 and 1393-8 which has a similar clogging effect.

In the film there is a deliberate and total inversion of all this, playing down the woman and playing up the man and his exploit. The incident is made more dramatic and stirring (especially for a less sophisticated 1960s audience).[7] Many will prefer this to Apollonius' deflation and 'spoiling' of the fight, although some will object to it as dumbing down.

In *Jason and the Argonauts*, after the hydra is killed the crew head off up a cliff with the Fleece and Medea. Aeetes turns up, sends some of his soldiers after them and calls on Hecate to revenge herself on the Argonauts and deliver to him the hydra's teeth. Somewhat surprisingly for a goddess of the Underworld, she sends down from the sky thunderbolts which burn up the hydra. He orders the men with him to hack out its teeth and bring them to him, remarking ominously, 'Against the children of the hydra's teeth there is no protection.' On top of the cliff one of the soldiers pursuing the Argonauts shoots Medea in the back with an arrow and kills her, but Jason pops the Fleece on to her and promptly revives her with it.

Aeetes now makes it to the top of the cliff and calls on Jason to halt, which he obligingly does. The king now tells his men to keep back or they may be killed along with Jason and his pirates. He throws the teeth on to the (hard, stony, unploughed) ground, saying rather portentously, 'Rise up, you dead, slain of the hydra, rise from your graves and avenge us! Those who steal the Golden Fleece must die.' While Aeetes 'sows' the teeth, Jason tells one of his men to take (the mere woman) Medea off to the ship with the Fleece, and he and another two comrades stay, swords and shields at the ready to face the danger. Amid ominous music seven skeletons pop up from the ground, also armed with swords and shields, and the king shouts out dramatically (and rather repetitively), 'Destroy them!' and 'Kill, kill, kill them all!' The dutiful skeletons slowly advance on Jason and his companions (who slowly retreat), and then they let out a high-pitched shriek and charge.

The unsporting skeletons take full advantage of their superior numbers and give every appearance of being invulnerable (they can be knocked down, but promptly bounce back; a sword through the ribs of one only discomforts it momentarily; another has its skull lopped off and wanders around like a headless chicken, but soon returns to the fray). The fight carries on for several minutes, amid exciting music, with lots of action and lots of movement to and fro, as weapons are lost in the cut and thrust and are then recovered, gaps between walls are vaulted just above slashing swords, and so on. Finally Jason's two men are killed and he is left to face the enemy alone on the edge of the cliff. They gang up on him and rush him, but he has acquired a spear from somewhere, throws it at them and then leaps off the cliff down into the sea far below. Quite carried away, and making no bones about it, the skeletons jump after him. This proves to be a bad move, as for some reason they disintegrate in mid-air and plop into the water harmlessly. Jason swims back to the ship and is reunited with Medea. The film ends with Zeus looking down from heaven and announcing that there are other adventures for Jason in the future (very true – like committing bigamy and seeing his family murdered by the vengeful Medea!).

With a systematic rewriting of Apollonius the film attempts to re-establish Jason as a real warrior and this fight as a splendid accomplishment. So far from helping Jason and telling him what to do, here Medea has to be hustled off to safety (and she has been recently helped by Jason herself, with the reviving Fleece). There is nothing to slow down or distract us from all the action (which is in fact enhanced by the energetic music). These opponents for Jason are meant to be formidable: skeletons rather than men are more scary for a modern audience; there is no trick with a boulder to divert their aggression; and it is they rather than Jason that seem to be supernaturally indestructible. The hero has to fight long and hard, and his victory is far from easy. This time Jason is an excellent swordsman and actually hits the enemy, regularly. He seems all the greater because he survives in contrast to his two (only two) companions. And he ends up facing all the skeletons on his own, is nearly overwhelmed by them, and only escapes thanks to some quick thinking (a ruse that he comes up with himself).[8]

There is another episode in *Jason and the Argonauts* and in the *Voyage of Argo* which involves monsters, and that is when the Argonauts help Phineus by driving off the Harpies that plague him. For discussion of the poetic account see pp. 63ff. above. Analyse the cinematic version of this incident, paying particular attention to differences from Apollonius.

10

Fighting with Monsters (1)

The Second Labour of Heracles: the Hydra of Lerna

In atonement for murdering his wife and children in a fit of madness, the mighty hero Heracles (Hercules) was ordered by the oracle of the god Apollo to serve a Greek king called Eurystheus for twelve years and to do whatever the king told him. Eurystheus set him twelve arduous tasks (known as the Labours). Several of these involved fighting with a monster. So for his second Labour Eurystheus ordered Heracles to kill the Hydra of Lerna, a monstrous watersnake which had been bred in the marsh of Lerna (in southern Greece) and used to emerge from there on to dry land, ravaging the cattle and the countryside. The Hydra had a huge body with nine heads (eight of which were mortal, while the one in the centre was immortal). Heracles made his way to Lerna on a chariot with his nephew Iolaus and arrived at the swamp. He went up to the creature's lair, and shot fire-arrows at it, forcing it to emerge. When it did, he seized it in a firm grip. But it wound itself around one of his legs and clung on tightly. He smashed its heads with his club but achieved nothing: as soon as one head was smashed, two grew in its place. Also a huge crab came to its assistance by biting his foot. So he killed the crab and called for help himself, from Iolaus, who set on fire part of a nearby forest and used blazing branches from it to sear the stumps and stop the heads from regrowing. When he had disposed of the regenerating heads in this way, Heracles cut off the immortal one, buried it and placed a heavy boulder on it. He then ripped open the dead Hydra's body and dipped his arrows in its gall, so that they would inflict an incurable wound.

There are many myths like this involving combat with a monster (in which a monster and an opponent confront one another and square up, each trying to prevail over the other). Such a combat myth provides one of the more common and meaningful roles for a monster; and for the opponent one way to achieve superior status is to grapple with and vanquish such a creature. Essentially what happens is that the opponent (generally male, and much more often a hero than a god[1]) fights with the monster (often seeking it out), almost always defeats it, and usually kills it too. Monsters tend to be formidable foes – for instance, they are terrifying to look at (part human and part beast, with multiple heads and bodies etc.); very strong, savage and quick; and possessed of preternatural powers, such as the ability to emit fire or fountains of venom and an impervious-

131

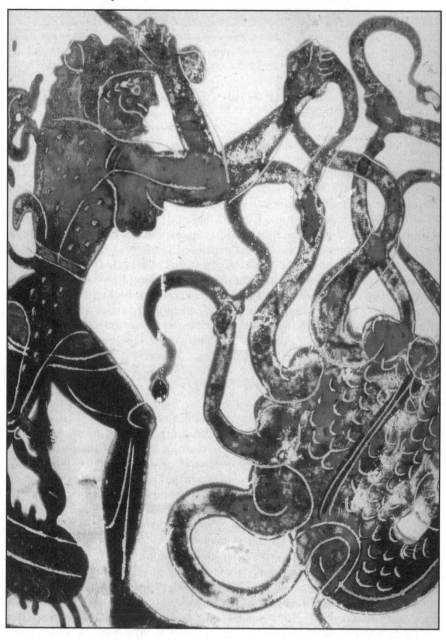

Heracles and the Hydra, from a black-figure lekythos by the Diosphos Painter, 500-490 BC. Louvre, Paris.

ness to weapons. To conquer them opponents need great courage, various fighting abilities, powerful weapons (like the thunderbolt, or Medusa's head whose gaze turns people to stone), often ingenuity rather than just brawn, and often assistance from human or divine helpers (e.g. directions, advice, provision of special equipment and even support in fighting).

Naturally in such narratives the focus is primarily on monsters and opponents, although there may be momentary highlighting of others, such as helpers (to provide relief and build anticipation) and victims (like the beautiful princess chained to a cliff as prey for a sea-beast), who bring out the pathos and horror. Naturally too such narratives contain much suspense and conflict (especially when the fight is presented at length, with attack, counter-attack, wounding and so on). Usually reversals of some kind are in evidence: the monster instead of killing and rampaging is killed and inert, fear gives way to relief, misery to celebration and so on. Frequently there is symmetry: the opponent returns to his starting point, the original situation before the depredations of the monster is re-established and so forth. Most often the victory has personal relevance for the opponent (who thereby performs a task, secures a prize, removes an obstacle or threat, recovers property stolen from him etc.), but sometimes it also has a more general application (like freeing a community from a beast's ravages).

Plot analysis: functions and stages

After that overview to provide general context it is now time to sharpen the focus.[2] One fruitful way to look at a narrative is to examine the plotting in it (which really helps one to take it apart, scrutinize separate components and see how the whole thing works). This becomes even more fruitful when one considers a narrative's plotting within the context of a group of similar narratives. The Russian literary critic Propp usefully broke stories down into 'functions', which are actions that are significant for the tale as a whole, that contribute to substantial movement from initial to final situation (i.e. not inconsequential stuff like putting the cat out, but important acts like crippling or killing an adversary).[3] These functions are the fundamental components or building blocks of a story, and by isolating them one strips a story down to its essentials. In a study of 26 Classical and 12 non-Classical myths of combat with a monster[4] I have found that 31 functions occur in 3 separate stages. None of these combat myths contains all 31 functions, and not all of them contain all 3 stages – this is the overall group of possibilities from which such narratives are constructed.

My findings can be conveniently laid out as follows, although the functions need not appear in narratives exactly in this order:

133

STAGE 1. PRELUDE (events immediately before the combat which bear directly on it):

MOTIVATION (the Opponent is sent against the Monster by another, wants revenge on the Monster or to recover property stolen by the Monster, tries to rescue a victim from the Monster, and so on)

PREPARATIONS (planning, acquisition of Helpers, arming etc.)

HELP (e.g. assistance with transportation, directions, provision of equipment)

JOURNEY (to the scene of combat)

ARRIVAL (the Opponent/ Monster arrives at the scene of combat)

STAGE 2. CONTACT (the actual combat):

PHYSICAL APPROACH (the Opponent goes right up to the Monster, or vice versa, for the combat)

OPPOSITION (the Opponent/ Monster opposes, defending a victim etc.)

VULNERABILITY (the Monster is/ falls asleep, the Opponent falls ill)

PREPARATIONS (planning, arming etc.)

FIGHTING (attack, defence, counter attack, blows/ wounds inflicted/ evaded, debilitation, recovery and so on)

CONTENTION (some other form of combat – e.g. magic)

HELP (information, guidance, support in fighting and so forth)

FLIGHT (the Opponent/ Monster flees)

PURSUIT (the Opponent/ Monster pursues)

CONCEALMENT (the Monster/ Opponent hides, is/ is not detected)

ESCAPE (the Monster/ Opponent escapes)

VICTORY (the Opponent defeats the Monster)

DEATH (the Monster/ Opponent dies)

STAGE 3. AFTERMATH (subsequent events directly linked to the combat):

TREATMENT OF CORPSE (the Monster's corpse is viewed/ mangled/ shunned/ utilized)

PUNISHMENT (e.g. the Opponent is threatened with punishment or actually punished for fighting, the Monster is punished)

FORGIVENESS (the Opponent is forgiven for fighting)

REWARD (for Opponent is promised/ given/ refused)

SACRIFICE (e.g. in thanksgiving, appeasement, to win divine protection)

EXPLOITATION OF VICTORY (victim released, stolen property recovered, obstacle posed by monster removed, prize taken etc.)

CELEBRATION OF VICTORY (vaunting by the Opponent, praise for the Opponent and so forth)

HELP (with advice, seizing prize)

ASSAULT (the Monster assaults the Opponent)

DEPARTURE (the Opponent departs)

JOURNEY (by the Opponent)

PURSUIT (on departing the Opponent is pursued)

ESCAPE (the Opponent escapes assault or pursuit)
ARRIVAL (the Opponent arrives at the final destination)

To give a concrete example of the way this kind of analysis works, the story of Heracles' combat with the Hydra outlined at the start of this chapter can be broken down as follows:

(Stage 1) MOTIVATION (Eurystheus orders Heracles to kill the Hydra), PREPARATIONS (Heracles acquires Iolaus as a Helper), JOURNEY (Heracles travels to Lerna) and ARRIVAL (he reaches the Hydra's swamp);
(Stage 2) PHYSICAL APPROACH (as he goes right up to its lair and it emerges), FIGHTING, HELP 1 (the crab helps the Hydra, until it is killed), HELP 2 (Iolaus sears the stumps), VICTORY and DEATH (as he kills the Hydra); (in stage 3) TREATMENT OF CORPSE (as its gall is utilized for Heracles' arrows).

One of the valuable things that this type of analysis does is to highlight any skimming or omission of functions and stages. There is the famous story of Theseus killing the Minotaur (see Chapter 6). Theseus went as part of the human tribute that the Athenians had to offer to the king of Crete to be thrown to the Minotaur (a half-man and half-bull monster) in the inextricable maze known as the Labyrinth, but he overcame the monster. In Catullus' version[5] FIGHTING with the Minotaur is passed over very quickly, downplaying the achievement of Theseus, who in Catullus is not a figure of romance but a rather dubious adventurer who carries off the Cretan princess Ariadne, who had helped him defeat the Minotaur, and then cruelly abandons her despite her help and his promises of marriage (compare pp. 79ff. above). So too the VICTORY and DEATH functions are treated very briefly in Diodorus Siculus in connection with Heracles' combat with the dragon guarding the golden apples of the Hesperides (which he had to fetch for one of his Labours), implying that for the greatest of the Greek heroes the conquest of this ferocious creature was easy.

This isolating of functions and stages also facilitates perception of significant expansion. So in Apollodorus, when Perseus goes to kill and bring back the head of Medusa (a savage female monster with snakes for hair and eyes that turn onlookers to stone), he receives extensive HELP (guidance from two gods, directions, winged sandals, a wallet to hold Medusa's head, a cap to make him invisible and a sickle of the hardest of metals [adamant] to cut off the head). Much of that HELP was from divinities, which marks Perseus out as a favourite of heaven, and the fact that so much HELP was necessary stresses the difficulty of the task and builds up the magnitude of Perseus' feat. Similarly when he returns from killing Medusa Perseus rescues a beautiful princess who had been chained up for a sea-beast to devour, and in Ovid and Manilius the FIGHTING with that beast is handled at great length, making for drama and excitement,

135

and building the combat into a truly epic contest and a major achievement for the hero.

This system clarifies norms in connection with functions, and abnormalities too, which often have point. So Catullus' account of Theseus and the Minotaur in his poem 64 is the only one of such narratives which does not directly describe the FIGHTING. Instead the poet uses a simile, likening the Minotaur being brought low to a tree on the top of a mountain being uprooted by a storm wind. He thereby takes the focus off Theseus at this important point and reduces his role. Claudian in his poem on the battle between the gods and the Giants achieves a certain impact and interest by means of unique variants on the DEATH function: one of the monsters endures a double death, as he himself is killed by a sword and the snakes that are an appendage of his are turned to stone by the gaze of Medusa's head; and another of the monsters suffers only a partial death, as the giant part of him dies but his serpent legs live on, hissing revenge and trying to attack the victorious Opponent.

Propp's approach facilitates analysis of the simplicity or complexity of plotting too. In the majority of these cases it is simple, with the exception of most of the stories about Heracles, which involve combats (with monsters or others) in addition to the main combats, other adventures and incident-packed journeys out and back (see further below). Similarly in Ovid's version of the Perseus tale there are two fights with monsters (Medusa and the sea-beast), presented in reverse chronological order, and with additional exploits and combats foregrounded. The complexity and temporal dislocation is even more pronounced in Catullus poem 64: he begins with Ariadne abandoned on the island; then he presents a flashback to the origin of the Athenian tribute, Theseus' decision to put an end to it, his journey to and arrival in Crete, Ariadne's help, his victory over the Minotaur and their departure; then he returns to Ariadne on the island, whose prayer that Theseus should be punished is granted, as he is made to forget to change his sail by Jupiter; then there is another flashback – to Aegeus' instructions to his son about altering the sail as Theseus left for Crete; finally Aegeus sees the black sail and leaps to his death, Theseus arrives back in Athens, and Dionysus turns up on the island to claim Ariadne as his bride.

Filling out the story

Functions provide the bare bones of a story, and it is now time to consider how authors fleshed out and gave life to that skeleton. Some of the functions (if at all developed) in themselves add body and have impact. MOTIVATION, for instance, can really involve readers and prejudice them against the Monster, so that they want to see it defeated; and PREPARATIONS can raise expectations and increase tension. There is also meat in an unusual, lively or striking expression of a function. Consider, for example, the PHYSICAL APPROACH of Hesione's monster which Heracles battles in Valerius Flaccus (after a great roar down in the gulf that is its home, the dragon appears far off at sea, with eyes that flash like stars, with a bellow like thunder coming from the mouth that has a triple row of fangs, and with a thousand vast coils covering the water, and it charges forward at great speed, driving the waves before it so violently that it causes a fierce storm at sea). Then there is Apollonius' version of CONTEN- TION, when the witch Medea uses magic on the bronze giant Talos, invoking the Spirits of Death (who feed on souls and swoop down on the living), bewitching the giant's eyes with her malignant glance, gnashing bitter rage at him and in a frenzy of anger sending deadly phantoms against him. FIGHTING is often given a dramatic and sensational form. In Ovid's lines on Perseus versus the sea-beast the latter is so savage (and short-sighted) that when Perseus soars into the sky at its approach and his shadow falls on the water, it viciously attacks the shadow. In Nonnus' passage on the struggle between Zeus and Typhos the Monster has a hand lopped off, but the hand continues to fight on its own, rolling along the ground manically and hurling a rock at the Opponent. And in Nonnus' depiction of the fight between the giant Damasen and a monstrous snake the latter hisses battle, wraps two coils around Damasen's feet, whips other coils about his body and opens wide its frenzied, cavernous mouth, rolling its wild eyes, breathing death, spitting fountains of poison and shooting a long gout of greenish-yellow foam into the giant's face, but the massively powerful Damasen throws the snake off and smashes an up- rooted tree down on its head.

Of course, narratives of combat (like all narratives) are also filled out by material other than functions (formal introduction, characterization, setting, similes and much else), to give them clarity, colour, logical coher- ence and so on. In connection with combat myths description is typical and important. By describing the Monster itself, its lair or activities a writer can show the odds against the Opponent, build tension, atmosphere, horror etc. (compare pages 29ff.). So Ovid pictures the home of Medusa as surrounded everywhere by immobile figures of beasts and men changed into stone by her gaze, and Hesiod depicts Typhos with a hundred snaky heads flashing forth fire and weirdly uttering all kinds of sounds (hisses, the speech of the gods, the bellow of a furious bull, the roar of a pitiless lion and the yelping of puppies). So too Statius portrays the depredations of the Monster subsequently killed by Coroebus (which glided into bed- rooms at night, snatched new-born babies from the breasts that suckled them, carried them off with hooked talons and iron nails fixed fast in their hearts and entrails, and then gorged on them with blood-stained fangs).

Sometimes there are exotic and bizarre touches to add vitality (like the three old crones called the Graeae who share and pass between them a single eye and a single tooth), and sometimes there is even humour (as when Perseus, while returning with the severed head of Medusa, catches sight of the half-naked Andromeda chained up for the sea-beast and is so staggered by her beauty that he nearly drops Medusa's head).[6] Also enlivening are abnormalities in material other than functions. So in the combats with the dragon guarding the Golden Fleece and with the bronze giant Talos it is (piquantly) the female Medea who is the Opponent, while Jason (a rather ordinary hero) is reduced to the role of Helper; and Bellerophon fights one Monster (the Chimaera) with help from another (he rides the winged horse Pegasus); and Heracles faces two Monsters in one – the Molionides, gigantic Siamese twins appointed as joint commanders (literally) of an army facing him.

The Tenth Labour of Heracles: Geryon and Cacus

The above general survey will now be followed by a demonstration of this analysis in action, homing in on a prominent figure in these combat myths – Heracles. He is much greater than other Greek heroes, and his super-heroic status is well brought out in these stories. He appears in 10 of the 26 Classical examples (far more frequently than anybody else[7]), sometimes faces very difficult monstrous foes (e.g. the invulnerable Nemean Lion and the Hydra with its multiple heads, which grow back double when cut off) and often has to fight several Monsters and/or other enemies in succession. Yet, unlike many other Opponents, he does not need special weapons (and in fact frequently uses just his bare hands). He does receive some help, but not with the actual fighting, and he himself figures as a Helper for the gods (in their battle with the giants). The greater complexity of plot in his combats with Monsters also marks him out as different.

A translation of the account in Apollodorus[8] of Heracles' tenth Labour follows, with functions signposted in advance in square brackets.

STAGE 1

[MOTIVATION:] As a tenth Labour he was ordered to fetch from Erytheia the cattle of Geryon. Erytheia was an island lying near the Ocean; it is now called Gadeira. Geryon lived there, the son of Chrysaor and the Oceanid Callirhoe. He had the bodies of three men grown together, joined into one at the stomach, but divided into three from the flanks and thighs down. He had red cattle, with Eurytion as herdsman and Orthus as watch-dog (the two-headed hound born by Echidna to Typhon). [JOURNEY:] So Heracles travelled through Europe after the cattle of Geryon and killed many wild animals on his way. He arrived in Libya and went on to Tartessus, and as memorials of his journey he erected two pillars standing opposite each other on the borders of Europe and Libya. In the course of his journey he was made hot by the Sun and bent his bow at the god. [HELP:] In admiration of his courage the Sun gave him a golden goblet, in which he sailed over the Ocean. [ARRIVAL:] When he reached Erytheia, he encamped on Mount Abas.

138

Heracles and Geryon, from a black-figure amphora by the Inscriptions Painter, 540 BC. Bibliothèque Nationale, Paris.

STAGE 2

[PHYSICAL APPROACH, FIGHTING, DEATH, VICTORY:] The dog spotted him and rushed to the attack, but Heracles hit it with his club; [HELP:] and when the herdsman Eurytion came to help the dog, Heracles killed him too. [HELP:] Menoetes, who was there pasturing the cattle of Hades, told Geryon what had happened. [PHYSICAL APPROACH, FIGHTING, DEATH, VICTORY:] Geryon caught up with Heracles beside the river Anthemus, as he was driving the cattle away, and fought with him, but was shot dead by an arrow.

STAGE 3

[EXPLOITATION OF VICTORY:] Heracles put the cattle into the goblet. [DEPARTURE, JOURNEY:] He sailed back across to Tartessus and returned the goblet to the Sun. He passed through Abderia and came to Liguria, where Ialebion and Dercynus (sons of Poseidon) tried to rob him of the cattle, but he killed them and went on his way through Tyrrhenia. But at Rhegium one bull broke away, quickly plunged into the sea and swam across to Sicily. Then it passed through the neighbouring land (which was named 'Italy' after it, as 'italus' was the Tyrrhenians' word for 'bull') and came to the plain of Eryx, who was king of the Elymi and a son of Poseidon, and who merged the bull into his own herds. [HELP:] So Heracles entrusted the rest of the cattle to Hephaestus and rushed off in search of the bull. He

139

found it in Eryx's herds, and when Eryx refused to hand it over unless Heracles beat him at wrestling, Heracles beat him three times and killed him in the wrestling bout. He then took the bull and drove it with the rest of the cattle to the Ionian Sea. But when he reached the sea's inlets, Hera sent a gadfly to attack the cattle, which scattered among the foothills of the mountains of Thrace. He went after them, caught some of them and drove them to the Hellespont, while those that were left behind were wild from then on. Heracles blamed the river Strymon for his difficulties in collecting the cattle together. This river, long navigable, he made unnavigable by filling it with boulders. [ARRIVAL:] He then took the cattle and handed them over to Eurystheus, [SACRIFICE:] who sacrificed them to Hera.

Apollodorus' chapter may be only a summary of earlier authors and only an outline, but it is still a narrative and it does illustrate the usefulness of this approach.

In the first stage the JOURNEY function receives the most development and rapidly raises the Opponent's standing: in the course of a long journey to a really remote place, which requires an extraordinary form of transport (the Sun's goblet), there are various parerga or incidental feats (including the erection of the famous pillars), and Heracles wins help from a god (whom he actually threatens).

The second stage is the briefest, but it contains the most functions and a flurry of activity (the individual combats may be skimmed, but there are three of them – two against Monsters, and one with Eurytion). Fighting with two monsters in close succession is most unusual, as is the twofold repetition of the sequence PHYSICAL APPROACH, FIGHTING, DEATH and VICTORY.[9] HELP for a Monster is uncommon, and the double HELP for the Monster is unique, while Heracles is the only Opponent who fights with such a Helper. All these rare features add interest and also present Heracles as a truly exceptional Opponent.

The third stage is the one that receives the most stress, and in it the JOURNEY function gets extensive treatment and is full of incident (this combat myth is far from over after the fights with the Monsters). Such dwelling on the JOURNEY back and all the action in it are most unusual. Here again vast distances are covered, there are even more incidental achievements, Heracles receives help from a god again, and there are still more fights (against sons of gods). He has lots of problems here, but deals with them all (even when divinely inspired) in an eventful narrative that depicts him not just as the killer of Geryon and procurer of his cattle but as a great traveller and great fighter generally (against numerous, impressive enemies).

There is also quite extensive patterning. Stages 1 and 3 receive more textual prominence than the second stage, and there are parerga in the JOURNEY back as in the JOURNEY out, and in those JOURNEYS Heracles gets help from a god and the Sun's goblet is given and returned. The number three recurs – Geryon's three bodies, the three enemies beaten in the course of Heracles' return and the three victories over Eryx in wrestling. There is symmetry too in Heracles being back again with Eurystheus at the end of the passage.

There is also some looseness and complexity of plotting here, with so many characters and so much incident worked into the narrative in a succession of episodes (often with their own climaxes). In particular this tale of the combat with Geryon also includes combat with another Monster, and combats with other foes too. And there is more complexity when one takes into account the adventure with Cacus, as related by Virgil and other authors who place it in Heracles' journey back: for then there is yet another embedded fight with a Monster (and yet another figure trying to rob cattle from the cattle-robber Heracles).

Virgil's version of the interlude with Cacus is worth considering now especially because a poet (as opposed to a mythographer like Apollodorus) demonstrates well how flesh can be added to the bare bones of such a narrative. In Virgil *Aeneid* 8.185ff. king Evander (who lives where Rome will later be built) tells the Trojan hero Aeneas about the earlier encounter there between Cacus and Hercules (the Latin form of Heracles' name). While driving Geryon's cattle back to Eurystheus, Hercules came to the Aventine Hill (on the future site of Rome), where Cacus had his lair. That massive and monstrous son of Vulcan (god of fire) stole eight of the cattle, dragging them backwards into his cavern, so their tracks would not give the theft away. When Hercules discovered the robbery, he charged up, club in hand, and Cacus fled to his cave, dropping a huge rock to seal the entrance. Since he couldn't get in that way, Hercules went to the ridge above the cavern and tore off the crag that formed its roof, revealing the monster's den below. When Hercules bombarded him from above, Cacus belched out thick black smoke and fire, but Hercules rushed through it all unheeding, grabbed Cacus by the throat and throttled him to death.

Virgil there produces in about eighty lines of poetry a full-blown narrative of combat with a Monster, with three stages and functions such as ARRIVAL, MOTIVATION and PHYSICAL APPROACH. His account has a lot more vitality, texture, colour and impact than Apollodorus' bare summary, for various reasons. So, after Hercules makes his first PHYSICAL APPROACH (charging up, club in hand), Cacus' FLIGHT (to his cave) and Hercules' PURSUIT and second PHYSICAL APPROACH not only enhance Hercules' status but also act as a retarding device, holding back the FIGHTING and so building anticipation. The second PHYSICAL APPROACH is lively too, because it is vivid and involves a unique breaching of defences. Virgil's lines are worth quoting:

> At that the black bile of rage rose in Hercules and he
> blazed with fury. He seized his heavy, knotted club and other   220
> weapons and headed for the lofty mountain's heights at a run.
> That was the first time that our people saw Cacus frightened,

with fear in his eyes. He ran off at once to his cave,
swifter than the east wind – fear lent wings to his feet.
He shut himself in, breaking the iron chains (his father's   225
handiwork) holding up a monstrous boulder; that now crashed
down, blocking and firmly barricading the entrance.
Suddenly Hercules was there, furious, scanning every
approach, looking this way and that, and grinding
his teeth. Hot with anger, he went around the whole   230
Aventine Hill three times, tried the stone-blocked doorway
three times and sat down in the valley, wearied, three times.
There stood a jagged crag of flint, sheer on all sides,
soaring up on top of the cave, a dizzying sight,
and a suitable site for the nests of birds of ill omen.   235
It leaned forward from the ridge towards the river on its left.
Straining directly against it from the right, he shook it and
wrenched it loose from its deep base; then he suddenly
heaved. That thrust sent a crack thundering through heaven
and made the banks leap apart and the river recoil in terror.   240
But Cacus' cave and vast palace lost its roof and was exposed ...

So too the FIGHTING in Virgil is much more developed than it is in Apollodorus and is a good example of how some functions in themselves can make a strong impression; it is full, detailed, dramatic and animated, puts an apt stress on darkness and appeals to all the senses (sound, sight, smell, touch and taste):

Cacus is caught in the sudden, unexpected daylight,
trapped in his rocky den and howling as never before.
Hercules sends arrows hurtling down, then any kind of
missile, hurling branches and boulders as big as millstones.   250
As his only means of escape now, astonishingly
Cacus' jaws belch forth an enormous cloud of
smoke and envelop his home in blinding murk,
blotting it out from sight and massing together down in his
cave night-black smoke and gloom shot through with flames.   255
This was too much for the angry hero. With a headlong leap
he flung himself through the flames into the thickest wave of
the smoke as it seethed around the huge cave in a black cloud.

Directly after that the DEATH function receives arresting expression (as the massively strong superhero needs only his hands to kill this mighty monster). The three verses devoted to it are grimly graphic, and there is a fitting vigour in the second line (which is dominated by words for grabbing, clasping and choking):

Here, as Cacus in the darkness futilely belches out fire,
he seizes him in a knot-like embrace, clinging and throttling,   260
until his eyes burst out and his throat is drained of blood.

Of material other than functions two features in particular deserve mention. First, there is effective description of Cacus' den at 193ff. In just five lines Virgil deftly captures the monstrousness of the place and its inhabitant, suggestively emphasizes darkness and death and also works in the monster's earlier depredations and a sketch of Cacus himself (giving us an outline with just a few bold strokes and leaving us to fill in the rest ourselves):

> Here, receding a vast distance, was a cavern,
> occupied by the dreadful figure of half-human Cacus and
> never reached by the sun's rays; the floor was always warm   195
> with fresh blood, and nailed to its proud doors
> hung the faces of men, pale in disgusting decay.

One is drawn in and one wants to see Cacus stopped as a result of those vivid, lurid and repulsive lines, especially the constant butchery (making the floor slippery and reeking of blood), the grisly trophies on the doors ('faces' are more pathetic and horrific than 'heads') and the very last word in the passage – *tabo* (translated as 'decay' but actually denoting a viscous fluid consisting of putrid matter etc.).

Secondly, there is the economical simile at 243ff., when Hercules wrenches the crag off the top of the monster's lair:

> But Cacus' cave and vast palace lost its roof and was exposed,
> and the shadowy cavern came into view down in the depths,
> as if some convulsion made the earth gape down in the depths,
> uncovering the Underworld and revealing that dim domain
> loathed by the gods, and the monstrous abyss was visible   245
> from above, and the ghosts shuddered at the inrush of light.
> Cacus is caught in the sudden, unexpected daylight,
> trapped in his rocky den and howling as never before.

The simile suddenly and dramatically transports readers to the world of the dead.[10] In addition, with succinctness it likens Hercules to a violent force of nature which cannot be resisted, conjures up a picture of Cacus' huge, dark and monstrous cave far down below, hateful, lit up and inspected (like the Underworld), suggests Cacus trembling like a ghost and as powerless as one, and highlights Cacus' association with death – a killer, in his den of death, he is soon to be killed and become one of the dead himself (so that there is foreshadowing here to heighten anticipation).

With a poet like Virgil there is much more that could be added, but the above should be enough to make my point about how meat is added to a narrative's skeleton.

By way of an exercise, analyse the following account[11] of Hercules' combat with the gigantic Antaeus (son of the ancient goddess Earth, who produced various monsters). Isolate the stages and functions, noting which ones receive stress or are omitted (and why); identify other elements (ones which are not functions) in the narrative; and pinpoint anything unusual or effective. The speaker is an African peasant who is explaining why some local hills are traditionally known as Antaeus' realm.

'Still not past giving birth after producing the Giants,
in a cave in Libya Earth conceived Antaeus, a dread monster
who gave her even more cause for pride than Typhon, Tityus   595
and fierce Briareus. Mercifully she did not send him up to join
the Giants battling the gods in the Phlegraean Fields.
Earth gave her son vast strength, and more:
when his body became weary, it promptly recovered its
strength and vigour from contact with his mother, the earth.   600
That cave over there was his home. They say that he lurked at
the foot of that lofty hill and preyed on lions for his food.
When he went to sleep, he would not use animal skins or
leaves for bedding, but lay on the bare ground,
thereby regaining his strength. He killed Libyan farmers,   605
he killed anyone who landed on the coast here. For a long time
the mighty Antaeus did not need to fall and get help from
Earth while wrestling. He was so powerful that nobody could
beat him even though he stayed standing. Finally great-hearted
Hercules (who was then ridding land and sea of monsters) was   610
brought to Libya by widespread reports of this bloody ogre.
Hercules stripped off the skin of the Nemean Lion that he wore,
Antaeus stripped off that of a Libyan lion. Hercules poured
olive oil over his body like an Olympic wrestler; Antaeus,
not trusting in contact with his mother through the soles of   615
his feet alone, poured hot sand over his body as an aid.
They locked hands and arms, grappling repeatedly. Their
massive forearms tested the strength of the other's neck
without success: neither head moved, their brows didn't budge.
Each was amazed at finding his match. Hercules was unwilling   620
to employ all his strength at the start of the contest. Instead
Antaeus was worn down, as was evident from his frequent
pants and the cold sweat that dripped from his weary limbs.
Then his neck grew tired and trembled; then his chest was
shoved back by Hercules' chest; then his legs tottered, struck   625
by sidelong blows of Hercules' fist. Antaeus gave way, and the
victorious Hercules encircled his back; next he squeezed his
waist by gripping his flanks tightly, then thrust his feet
between the thighs, to part them, and brought him down, all of
him. The dry earth quickly absorbed his sweat; warm blood   630
replenished his veins, his muscles swelled, his whole body
hardened, and with new strength he loosened Hercules' grip.
The hero stood there, astounded by such great might, and more
afraid than he had been of the self-regenerating Hydra of
Lerna (and he had been an inexperienced fighter then).   635
They fought on as equals, Antaeus with Earth's strength,
Hercules with his own. Cruel Juno never had higher hopes of

144

Hercules' death, seeing his limbs and his neck (which never
sweated when he held up the sky) exhausted by his exertions.
Antaeus grew weary once more, and when Hercules grappled   640
with him, he fell down of his own accord, before feeling the full
force of his opponent, then rose up again, invigorated and more
powerful still, having received all Earth's vitality (so that she
felt the strain herself while her son wrestled).

When Hercules finally realized that Antaeus was being aided   645
by contact with his mother, he said: "You have to stay upright.
You won't be allowed to rely on the earth or to lie down on the
ground any more. You'll remain clasped in my embrace, and if
you fall, you'll fall on to me." He lifted his opponent high up as
he struggled to get to the ground. As her son died, Earth could   650
not send strength into his limbs: Hercules was between them,
gripping his enemy's chest (already sluggish and stiff with
cold), refusing to consign him to the ground for a long time.'

Fighting with Monsters (2)

These combats with monsters also demonstrate the flexibility of myth. People often think that there is just one version and one standard outline of a mythological story, but myth is not as rigid as that. There are, in fact, many variants, in connection with details, names, events, outcome and so on. For example, some maintained that the great hero Heracles slept with and impregnated each of the fifty daughters of king Thespius on fifty successive nights, while others claimed that he slept with and impregnated all fifty in one and the same night. Sometimes we find dissimilar local traditions (different versions of the same tale in different places), and sometimes variations will be due to oral tradition (where stories were passed on by bards and by word of mouth and did not have a fixed, written form). Writers were also responsible for this dynamic quality of myth, as they produced their own modes of narrative, with their own aims, point of view, tone, emphasis etc. This chapter explores some of the differing ways of telling the same tale evident in written accounts of combats with monsters (although its approaches and observations are equally applicable to any narrative).

Typhos

Typhos (also known as Typhon, Typhaon and Typhoeus)[1] was a huge and immensely strong monster with multiple snaky heads, who fought with and was defeated by Zeus (most often because Typhos tried to take over as ruler of the universe) and was then imprisoned beneath the earth. Some authors depicted Zeus as winning without too much trouble (thanks to his awesome thunderbolt). In other authors there are more difficulties. Sometimes the gods, with the exception of Zeus (and occasionally Athena), flee from Typhos' attack all the way to Egypt, and are pursued by him, but finally escape by altering their appearances to those of animals, while Zeus battles with Typhos using his thunderbolt (and in some cases a sickle). Sometimes Zeus is weakened and immobilized, losing to Typhos his thunderbolts, sickle and even his sinews, until they are returned by one or more helpers and he is finally victorious over his enemy.[2]

The early Greek poet Hesiod wrote a poem called the *Theogony* in which he explained the origin of the gods and the succession of rulers in heaven. At 820ff. he solemnly exalts the victory of Zeus (civilization) over Typhoeus

11. Fighting with Monsters (2)

(savagery).[3] After beating some gods called the Titans (with help) Zeus now wins again (without help this time), here maintaining the supremacy gained against the Titans, and after this combat he is made ruler (at 881ff.). So there is a full account here, as this is the climax of Zeus' feats and the crowning instance of his invincibility.

But after Zeus had driven the Titans out of heaven,   820
through golden Aphrodite ample Earth made love with
Tartarus and bore her youngest child – Typhoeus.
He was a mighty deity, whose hands possessed strength
and vigour, whose feet were untiring. From his shoulders
grew a hundred snake heads, dread dragon heads,   825
with dark, darting tongues; from under the brows
the eyes in his awesome heads flashed forth fire:
fire blazed from all of his heads as he glanced around.
In all of those dreadful heads there were various voices which
uttered all kinds of unspeakable noises – sometimes speech   830
that the gods could understand, sometimes the roar
of a proud bull bellowing loudly in irresistible fury,
sometimes that of a lion that has no pity in its heart,
sometimes an astounding sound like a pack of puppies;
and sometimes he hissed, and the lofty mountains re-echoed.   835
On that day a thing beyond all undoing would have happened,
and he would have become king of mortals and immortals,
if Zeus, father of gods and men, had not been quick to see that
and thundered harsh and mighty. The earth around
resounded terribly, and so did the wide sky above   840
and the sea and Ocean's streams and Tartarus below.
As the lord rushed forth, great Olympus shuddered under
his immortal feet, and the earth gave a groan.
The violet sea was seized by heat from them both –
from Zeus' thunder and lightning and the monster's fire,   845
from scorching gales and blazing bolts.
All the land and sky and sea boiled.
Towering waves raged all along the coast at the charge
of these immortals and the ground was continually convulsed.
Hades, lord of the dead down below, trembled,   850
and so did the Titans with Cronos down in Tartarus
because of the continual clamour and that formidable combat.
Zeus heaped up his strength, seized hold of his weapons
(thunder and lightning and smoking bolt)
leapt on him from Olympus and struck. He completely   855
incinerated all the awesome heads of that dread monster.
He conquered him, lashing him with lightning-strokes,
hurling him down crippled, and the ample earth groaned.
Flames leapt forth from lord Typhoeus
in the craggy mountain's dark glen where he was   860
struck by the thunderbolts. The awesome blast set on fire a

147

large tract of the ample earth and melted it, as tin melts
when heated by craftsmen in pierced crucibles,
or as iron (which is the strongest of all things)
when overcome by burning heat in a mountain glen   865
is melted in the divine ground by the violence of the flames –
so the earth was melted by the bright, blazing fire.
With rage in his heart Zeus flung him into broad Tartarus.
From Typhoeus come boisterous rain-bringing winds –
not Notus or Boreas or clearing Zephyrus, for they   870
are descended from the gods and are a great blessing to men –
but the others, reckless gusts that blow on the ocean.
They fall upon the misty sea, a calamity
for mortals with their raging, ruinous gales.
They blow differently at different times, scattering ships   875
and killing sailors. Men who meet with them
at sea have no defence against their malevolence.
Others over the limitless, flower-filled land
lay waste the lovely fields of earthborn humans,
filling them with dust and a dreadful din.   880

This is a conventional expansive account in high style of a massive power struggle between divinities. Dramatic and stirring, it reverently celebrates what is presented as a decidedly epic exploit. The actual FIGHT-ING and (rapidly successive) VICTORY are handled quite briefly (at 855ff.), implying that even such an enemy as Typhoeus was no match for Zeus' great might. But there is still impact, thanks especially to the emphasis on elemental violence and horror in the PHYSICAL APPROACH of the two charging combatants, the effects of their weapons and the description of the monster. That description (823ff.) at an early point in the narrative highlights the danger, raises the tension and magnifies the subsequent achievement, stressing via repetition the creature's strength, multiple heads, menace, fire and variety of voices (coming from the hundred heads). The latter touch in particular is strange and memorable. Most of the voices intimate strikingly Typhoeus' divinity, power, arrogance, fury, pitiless-ness, deadliness and so on, while the last (puppy-like) sound is especially weird and unexpected (and also foreshadows the monster's weakness in comparison to Zeus).

About two hundred years later the fifth-century BC Greek tragedian Aeschylus wrote a tragedy called *Prometheus Bound*. In it the god Prometheus is punished for defying the newly established king of heaven (Zeus) by championing mankind. He is chained to a remote and lofty crag; he then receives various visitors, prophesies that Zeus will fall from power (unless he receives from Prometheus information about what exactly would bring that about), when pressed refuses to reveal the secret and is therefore plunged into the depths amid a raging storm. Among the early visitors is the god Oceanus, who offers to intercede with Zeus if

Prometheus will moderate his proud and rebellious attitude. Prometheus declines his offer and tells him to do nothing on his behalf, but to look out for his own safety, adding at 347ff.:

> My own adversity does not make me want
> as many others as possible to suffer too.
> Far from it. For the fate of my brother Atlas
> wears me down. Off towards the west   350
> he stands, supporting on his shoulders the pillar
> of heaven and earth, a scarce-bearable burden.
> I also felt pity for the earth-born inhabitant of Cilician
> caves, that deadly, hundred-headed monster,
> furious Typhos, when I saw the violence used   355
> to conquer him. He confronted all the gods,
> hissing forth terror from his formidable jaws,
> and he flashed from his eyes a grim-glaring lightning,
> intending to terminate the tyranny of Zeus forcibly.
> But Zeus' sleepless weapon came at him,   360
> the swooping, fire-breathing thunderbolt,
> and blasted him out of his high-sounding,
> boasting words. He was hit right in the heart and had
> his strength scorched and thundered out of him.
> Now he lies near the sea-straits,   365
> an ineffectual, sprawling form,
> pinned beneath the roots of Mount Etna,
> while up on the summit, hammering red-hot iron, sits
> Hephaestus. One day rivers of fire will burst forth
> from there, devouring with savage jaws   370
> the level fields of fruitful Sicily –
> such will be the fury that Typhos will send boiling out
> in blazing shafts of unapproachable, fire-breathing spume,
> despite being burnt to a cinder by Zeus' thunderbolt.

Point of view is very important here, as Zeus' enemy Prometheus obviously sympathizes and identifies with Typhos (who also suffers at the hands of Zeus and is also a rebel forcibly overcome and confined by him at a mountain in punishment, but not completely subdued). Hence the brand new and most unusual tone of pity for Typhos (overtly enunciated in 353, at the very start of the lines about him, and implicit throughout those lines). Typhos is represented as (after Prometheus and Atlas) a third victim of a violent and ruthless king of heaven, and what was in Hesiod a splendid exploit is here turned around and becomes something more questionable. So too Aeschylus has Prometheus produce a much shorter and more selective version of the combat, to minimize it and play it down. Like Hesiod, Aeschylus goes beyond the fight to something produced by Typhos beneath the earth, but here (at 369ff.) instead of winds there is something more significant – the eruption of Etna. The description of that receives more lines than any other element in this passage and seems to be symbolic (the fire of rebellion is still smouldering in Typhos, and he is still able to inflict some damage, as is true of Prometheus too).

On the other hand the surface impression of Zeus here and throughout the play is surprising (elsewhere in Aeschylus he is a god of justice and wisdom), and lines 191-2 indicate that Zeus and Prometheus would be subsequently reconciled. Many scholars believe that the *Prometheus Bound* was part of a trilogy (a group of three plays produced together) and that this reconciliation would have taken place later on in the trilogy, when circumstances had changed and Zeus was no longer young, new in power and threatened (and so harsh and arbitrary), but had acquired some experience and stability. In any case Aeschylus here also deftly allows readers to discern that there might be another side to Prometheus' version of events: one is, of course, aware that the speaker is partisan; even he brings out (at 354ff.) Typhos' monstrosity, menace and violence; and lines 358 and 359 permit the inference that Zeus was only using fire against fire and force against force.

Round about the time that Aeschylus produced that play the Greek lyric poet Pindar wrote his *Pythian Odes* 1.[4] This poem was a victory ode, to celebrate the success of the Sicilian tyrant Hieron in the chariot race at the Pythian games of 470 BC. There he had himself proclaimed Hieron of Etna, to honour that city, which he had recently established near the volcano Etna and entrusted to his son to rule, and the town figures prominently in Pindar's piece. It was customary in such victory odes to include information about the victory and the victor, and also moralizing (maxims, advice, etc.) and the narration of a myth in some way apposite to the winner. In *Pythian Odes* 1 the moralizing and the myth are related to the government of the new town of Etna, and Pindar holds out a desirable course with its rewards and an undesirable course with its punishments. Essentially the message is that goodness and great achievements should be aimed at (for they result in prosperity, praise and glory), and evil and the illegitimate use of force should be avoided (since they lead to disaster, criticism and infamy).[5] As one of his examples of the latter type of conduct Pindar cites Typhos at 13ff.:

> But when the Muses' ringing voices reach beings that Zeus
> does not love, they're distraught, on land and raging sea,
> and that includes the one who lies in terrible Tartarus,   15
> hundred-headed Typhos, the foe of the gods.
> The far-renowned Cilician cave once nurtured him, but now
> Sicily and the sea-fenced heights above Cyme crush his shaggy
> chest, and a sky-high column holds him fast, painfully –
> snowy Etna, year-long nurse of cold, bright snow.   20
> Purest founts of unapproachable fire belch forth from its
> depths; during the day its torrents pour out a gleaming
> stream of smoke, while in the dark with crashes the crimson,

rolling flame carries rocks right down to the deep, flat sea.
That serpent sends up truly awesome flaring fountains; it's an   25
amazing marvel to see and it's amazing to hear when present
what a creature is pinioned by Etna's leaf-black peaks and
plain, with all its outstretched back gashed and torn by its bed.

This severely stripped down and typically concentrated account contains only one stage (Aftermath) and only one developed function (PUNISHMENT). Pindar, who is simply not interested in telling the story as such, boldly omits much material (such as the actual combat) and homes in on and dwells on just the end, thereby achieving a tight focus and sombre impact. The poet streamlines his narrative in this way to keep it closely tied in to his point about wickedness and the illicit use of force leading to punishment. So, for example, he does not care (or need) to specify Typhos' motivation, and he does not want to show Typhos being at all formidable or causing Zeus any problems in the PHYSICAL APPROACH or FIGHTING. For his purposes he wants to stress the disaster suffered by a crushed Typhos (and depict this representative of the incorrect course of conduct as an unappealing figure). He does this in prominent positions at the start and end, and by way of reinforcement at other points in between. So at 13ff. we are shown Typhos hated by Zeus himself and punished by him, distraught and imprisoned in terrible Tartarus; there is also emphasis on punitive constraint at 18-20; confinement and agony are highlighted at 27f. as well; and Pindar also works in references to Typhos' impiety and monstrosity at various points. This is a powerful way of putting across how horrible the representatives of violence and wickedness are, and how dreadful the retribution inflicted on them is.

Like Aeschylus, Pindar describes Etna's volcanic activity caused by Typhos. But Pindar puts the description in the middle of his passage, to split it up and give it an enlivening factual core. He also makes it more graphic, appealing to all the senses, letting fire and smoke and colour permeate the lines, and using contrasts (such as flame at night) to make details stand out. This vividness, together with the drama and spectacle, makes the poet's advice more memorable. After this sketch of Typhos in action the mountain (closely linked to the town by name and location) would always be a visible symbol and reminder of Pindar's message for the town's rulers, intimating that the terrible and destructive evil forces are real and close and have always been a threat, even back in the remote past.

Nearly five hundred years after that abbreviated and split up account the Latin poet Ovid produced a version that was similarly truncated and still more fractured (told in two parts, with a break between the two speakers). He made some changes to the story as well, and injected much ingenuity. In all of these ways he added novelty and interest to what was by then an old story.

In book 5 of his *Metamorphoses* an unnamed member of the Muses (goddesses of song) tells Minerva (= Athena) how the arrogant daughters of king Pierus had challenged the Muses to a musical contest. One of the daughters had begun by singing of Typhoeus, following (and embellishing) the tradition in which Jupiter (= Zeus; also identified with Ammon) and the gods had real problems with Typhoeus and changed themselves into animal forms to escape him. In her response Calliope (another one of the Muses) had sung of the abduction of Persephone (daughter of the agricultural goddess Ceres): her abductor, the god of the Underworld, had been shot with an arrow by Cupid and made to fall in love with her when he was roaming the earth after checking that Typhoeus' struggles to escape from the weight of Sicily had not opened up any fissures in the ground. The first Muse is telling Minerva the story at 318ff.:

'Then, without drawing lots, the one who set up the contest
sang first, of the wars of the lords of heaven (unfairly
honouring the Giants, and belittling the mighty gods' feats),　　　320
and how Typhoeus sprang from the lowest depths of the earth
and frightened the gods, and how they all turned their backs
and fled until in an exhausted state they reached the land
of Egypt and the Nile with its seven separate mouths.
She told how earth-born Typhoeus also arrived there, and the　　　325
heavenly ones concealed themselves by taking on lying forms.
"Jupiter became a ram, leader of the flock," she said, "and so
Libyan Ammon even now is depicted with curving horns.
Apollo hid as a raven, Bacchus as a goat,
Diana as a cat, Juno as a snow-white cow,　　　330
Venus as a fish, and Mercury as a winged ibis."
So she sang, to the accompaniment of a lyre;
then we Muses were called – but perhaps you are too busy
and don't have the time to listen to our song?'
'Don't hesitate, tell me your song in its proper order,'　　　335
said Minerva and sat down in the grove's shifting shade.
The Muse replied, 'We chose one to represent us all in the
contest – Calliope. Her flowing hair bound by an ivy wreath,
she rose, tested the plaintive strings with her thumb and sang
the following song, accompanying herself on her lyre:　　　340
"Ceres was the first to cleave clods with a curving plough,
the first to give the world corn and civilized sustenance,
the first to give laws; everything is Ceres' gift.
She must be my subject. If only I could sing a song worthy
of the goddess! The goddess is surely worthy of a song.　　　345
Huge Sicily was heaped on the gigantic body of Typhoeus,
who for daring to hope for a home in heaven had been
placed beneath the island and was crushed by its vast mass.
He really struggled and often fought to rise again,
but his right hand was placed beneath Pelorus near Italy,　　　350
the left beneath Pachynus, his legs were pinned by Lilybaeum,
and Etna lay heavy on his head. Beneath it, on his back,

152

savage Typhoeus belched out sand and spewed up flames.
He often strained to heave away the weight of land
and to roll off from his body the towns and massive mountains.   355
Then the earth quaked, and even the king of the silent dead
was afraid that the ground would split and gape wide open
and daylight would stream in and terrify the trembling ghosts." '

In this version there is no Stage 1 (Prelude) and Stage 2 (Contact) is incomplete, with the FIGHTING and VICTORY functions notably absent. Each of the two storytellers has her own agenda and concentrates only on material relevant to that, firstly belittling the gods, and then counteracting that slur.

Pointedly the daughter of Pierus includes just Typhoeus' PHYSICAL APPROACH, the gods' FLIGHT, Typhoeus' PURSUIT and the gods' CONCEALMENT (functions which show the deities in a bad light and the monster in a good light) and puts most stress on the demeaning FLIGHT and CONCEALMENT. She makes all the gods flee, including Jupiter and Minerva (who elsewhere face Typhoeus), in such headlong panic that they become exhausted, and she underlines the disgrace of the gods hiding in lying forms by citing several examples of these alterations, beginning with Jupiter himself (who everywhere else remains unchanged to do battle with the monster). It would appear from line 332 that the woman's narrative is complete at 331, in which case she omitted FIGHTING and VICTORY in Stage 2 and all of Stage 3. This would mean that she was an unreliable narrator, breaking off early and ending with Typhoeus apparently triumphant and the gods worsted and skulking in an outrageously distorted and blasphemous new version of the myth.[6]

Calliope's answering song is concerned with Ceres and the abduction of her daughter, but she dexterously inserts Typhoeus near the start to slyly correct the daughter of Pierus in passing. In a manner reminiscent of Pindar she focuses solely on Typhoeus' PUNISHMENT for this purpose. As part of her riposte she brings out the totality of his downfall by remarking on the many heavy masses piled on him to imprison him completely and emphasizes the unpleasantness of his penalty by depicting him at 349ff. as fretful and in distress.

There is further subtlety and wit here. Although we can see that at 346ff. Calliope is responding to the earlier singer's depiction of Typhoeus, the precise relevance of those lines to Ceres (announced as the song's subject at 341ff.) is initially quite a puzzle, and teasingly the reader is kept in the dark about that for quite some time. One must also bear in mind that the unnamed Muse telling the story of the contest is relating the woman's account of the discomfiture and disgrace of the gods to a goddess – Minerva (who according to others actually withstood Typhoeus). And there is another entertaining piece of complexity: the daughter of Pierus who insolently set up the contest here celebrates Typhoeus (who also challenged gods), omitting his defeat and punishment and mocking the altered state of the gods, when she herself will soon be defeated (the Muses won the contest) and be punished for similar impiety with an altered state (the daughters were changed into magpies).

Perseus, Andromeda and the sea-monster

It is also interesting and instructive to compare and contrast two versions of another famous combat with a monster (Perseus' rescue of Andromeda from the sea-beast) as they appear in Manilius' *Astronomica* and Ovid's *Metamorphoses.*[7] Here tone is particularly important. The myth in surviving literature down to this time can be summarized as follows. Cassiope, wife of Cepheus (an Ethiopian king), boasted that she was more beautiful than the sea-nymphs. As a punishment her daughter Andromeda was chained to a cliff to be devoured by a ferocious sea-monster sent by the angry god of the sea Neptune (as decreed by an oracle of Ammon in Ovid, after the kingdom had been flooded in Manilius). Perseus arrived, on his way home from slaying the Gorgon Medusa, and when the monster appeared he fought and killed it (in Ovid and Manilius after bargaining with her parents for her hand in return for rescuing her). He married Andromeda, and subsequently she was set among the stars as a monument to Perseus' feat.

In the fifth book of his *Astronomica* (a poem on astronomy and astrology) Manilius includes a lengthy digression to explain the origin of the constellation Andromeda. He produces an affecting and exciting narrative, in which he depicts the heroine Andromeda as a figure of beauty and pathos, Perseus as a great warrior, the monster as a terrifying foe, and the rescue of the princess in peril as a splendid heroic exploit.

> Next the constellation of Andromeda's golden light appears
> in the right-hand sky when the Fishes have risen to 12 degrees.
> Her dreadful parents' crime once doomed her to punishment 540
> at the time when an entire hostile sea covered the whole
> kingdom, the land was shipwrecked and fluid, and the king's
> territory was now ocean. Only one way of averting that evil 514
> was proposed – to give up Andromeda to the raging sea 543
> so that a monster could devour her tender body.
> In this wedding her private hurt relieved the public hurt. 545
> In tears she was adorned as a victim for the avenging beast,
> putting on a bride's dress not intended for such a sacrifice,
> and then the girl was hurried off, a living corpse.
> As soon as they reached the shore of the hostile sea,
> her soft arms were stretched out on a hard crag, 550
> they fixed her feet to the rocks, chaining her, and there,
> crucified and doomed to die, the young virgin hung.
> Even while punished she maintained facial control.

Andromeda by Joachim Wtewael (1532-1603). Louvre, Paris. Perseus is
about to attack the sea-monster in the background.

Her suffering added to her attractiveness. She gently inclined
her white neck and was seen to be in charge of her expression.   555
Her clothes slipped down from her shoulders and fell from
her arms, her streaming hair clung to her shoulder-blades.
Andromeda, halcyon-birds flew around you, mourning
and lamenting your fate in their pitiful song,
their wings overlapping to make shade for you.   560

The sea stayed its waves to gaze at you
and for once stopped breaking on the cliffs.
A sea-nymph raised her face above the surface and,
pitying your plight, drenched the waves with her tears.
A breeze blew gently over you as you hung there, refreshing   565
you and sighing sadly along the edge of the cliff.
It was a happy day that finally brought Perseus to that shore
on his way home after defeating the monstrous Gorgon.
Although undaunted by the sight of Medusa, when he saw
the girl hanging there on the crag, he stiffened and nearly   570
dropped the severed head, and the vanquisher of Medusa
was vanquished by Andromeda. He envied the rock itself
and called the chains fortunate because they held such a body.
He learned from the girl herself the reason for her punishment
and resolved to win her hand by battling the sea-beast,   575
unafraid if even another Gorgon came against him. He quickly
flew to Andromeda's weeping parents and brought them
relief by promising to save her life if he could then wed her.
He returned to the shore. By now a heavy surge had begun
to rise, and in a long line wave after wave was fleeing from   580
the thrust of the mass of the monster. As it cleaved the ocean,
its head emerged, spewing spume; it bore along in its jaws
swirling water, and the sea seethed loudly about its teeth.
Behind it rose its massive coils in an immense chain, and its
back covered the deep. The waves everywhere were in uproar,   585
even the cliffs and crags were terrified as it rushed up.
Poor girl, although you had such a splendid defender,
there was then absolute horror on your face, you panted in
quick gasps and went pale all over, as from the hollow
in the rocks you saw with your own eyes your doom –   590
the avenging sea-beast swimming towards its tiny prey
and driving ocean before it. At that Perseus, wings fluttering,
flew up and hurled himself from the sky at his enemy,
driving home his sword stained with the Gorgon's blood.
The beast sprang up to meet him, wrenching its head   595
from the water, rearing up aloft, its whole body
towering on high, supported on its twisted coils.
But again and again, the higher it hurled itself from the deep,
the higher Perseus flew, fooling it, the length and breadth
of the sky, hacking its head as the creature sprang up.   600
It didn't give in, it went for the upper air, biting viciously,
but its teeth snapped together uselessly, without wounding.
It spouted ocean into the sky, drenching the flier with a
bloody spray, spurting seawater right up to the stars.
The girl they were fighting over watched them fighting   605
and forgot her own plight in her fear for her mighty champion.
She sighed, hanging there, and hanging upon Perseus.
At last the beast, riddled with wounds, filled with water
and sank, then floated back up to the surface again,

its colossal corpse covering a huge expanse of ocean,   610
fearsome even in death, and not a fit sight for a girl's eyes.
Perseus bathed his body in clear water and, a
greater hero now, flew from the waves to the lofty crag
and freed from the binding chains his bride to be, who was
betrothed by combat and had rescue as her wedding present.   615
He won her a place in the sky and enshrined her among the
stars, the prize of that great battle, in which a monster as
formidable as the Gorgon herself died, to the sea's relief.

Manilius begins by introducing Andromeda and arousing great sympathy for her. Initial impressions are important. First of all we are shown an innocent victim (540), and the princess's youthful, fearful and vulnerable femininity also receive early stress, at 544, 546 and 548 (and are subsequently reinforced by repetition). Beauty and bravery are added for further appeal at 553ff. Attention is especially drawn to poor Andromeda in her crucified state by the address to her and the strange (and so arresting) tableau at 558-66, where (even though an offence against the sea-nymphs is being punished by the god of the sea) sea-birds, a sea-nymph, the sea itself and a sea-breeze are affected by the sight of Andromeda. In all of these ways Manilius builds up a prolonged and langorous pathos, making us eager to see the victim rescued.

He then brings on the rescuer. Perseus is another sympathetic character, a combination of the warrior and the lover. The first mention of him (at 567-9) indicates his status as a great hero and alludes to his bravery and tactical abilities. Then, at 570-6, his heroic qualities figure again, but simultaneously his lighter and more human side is brought out, as he immediately falls deeply in love (and there is even a bit of humour at 570ff., which makes for additional warmth). Readers should be rooting for Perseus, especially when the dreadful monster appears at 579ff. (on which see pages 30f.).

The monster is a powerful creation – terrifying, huge, mighty, ferocious and possessing snaky coils. And the fight with it is a thrilling, extraordinary and truly epic contest, described at length and in detail, and full of incident, conflict and fluctuation. The to and fro of battle is indicated by alternation of hero and monster as focal point and by extensive movement through space (as the action shifts up and down, back and forth, far and wide). The two fighters are well matched (both possessing formidable weapons and showing great persistence), and there is real suspense at 603ff., where the bloody spray might blind Perseus and waterlog his wings, before he is finally victorious and frees Andromeda, as the narrative ends on a note of quiet triumph.

Ovid's account has much in common with this one. It is about the same length as Manilius' and the basic story line is the same in both. Ovid also has three stages, includes all of the functions found in Manilius[8] and like

157

him dwells on MOTIVATION and FIGHTING. Various individual details are shared too – Andromeda's arms chained to hard rocks, Perseus comically staggered at the sight of her, the hero eluding the monster's snapping fangs etc. However, there are also distinct and significant dissimilarities, due especially to the fact that Ovid's narrative has a very different thrust and tone. Ovid was not much interested in sympathy, epic grandeur, drama or spectacle; he was far more concerned with entertaining readers in other ways.

This is his version at *Metamorphoses* 4.663ff.:

Aeolus had shut up his winds in their prison under Etna,
and the morning-star had risen, high heaven's brightest,
reminding the world to work. Perseus picked up and put on his   665
winged sandals again, equipped himself with his curved sword
and cleaved the clear air with fluttering wings.
He passed countless peoples all around him and beneath him,
and then the Ethiopians and Cepheus' country came into view.
There unjust Ammon had ordered that innocent Andromeda   670
should be punished for what her mother had said.
When Perseus saw her, bound by the arms to the hard cliffs,
he would have thought her a marble statue, except that a slight
breeze stirred her hair and her eyes were wet with warm
tears. Immediately, and unwittingly, he burned with love;   675
stunned and overcome by the vision of beauty that he beheld,
he almost forgot to flap his wings in mid air.
He landed and said: 'Oh lady unworthy of bonds like these,
worthy rather of those that link passionate lovers together,
tell me the name of this land and your name and why   680
you are in chains.' The girl was silent at first, not daring
to address a man, and she would have modestly hidden her
face behind her hands, if she hadn't been shackled.
She did what she could – filled her eyes with welling tears.
When Perseus kept pressing her, in case he thought she'd done   685
something wrong and wouldn't confess, she told him her name
and the land's and how her mother had been too confident in
her beauty. Before she had finished speaking, the water roared
and a monster came out of the vast expanse of ocean,
looming up, its breast covering a broad stretch of sea.   690
The girl screamed. Her sorrowful father went to her, and so did
her mother – both miserable, the mother with better cause.
They had no help to offer, only tears in keeping with such a
moment and lamentation, and they clung to her fettered body.
The stranger said: 'You can have a lengthy time for mourning   695
later, there is only a little time left for helping her.
If I asked for her hand as Perseus, the son of Jupiter and
Danae (who Jupiter impregnated in a fertile shower of gold),
as Perseus who vanquished the snake-haired Gorgon,
and dared to fly through the sky on beating wings,   700

158

I'd surely be first choice as son-in-law. I'm trying to add an
act of kindness to my endowments, with the help of the gods.
I propose that if she's saved by my valour she becomes mine.'
They accepted the conditions (who would waver?), begging his
help and promising him the kingdom too as a wedding present.   705
Look! As a swift ship with a beak at its prow ploughs through
the sea, powered by the young rowers' sweating arms, so the
beast came on, parting the waves with its thrusting chest.
It was only as far from the cliff as the distance that a lead shot
can be hurled through the air by a Balearic sling   710
when young Perseus pushed off from the ground and
soared into the clouds. The beast saw his shadow
on the surface of the sea and savaged his shadow.
As Jupiter's eagle, on seeing a snake sunning its livid
back in a deserted field, seizes it from behind   715
and fixes its eager talons in the snake's scaly neck,
to stop it twisting around with its vicious fangs,
so the hero swooped headlong through the empty sky and
attacked the beast's back, burying his sword up to the
curved hilt in its right shoulder and making it bellow.   720
In pain from this serious wound it first reared up high in the
air, then plunged beneath the waves, then whirled about, like
a fierce boar terrified by a pack of hounds baying all around it.
Perseus flew quickly away from its greedily snapping jaws.
Wherever it was exposed, he struck repeatedly with his curved   725
sword – now at the back covered in barnacles, now at the ribs,
now at the point where the tapering tail ended in fins.
The beast vomits seawater mixed with crimson
blood; the spray soaks his wings and weighs them down.
He doesn't dare trust the drenched feathers any more,   730
then he catches sight of a rock whose summit projects when
the waves are still but is covered by the sea when it surges.
Resting on that and holding its topmost ridge in his left hand,
he drives his sword repeatedly through the creature's groin.
Shouts and applause fill the shores and the homes of the gods   735
in heaven. The delighted parents, Cassiope and Cepheus,
greet Perseus as their son-in-law and call him the protector
and saviour of their house. Freed from her chains, the girl
comes forward, the reward and reason for his efforts.
The victor himself drew water and washed his hands   740
and, so as not to damage the snaky head on the hard sand,
he made a soft bed of leaves on the ground, strewed seaweed
on it and placed there the head of Phorcus' daughter, Medusa.
The fresh weed was still alive, with a porous core, and it
absorbed the monster's power and hardened at its touch,   745
and the stems and fronds acquired a strange stiffness.
The sea-nymphs tried out this miracle on more sprays of
seaweed, were delighted that the process repeated itself
and spread the substance by scattering its seeds on the sea.

Even today coral is still the same: it hardens when   750
touched by the air, and what was a tendril in the
water is turned to stone when brought above the surface.
Perseus builds three altars of turf to three divinities –
the left one to Mercury, the right to warlike Minerva,
the central one to Jupiter. A cow is sacrificed to Minerva,   755
a calf to winged Mercury, a bull to the greatest of the gods.
Immediately Perseus takes Andromeda, without a dowry,
as the reward for his great exploit. Hymen and Cupid wave
the marriage torches in front of them …

There are minor differences of various kinds between the two narratives. For example, Ovid excludes some of the details found in Manilius
(the flooding of Cepheus' kingdom; nature and the sea-nymph affected at
the sight of Andromeda etc.); Ovid also includes some things that are not
found in Manilius (such as similes and quotation of people's words in direct
speech); and Ovid has dissimilar emphases (e.g. he has much more on the
conversation between Perseus and the parents; and he moves quickly to
the point where Perseus catches sight of the princess, providing a lot less
background).

More important are the major differences, which are closely connected
with the mood and purpose of the passage in the *Metamorphoses* (where
Ovid is providing a narrative of the combat with a brand new twist – in
place of a serious account of a grand exploit his subversive version is
characterized by (often subtle) wit and humour and constantly deflates
and debunks the epic hero Perseus[9]).

So, because he is not much interested in pathos, Ovid's Andromeda is
not the major character that she is in Manilius[10] nor anything like as sad
a figure. In fact she is more a figure of fun. At 681ff. her modesty when
about to be devoured by a ravening sea-beast is quaint, her tears in the
presence of the man who will rescue her are comically inappropriate (and
hardly conceal her), and her admirer's persistent questions put her in an
amusing bind (speaking to a man would be immodest, but keeping quiet
may make her seem guilty of some offence). It is also a droll touch that,
whereas the hero is thunderstruck at the sight of her, she doesn't even
seem to register the fact that there is a man with extraordinary winged
sandals hovering in mid air in front of her. Andromeda is also employed to
mock Perseus. It is thanks to her and her effect on him that he almost
forgets to flap his wings, comes out with his flowery speech to her at 678ff.,
bargains with her parents for her hand even as the monster approaches
(choosing his moment perfectly for what is the longest speech in the whole
passage!) and in his attempt to impress them is rather bumptious and
pompous.

The same considerations operate in connection with Ovid's monster.
Manilius makes more of the creature and gives it more impact. He devotes
a larger number of lines to it; he makes it more vivid (especially in the

PHYSICAL APPROACH at 579ff.); he stresses its horror, ferocity, size and strength more; and he makes it more active and threatening, giving it many more verbs (especially vigorous verbs) and epithets (particularly ones that bring out its vastness and monstrousness). Ovid by means of his monster does create some excitement, but he also wants to keep the tone light, and he is careful not to build Perseus up by creating a really formidable foe for him. Ovid uses the monster as well for humour and to undercut the hero's achievement, aims which would be undermined by too terrifying a sea-beast.

That is why the FIGHTING in Ovid is rather one-sided and has its comic aspects. Perhaps not all that heroically, Perseus really exploits his flying ability to give himself a distinct edge over his enemy. The dumb beast is visually challenged (it doesn't see Perseus fly up into the air and attacks his shadow instead of the man himself). It is also slow on the uptake (it doesn't know what hits it as Perseus attacks from above and behind). Very soon it is severely wounded (although Perseus also, for some reason best known to himself, attacks its tail). The nearest it gets to touching the hero is throwing up on him, making his wings soggy. When he lands on the rock, the stupid creature conveniently swims up and obligingly stays still while he polishes it off with several blows, exposing itself and taking wounds in the groin.[11] The round of applause in 735 is whimsically amusing (especially after such an easy victory), and the reference at 741ff. to the Gorgon's head (which Perseus could have used simply to turn the monster to stone) is deflating (whether he just forgot about it or was deliberately not using it so as to show off).

Perseus and Medusa

Factors such as purpose and tone always affect story-telling and often result in disparate versions of what is essentially the same myth. Bear that in mind as you examine the following three passages on an earlier adventure of Perseus (the killing of the Gorgon Medusa, whose terrible petrifying eyes had to be avoided). The first two passages relate the whole incident. Compare and contrast them, paying attention to aspects such as length, clarity, vividness, pace (slow or fast) and impact.

First, there is *Library* 2.4.2 by Apollodorus (the name given to a mythographer who apparently tried to provide general readers with a reliable summary in prose of the most important myths as they had appeared in earlier writers):

Under the guidance of Hermes and Athena Perseus made his way to the daughters of Phorcys – namely Enyo, Pephredo and Deino. They were old from birth, sisters of the Gorgons, born to Phorcys by Ceto. The three of them had a single eye and a single tooth, which they passed on to one another in turn. Perseus got possession of the eye and the tooth, and when they asked

Perseus Turning Phineus and his Followers to Stone by Luca Giordano (1634-1705). National Gallery, London.

for them back said that he would hand them over if the sisters would tell him the way to the nymphs. These nymphs had winged sandals and the kibisis, which they say was a leather pouch. They also had the cap of Hades. When the daughters of Phorcys had told him the way, he returned to them the tooth and eye, then went to the nymphs and got what he was after. He slung the kibisis around his neck, fastened the sandals to his ankles and put the cap on his head. While wearing this he saw whoever he wanted to but was not seen by others himself. He also received a scimitar of adamant from Hermes and then flew to Ocean and caught the Gorgons sleeping. They were Stheno, Euryale and Medusa. Only Medusa was mortal, which was why Perseus was sent to fetch her head. The Gorgons had scaly snakes coiling around their heads, great tusks like pigs', hands of bronze and wings, with which they flew. And they turned to stone those who looked on them. So Perseus stood over them as they slept, and, while Athena guided his hand, he turned away and looked into a bronze shield, in which he saw the reflection of the Gorgon, and beheaded her. After the head had been cut off, from the Gorgon were born Pegasus the winged horse and Chrysaor the father of Geryon. She bore these to Poseidon. So Perseus put the head of Medusa into the kibisis and returned, but the other Gorgons got up from their sleep and tried to pursue Perseus. But they could not see him because of the cap, which concealed him.

11. Fighting with Monsters (2)

Secondly, there is *Metamorphoses* 4.772ff. (part of the complex of stories in which Ovid divests Perseus of much of his glamour). There at his wedding to Andromeda Perseus is asked how he won Medusa's head and tells the tale (rather late in the whole Perseus narrative, so that it almost seems like an afterthought):

> Perseus told of a cavern lying beneath chilly Mount Atlas,
> securely protected by the mass of solid rock.
> In its entrance-way lived the daughters of Phorcys, two
> sisters who shared the use of single eye, he said.   775
> With skill and cunning by stealthily interposing his hand he
> stole the eye while it was passed from one to the other. He
> travelled across very remote and pathless regions and rock
> overgrown with rough woods and finally reached the Gorgon's
> home. Everywhere in the fields and paths he saw statues of   780
> humans and animals changed to stone by gazing on Medusa.
> But he himself looked on her dread form reflected in
> the bronze of the shield which he bore in his left hand,
> and while a deep sleep held fast Medusa and her snakes
> he hacked off her head from the neck. From her blood   785
> were born swift-winged Pegasus and his brother Chrysaor.

Finally there is a passage which refers to just one part of this same episode. This is the epic *Shield of Heracles* 216ff., which describes some of the ornamentation on a great shield made for the hero's use in battle by the god Hephaestus, a marvellously skilled worker of metal who on one part depicted in gold, silver and adamant (the hardest of metals) Perseus fleeing with the severed head of Medusa and pursued by the other Gorgons. Consider why the poet tells only part of the story, why he chooses that particular part, how well he catches it, and what elements he highlights:

> On it also was the horseman Perseus, the son of Danae of the
> lovely hair. He did not touch the shield with his feet but stood
> out from it a little, completely unsupported – a truly
> marvellous sight. That was how glorious Hephaestus fashioned
> him in gold. On his feet he had winged sandals. His   220
> black-sheathed sword was slung across his shoulders in a
> bronze cross-belt. He was flying along like a thought.
> His entire back was covered by the head of the Gorgon, that
> dread monster, enclosed in a kibisis of silver (a marvellous
> thing to see), from which there hung down glittering golden   225
> tassels. On the head of that lord lay the dread cap
> of Hades, which had the terrifying darkness of night.
> Perseus himself, the son of Danae, was at full stretch,
> like somebody rushing off in horror. The awful,
> unspeakable Gorgons were charging after him,   230
> longing to seize him. As they moved on the pale adamant,

163

the shield rang out, piercing and clear, with a
great clang. On their girdles two snakes
hung down, with heads that arched forward.
Their tongues were flickering, their fangs were snapping   235
savagely and they were glaring fiercely. On the dread heads
of the Gorgons mighty Terror menaced.

12

Polyphemus

This chapter concerns one of the most famous of ancient monsters, the one-eyed, man-eating giant Polyphemus. His fame in fact extended far beyond the Classical world: he figured in music by Handel and in paintings by Raphael, Poussin and Moreau; a story originated in the fourteenth century that his skeleton had been found on Sicily, over 330 feet tall, seated on a mountainside, with one hand resting on a club as long as a ship's mast, and that the bones crumbled when touched, but the skull with its single eye was preserved and was exhibited in a local church for many years; and even today on the coasts of Sicily and south Italy there are various caves called the 'cave of Polyphemus' with huge rocks nearby supposedly hurled by the monster. Polyphemus was a Cyclops (i.e. a member of the race of giants called Cyclopes),[1] and there are two main stories told about him – his blinding by the Greek hero Odysseus[2] and his love for the sea-nymph Galatea. This chapter provides a brief history of the Classical Polyphemus, concentrating on major treatments of those two stories by various Greek and Latin writers,[3] and tracing his development over the course of nearly one thousand years.

Odysseus and Polyphemus

In the first story essentially what happens is that the Greek hero Odysseus (early on in his voyage back to Greece after fighting at Troy in the Trojan War) is trapped with some of his men in the cave of Polyphemus, who devours two of the Greeks at a time for his meals, until Odysseus gets him drunk and blinds him and then escapes from his cave and continues his journey.

The earliest surviving account of this story is found in Homer's epic poem, the *Odyssey* (eighth century BC). Homer makes this into a truly heroic episode, allocating most of book 9 to it (nearly 500 lines of poetry) and working in standard epic features such as the despoiling of the opponent and vaunting over him. This is a classic confrontation between two well matched, strongly developed and diametrically opposed characters, who receive almost all of the focus and who arouse powerful emotions in readers. There is violence and gore, horror and excitement in this tale of high adventure (concerning a literally life and death situation) in a remote and mysterious setting (Odysseus had been blown far off course

165

into a never-never land). And the account gains in colour and animation by being put in the mouth of Odysseus himself: he is here recounting his earlier experiences to the Phaeacians (who have taken him in and given him hospitality later on during his journey home) and in so doing he exultantly highlights the odds facing him and the qualities that helped him win through.

At *Odyssey* 9.106ff. Odysseus begins as follows:

> We came to the land of the lawless, overbearing
> Cyclopes, who don't lift a hand to plant or
> to plough but just trust to providence.
> Yet without sowing or ploughing everything grows for them –
> wheat and barley and vines, which are watered by   110
> Zeus' rain and yield wine from their fine grapes.
> The Cyclopes have no assemblies for council and no laws.
> They live on the peaks of lofty mountains in
> hollow caves; each lays down the law for his wife
> and children, and none of them cares about his neighbours.   115

Those lines indicate from the start that the Cyclopes (as opposed to the Greeks) are on a very low cultural level, ignorant of law, morality, agriculture, political life and social relations, and later Polyphemus is repeatedly depicted as more beast than man. This is the story of the triumph of civilization and the intellect over primitive savagery and brute force.

Homer next spends over fifty lines on an island that is not far off from the land of the Cyclopes but not occupied by them, a beautiful and fertile island filled with wild goats that has a safe harbour and at its head a cave with a spring of bright water. Miraculously the Greeks sailed right into that harbour in the midst of blackest night (guided by some god). On the following morning they killed lots of goats, and then for the rest of the day they feasted on them and drank wine until it was time for sleep.

Here we see the start of all the realism and incidental detail in this episode that enables us to suspend disbelief (we know that in actuality there is no such thing as a Cyclops, but we are prepared to accept all this because the overall world of the story is so credible). The expansiveness here amplifies, contributing to the feel of an epic adventure, and this leisurely opening amounts to the calm before the storm (this is an idyllic beginning to what is in fact a horrific incident, one whose horror is heightened by the contrast with these lines). There is foreshadowing as well, adding to the strangeness of this tale, with a rather eerie rehearsal for what will shortly follow: several elements (e.g. the goats, cave, killing, feasting and wine) which appear in a non-threatening light here will shortly recur in a very threatening context.

There is also the start of a build-up here: the description of the Cyclopes at 106ff. should have piqued interest and aroused expectation, but now the narrative is tantalizingly slowed by all the lines on the island; so too in the subsequent verses there is a similar slow pace combined with ominous touches that arouse foreboding, like the reference to Polyphemus, the owner of a cave that they see (at 187ff.):

> That was the den of a monstrous man who pastured
> his sheep on his own, far from everyone, a lawless
> loner who didn't go about with the others.
> He was an appalling monster, built like no man who   190
> eats bread, but like some wooded peak in a high
> mountain-range that stands out on its own from the others.

In those subsequent verses Odysseus decides to visit the land of the Cyclopes beyond the island and sails off with one of his ships. He sees the cave just mentioned, home of the monster and his flocks of goats and sheep, and goes to investigate it, taking with him twelve of his crew and a wineskin containing a sweet and extremely strong wine (because of a premonition that he might meet some lawless savage). Polyphemus is off pasturing his sheep but Odysseus and his men enter his cave and have a look round. The men beg Odysseus to take some of the cheese there and leave, but he wants to meet the owner and try to get hospitality from him. The monster returns, to their horror, drives in his sheep and blocks the entrance with an enormous rock. He milks his sheep, lights a fire and then catches sight of the Greeks.

Homer has very effectively put us in Odysseus' shoes so that we will identify with him (landing us on the island, then taking us to the Cyclopes' country and finally into Polyphemus' cave, and making us wait there until the monster enters). At this point Homer begins the numerous verbal exchanges that do so much to add immediacy to his account and bring out the contrasting characters of the hero and the monster. In what follows Odysseus, the swashbuckling adventurer (though perhaps a bit too bold and curious), becomes a still more sympathetic figure with numerous qualities (especially intelligence, resourcefulness and bravery), while Polyphemus is seen to be a hateful ogre with many failings (impious, inhospitable, savage, stupid, possessed of a low, lumbering cunning etc.) and is really brought alive and made memorable by various distinctive touches.

Polyphemus asks who they are – pirates perhaps? Odysseus explains that they are on their way home from Troy and begs for hospitality out of reverence for Zeus, god of suppliants and strangers. The monster replies that Cyclopes care nothing for Zeus or the other gods as they are much stronger than them, then enquires where their ship is. Odysseus is not taken in by this rather obvious ploy and protects his ship and the rest of his crew by pretending that he has been shipwrecked. At this point the bestial Polyphemus, instead of offering food to guests in need as civilized custom prescribed, does quite the reverse:

Pitiless Polyphemus did not reply. Instead he leapt up and
lunged for my men. He seized two of them at the same
time and smashed them on the ground as if they were
puppies. Their brains ran out on to the earth, soaking it.   290
He ripped them apart limb from limb for his supper
and ate them, like a mountain-lion, every last bit
of them – entrails and flesh and bones, marrow and all.
We wept, holding up our hands to Zeus in appeal,
as we witnessed this act of barbarism, feeling helpless.   295

The tension is now increased: how can the hero get out of the cave with the
immovable boulder in its mouth; how can he stop the killing; if he murders
Polyphemus how does he escape; will he be able to come up with a plan
before he is eaten himself?

After watching the monster wash down his repulsive meal with a drink
of milk, Odysseus reluctantly concludes that he cannot kill him with his
sword because then they would be trapped. The next day Polyphemus eats
two more men for breakfast, drives his flocks out of the cave, puts the huge
boulder back in the entrance and then takes his sheep off to pasture,
whistling cheerfully. Odysseus decides to blind the monster in his sleep,
sharpens a great stake of olive wood for that purpose and conceals it under
some dung. Polyphemus returns with his animals and eats two more men.
Odysseus now approaches him with a bowl of the very strong wine that he
had brought and offers it to him. The monster drains it, then requests another
bowl of the delicious drink and asks the hero to tell him his name, so that he
can give the hero a gift. After watching Polyphemus befuddle his wits with a
second and then a third bowl, Odysseus tells him that his name is Nobody,
and the giant then says that as his gift to Nobody he will eat him last.

As part of the lively mixture of mood in this account, the humour here
(in the Cyclops' clownish joke, and in him being tricked by Odysseus while
trying to trick the hero himself) is well judged: it effectively releases the
tension for a moment, so that there is more impact when the emotional
pitch is screwed up again in what follows (where Homer is careful to show
Polyphemus at his most repulsive before he is blinded).

With that he toppled over and fell on his back. There he lay,
his massive neck twisted around, as all-conquering sleep
seized him. Wine and bits of human flesh came
spurting from his throat, as he vomited in his drunken stupor.
Then I drove the stake deep into the fire's ashes,   375
to get it hot, and rallied all of my men
so that nobody would shrink back in fear.
When the olive-wood stake was on the point of bursting
into flames and was glowing terribly even though it was green,
I brought it over from the fire. My comrades stood around   380
me and some god breathed great courage into us.
They took the sharp-pointed stake of olive wood and

12. Polyphemus

drove it into his eye, while I pressed down from above
and twisted it round, like a man boring through a ship's
timber with a drill which his mates below keep twirling   385
continuously with a strap that they hold at either end.
Just like that we took the fiery-tipped stake and twisted it
round in his eye, and the blood gushed about its heated point.
The scorching blast singed all his eyelid and all round his brow,
while the eyeball burned and its roots crackled in the heat.   390
His eye sizzled around the olive-wood stake
as a glowing adze or great axe hisses loudly
when a smith dips it in cold water,
tempering it to strengthen the iron.
He gave a terrible great wail, making the cave ring,   395
and we ran off in fear. He wrenched the stake,
drenched and streaming with blood, out of his eye
and flung it from him in a frenzy.

At this point some more humour is introduced to briefly lighten the mood, as Polyphemus calls for help to the other Cyclopes, they turn up outside his cave and ask him what is wrong, he says that Nobody is killing him and they reply that if nobody is attacking him then he must be mad, and flounce off in a huff. The Cyclops now removes the rock in the cave mouth and sits there with his hands outstretched to catch anyone who tries to leave. The wily Odysseus comes up with a plan to elude this obvious ruse. He ties the large rams together in groups of three with one of his men under each group, and when dawn arrives and the animals go out to pasture, the blind giant feels along the backs of the sheep but does not realize that there are men tied beneath them. Odysseus himself grabs hold of the shaggy fleece of the biggest of the rams and curls up underneath it. This ram is the last to leave, and when Polyphemus realizes this, he speaks to the animal, and his speech is at times rather affecting:

'Dear old ram, what's this, why are you the last of the flock to
leave the cave? You've never lagged behind the sheep before;
with your long strides you're always easily the first to graze on
the tender shoots of grass, the first to reach the river,   450
and the first to long to return to the fold of an
evening. But today you're the last of all. You must be upset
about your master's eye, put out by that criminal and his
cowardly men after he befuddled my wits with wine – I
mean Nobody, who hasn't escaped death yet, I swear.   455
If only you possessed intelligence like me and the power of
speech to tell me where he is hiding from my fury.
I'd smash him on the floor, dash his brains all over
the cave, to console myself for the suffering
that good-for-nothing Nobody has caused me.'   460

169

Having built up Polyphemus into a repulsive ogre, now that he has been defeated, Homer shows some feeling for him and fills out his depiction with an extra dimension by bringing out briefly a more sympathetic side – in his closeness to the ram and in the pathos of his blinding. But it is only with an animal that the bestial Polyphemus can feel any affinity, and he is still dangerous and menacing. And if you picture the situation, you will see that there is also irony and humour here, which the narrator Odysseus is no doubt savouring: the monster says that the ram would tell him where the hero is hiding when in fact he is hiding directly underneath the ram; he imagines that the ram would help him to catch the hero when it is actually helping him to get away; and he maintains that the hero has not escaped destruction when the ram is enabling him to do just that.

After this speech Polyphemus lets the ram go, Odysseus (now free) unties his men, drives off the animals as spoil back to his ship and sails away.

Anybody who thinks that the story is over at this point is in for a surprise. The Greeks' escape would have made an easy and obvious ending, but Homer added more, winding up the tension again, bringing out the sense of triumph (by means of Odysseus' vaunting), adding to that some darker, more disturbing elements, and amplifying the importance of the episode (for here we see the origin of the wrath of Poseidon, which dogged Odysseus on the rest of his way home).

When the Greeks had rowed to a distance at which Odysseus could still be heard by the Cyclops if he raised his voice, he shouted out that it was clear now that he was no weakling and that Polyphemus had been justly punished. Enraged, the monster hurled in the direction of the hero's voice a great pinnacle of rock, which landed just ahead of the ship's bows. The backwash drove them into shore and Odysseus had to push them off with a pole and get his men to row hard to get them clear of danger. When they had rowed out to twice the previous distance, despite his men's pleas for him to keep quiet, the angry hero made sure that the Cyclops knew who had beaten him by shouting out to him his real name. The giant groaned and recalled that a prophet had told him that he would one day be blinded by a man called Odysseus, but he had always imagined that this Odysseus would be a big and mighty man. He then prayed for revenge to his father Poseidon (god of the sea), asking him to plague Odysseus on his voyage home; and Poseidon heard his prayer. Polyphemus hurled an even bigger boulder, which fell just behind the ship this time, making a wave that drove it off towards the shore of the nearby island. Odysseus duly landed on the island and was reunited with the rest of his ships there. He divided the spoil among his men and sacrificed the big ram to Zeus, but the god would not accept the sacrifice and must have been already planning the subsequent destruction of Odysseus' ships and their crews. They feasted and drank all day, and the next morning they sailed away, glad to have escaped death but grieving for the friends they had lost.

Subsequently several authors emphasized the lighter elements of the story, presenting it on stage in comedies and Satyr plays. One of the latter type has survived in its entirety – Euripides' *Cyclops*, which was written round about 400 BC. In fifth-century Athens dramatists regularly put on a group of three tragedies followed by a Satyr play, which consisted of a comic and ribald treatment of a myth to provide variety and light relief from the tragedies, and which contained a chorus of Satyrs (minor gods of the countryside, part human and part animal in form, and very fond of wine and sex).

In Euripides' *Cyclops* the god of wine Dionysus had been carried off by pirates, and the Satyrs and their father Silenus had sailed away in search of him, been blown to Sicily and there fallen into the clutches of Polyphemus, who made them his slaves. Odysseus turns up with his men and begins bargaining with Silenus for food (which he is only too willing to hand over – in fact he offers all of Polyphemus' animals in return for the delicious wine which the hero has with him and lets him sample). When Polyphemus suddenly returns and catches him in the act of handing over food, the terrified Silenus pretends that the Greeks were thieves whom he had tried his best to fend off. The monster drives the men into his cave and eats two of them. Odysseus gives the Cyclops some wine, telling him that his name is Nobody, and sneaks out of the cave to enlist the aid of the Satyrs in blinding the monster. Polyphemus comes out and is given more to drink (while Silenus manages to pinch some of the wine) until finally he becomes amorous and drags Silenus into the cave to have his wicked way with him. Odysseus gets the stake ready, but now the cowardly Satyrs back out of giving him help (claiming suddenly sprained ankles and specks of dust in their eyes), so he blinds the monster with the help of his men. Polyphemus now stands at the entrance so that the Greeks cannot get out, but the Satyrs make him bang his head on a rock as they send him stumbling off in the wrong direction in search of the Greeks, who meanwhile escape from the cave. Finally Odysseus reveals his real name and the Greeks leave with the Satyrs and Silenus, while Polyphemus staggers off to get a boulder to hurl at them.

It will be clear from the above summary that Euripides followed closely the main lines of Homer's story and included many details from it. Most of the differences are due to the medium. For example, as this was presented on stage, the action had to be shifted to outside the cave, and as this was a Satyr play the Satyrs had to be added somehow. In fact the Satyrs and Silenus do much to bring out the humour: they are incongruous intruders and gods (albeit only minor gods) who are terrified of Polyphemus, have been made into slaves (forced to clean out the monster's cave, look after the sheep etc.) and are somehow powerless to escape, while Silenus is greedy and cunning, a liar and a coward, who will do anything for a drink of wine. There is lots of farce here, with a comic goriness, and although Odysseus retains most of his heroic status, Polyphemus has

171

become a bogey-man or fairy tale ogre and very much a figure of fun. He is a stern master, checking on his return that the Satyrs have done all their chores. In a more developed and amusing drinking scene the wine makes him belch, sing (badly), feel dizzy, see things and develop an erotic interest in ugly old Silenus, who he calls his 'Ganymede' (a very handsome young prince who became the boyfriend of Zeus). He expresses his contempt for Zeus crudely, saying that after a good meal he can fart louder than Zeus can thunder (unless the Greek at 327f. refers to masturbation and means that his pumping fist hitting the bedclothes makes more noise than Zeus' thunder). And this Cyclops is something of a gourmet: he fancies manmeat as a change from eating stags and lions, and he actually cooks his two Greek victims.

Writing shortly before the birth of Christ, the Latin poet Virgil was also much indebted to the *Odyssey* as part of a deliberate attempt to give his epic a Homeric flavour, but he produced a version of this story that also has significant differences from Homer and is generally darker and more melancholy and muted.[4] In Virgil's *Aeneid* the Trojan hero Aeneas (like Odysseus in the *Odyssey*) towards the end of a long voyage after the fall of Troy to find a new home tells someone who offers him hospitality (queen Dido) the tale of his experiences so far, which include an episode involving Polyphemus. While making their way to Latium in Italy (where they will find their new home) Aeneas and some other Trojan survivors come to Sicily, where they spend a night disturbed by the rumblings of the volcano Etna. The next morning one of Odysseus' men suddenly appears and begs them to rescue him, telling them of the danger from the Cyclopes there and explaining how the rest of the Greeks had escaped Polyphemus after the giant had been blinded but he had been left behind in the confusion. At that point they see the blind monster go down to the sea, where he washes his gouged-out eye, groaning. Terrified, they take the Greek on board and row off quickly, but Polyphemus hears them and makes for them. When he cannot catch them he lets out a great roar, at which the other Cyclopes flock down to the shore and stand there glaring helplessly as the Trojans hurriedly sail away.

It will be clear from the above summary that in the *Aeneid* this is something of a non-adventure, as nothing really happens to Aeneas and his men (unlike Odysseus and his) and for them there is just a brush with and flight from impotent Cyclopes rather than a dramatic close encounter with combat, and just terror and rapid escape without the suspense, relief and triumph. In addition this episode is much shorter than the one in Homer and comes after several earlier incidents in the *Aeneid* (one of which is developed at much greater length). Overall Virgil's account is low-key and rather unsettling and dispiriting. At this stage in the poem the Trojans, battered and buffeted by fate, are still in the shadow of their Greek victors, and for them the great exploits have not yet begun.[5] And Aeneas (who does not exult as he tells his story) is a much less glamorous,

flamboyant and forceful figure than Odysseus. But then again Aeneas is a
prudent and responsible leader who does not endanger his men's lives or
lose any of them (unlike the inquisitive and rather rash Odysseus); and we
also see here Aeneas' famous compassion, especially in his act of kindness
and mercy to a Greek enemy. In place of romantic appeal, we find a quiet
efficiency and feeling.

Whereas Homer had begun his account by speaking of the automatic
crops enjoyed by the Cyclopes in their mysterious never-never land and
had described the fertile island nearby, providing a misleadingly idyllic
setting, Virgil at *Aeneid* 3.569ff. locates the Cyclopes firmly in the real
world (by Mount Etna in Sicily) and goes for something more gloomy and
grim, bringing out the menace and the horror from the start. Also apt are
the references to hugeness (570, 579), belching (575), blindness (584ff.)
and a conquered and suffering giant (578ff., of Enceladus, who for making
war on the gods was struck by the thunderbolt and imprisoned under Etna
according to some authorities).

> Not knowing the way, we drifted to the Cyclopes' coast.
> There's a harbour there out of the wind. It is still and huge, 570
> but nearby Etna thunders and rains down its dread debris.
> Sometimes it shoots into the sky a black cloud of
> swirling pitchy smoke and white-hot ashes
> and sends up balls of flame to lick the stars.
> Sometimes it belches up boulders, tearing out its own 575
> entrails, hurling into the air a mass of molten stone
> with a moan and boiling over from its very foundations.
> The story is that the body of Enceladus, half-incinerated by a
> thunderbolt, is crushed beneath the huge mass of Etna,
> which breathes forth fire from its shattered furnaces, 580
> and whenever that giants tires and turns over, all Sicily
> rumbles and trembles, and the sky is veiled with smoke.
> We hid in the woods and endured a night filled with
> monstrous horrors, unable to see what was making the din
> (for there were no fiery stars to brighten the sky with 585
> their radiance, the heavens were obscured by clouds
> and the dead of night enfolded the moon in gloom).

As part of the darker mood Virgil builds up the pathos found in Homer,
beginning at 588ff. where Achaemenides, the comrade of Odysseus (or
Ulysses, to give him his Latin name) who was cheated of escape, makes
his appearance, pitifully emaciated and dirty, after several months cut off
from human contact and hiding in fear from the monstrous Cyclopes. He
tells the story of the Greeks' encounter with Polyphemus, and it is essentially the same story as in Homer, but it is put into the mouth of a brand
new character, one of the rank and file. His aims and circumstances differ
from those of his leader when he told the tale (Achaemenides has had even

more terrible experiences, is still somewhat in shock and is trying to win pity from the Trojans so that he can be rescued). This means that his version has a different perspective and flavour. He opens on a negative note and soon highlights the horrors that he and the rest endured. He does move on to the blinding, but that did not mean escape for him, and he adds a dampening note by immediately proceeding to dwell on the dangers of the Cyclopes and his own wretched existence there. In place of the triumph and elation evident in the *Odyssey* we find here something more miserable and bleak. Achaemenides[6] begins his speech in 613:

'I am Achaemenides from Ithaca, one of luckless
Ulysses' men. I went to Troy because my father Adamastus
was poor (how I wish that I had just stayed poor!).   615
In their anxiety to get away from the cruel cave-mouth my
comrades forgot me and left me behind here in the Cyclops'
enormous cavern. It's a house of gore and bloody banquets,
black and huge inside. He is tall, his head strikes the stars
on high (gods, don't let creatures like him plague the earth!),   620
he's a forbidding sight and nobody would dare talk to him.
He feasts on the flesh and dark blood of his poor victims.
With my own eyes I saw him seize in his great hand two of our
men and (while lolling on his back in the middle of the cave)
smash them on the rock, spattering and soaking the entrance   625
with blood. I saw him chew their bodies, oozing black gore,
and bring his teeth down on their warm and quivering limbs.
But he was punished. Ulysses of Ithaca did not put up with
such behaviour or forget who he was in that terrible crisis.
Full of food and dead drunk, the giant bowed his head,   630
laid it down and sprawled out the length of the cave,
belching up bile and bits of flesh and bloody wine as he
slept. We immediately prayed to the great gods, drew lots
for the parts we would play, poured around him all together
on every side and with a sharp weapon bored through the   635
huge single eye set deep under his grim brow,
as big as a Greek shield or Apollo's sun.
So we gladly avenged our dead comrades at last.
But get away from this coast, you poor men, get away,
cut your moorings!   640
As well as Polyphemus, who pens and milks his woolly flocks
in his hollow cave, there are a hundred other horrible
Cyclopes, just as cruel and colossal, living all along
these curving shores and roaming the high mountains.
There have been three full moons since I began dragging   645
out an existence in the woods among the dens and lonely
lairs of wild animals, watching the massive Cyclopes from crags
and trembling at the tramp of their feet and their voices.
The food that I eat is pitiful – berries and the stony fruit
of cornel-trees and the roots of plants that I tear up.   650

12. Polyphemus

I kept the whole area under observation, but yours are the
first ships I've seen landing. Whoever you are, I have
surrendered to you, just glad to escape the appalling Cyclopes.
Rather than facing them I'll submit to any death you like.'

Virgil is there also trying to outdo Homer. Throughout that passage there
are many words denoting the massiveness of Polyphemus and his home,
and at 619f. (compare 664f. below) he employs exaggeration to make him
tower aloft much higher than Homer's monster. In addition Virgil has gone
for the most horrific element in the lines in the *Odyssey* and heightened
its impact: he highlights the cannibalism at the start, with much on blood
and body parts and devouring, and with lurid expression in 618, 622 and
especially 626f. (where the graphic and gruesome picture is worse than
anything in Homer); he also condenses the Homeric account, omitting
much of the incidental detail, to produce more concentrated horror; and he
gets down to the cannibalism very quickly, with nothing on the Greeks
entering the cave or Polyphemus returning, no conversational exchanges
and so on.

Virgil also adds to Homer in the lines that follow the above passage,
where he shows us Polyphemus and his way of life after his encounter with
Odysseus. There as their first experience of the giant the Trojans catch
sight of a blind figure with a stick (quite different from the terrifying
monster that turned up at the cave which Odysseus and his men were
investigating). This Polyphemus is a diminished and rather pitiful character. After employing Achaemenides to bring out the horror, Virgil now
uses Aeneas as narrator to heighten the pathos. For, as someone who did
not suffer at the hands of the monster as Odysseus did, Aeneas (although
appalled) is not so hostile to Polyphemus and is (as often) more compassionate than Odysseus. He may also feel sympathy for the giant as a fellow
victim of the cunning and violence of the Greeks (especially of the hated
Odysseus[7]). The pathos extends over lines 659 to 664.

> He had scarcely finished speaking when we saw high up on the   655
> mountain the shepherd Polyphemus in person among his flock,
> his massive bulk in motion, making for the familiar shore,
> a horrific monster, hideous and huge, his eyesight gone.
> A lopped pine tree in his hand guided and steadied his steps.
> The woolly sheep were his companions. They were his sole   660
> source of pleasure and solace for his suffering.
> As soon as he reached deep water in the sea,
> he washed away the oozing blood from his gouged eye,
> groaning and grinding his teeth. Then he waded through mid-
> ocean, and still the waves didn't wet his towering flanks.   665
> Afraid, we hurried to get far away, taking on board the Greek,
> who deserved to be rescued, and silently cutting our cable.
> We swept the water with straining oars, bending forward.

He heard, and turned off towards the sound.
But he wasn't able to get hold of us, he couldn't keep up   670
as the Ionian Sea's current carried our ships away.
He sent up a tremendous roar, that got the ocean and all
its waves trembling, terrified Italy far inland
and made Mount Etna's winding caverns bellow.
The other Cyclopes were roused by it, rushed to the harbour   675
from the forests and high mountains and thronged the shore.
We saw them standing there helpless, those brothers from
Etna, with their glaring single eyes and heads towering into
the sky, a horrific gathering, like tall oak trees or
cone-bearing cypresses standing together with towering   680
tops, some soaring wood of Jupiter or grove of Diana.

Among numerous Homeric echoes with variation in this episode, at the end here the Cyclopes come flocking to Polyphemus' cry but with none of the clownish humour about Nobody, and in place of the final sight of the lone Polyphemus praying to Poseidon and hurling a boulder here there is the silent menace of massed Cyclopes who do nothing. That is a striking picture with which to close (the hundred huge giants packed together on the shore with their grimly glaring single eyes), another of the many weird events related in book three of the *Aeneid*. In particular this whole incident reinforces two recent adventures of the Trojans at 521ff. Shortly before arriving at Etna they had only just escaped the dreadful and deadly whirlpool caused by monstrous Charybdis, and immediately before that during a brief landing in south Italy they had seen four horses grazing, an omen of war and also of peace. These three passages on the Trojans' first experiences in the Italian area foreshadow the great war that the Trojans will soon fight in Italy and eventually win after much danger and diffi- culty, and in the lines on Etna and the Cyclopes the terror, horror, violence, savagery, suffering, death and pathos are all very appropriate. In this way Virgil's account has more resonance than Homer's.

Polyphemus and Galatea

The second main story about Polyphemus (his love for Galatea) presents a quite different picture of a love-sick Cyclops, but it has some details in common with the first story, also contains pathos and humour, and recalls the erotic incident with Silenus in Euripides and the tenderness towards the ram in Homer. This tale appears to originate with the Greek poet Philoxenus round about 400 BC. In one famous account we are told that he fell from favour with the Sicilian tyrant Dionysius I and was sent to the quarries by him as punishment for trying to seduce Dionysius' mistress (a woman called Galatea), and there to get his own back he composed a poem with a satirical edge in which he portrayed Dionysius (who supposedly had poor eyesight) as the monstrous Polyphemus, the woman Galatea as a sea-

176

Polyphemus, Acis and Galatea by Giulio Romano (*c.* 1492-1546).
Metropolitan Museum of Art (Rogers Fund, 1928.28.221).

nymph of the same name unsuccessfully loved by the giant (who apparently addressed a love song to her) and himself as Odysseus (who perhaps only blinded the Cyclops after he refused to release him from the cave in return for help to win over the sea-nymph).

That poem by Philoxenus has not survived, but we do have a poem on the giant's hopeless love by a Greek author called Theocritus, who wrote about a hundred years later. He sets this incident before Odysseus arrived (so that this is a prequel) but exploits that future event by means of various references to it. In his *Idyll* 11 he presents a version of Polyphemus' song

177

to Galatea which is both affecting and amusing, a delicate blend of sadness
and gentle humour. Theocritus has here largely suppressed the menace
and savagery of the Homeric Cyclops (except for a few allusions to the
Odyssey), and in place of a murderous and cannibalistic ogre he presents
an earlier version of Polyphemus who is a simple and uncouth shepherd,
so young that his beard is only just starting to sprout, so that we are more
likely to feel sympathy for him. The situation in itself is rather poignant –
the ugly, one-eyed lover deeply but hopelessly smitten with a beautiful
creature from a different world and having absolutely nothing to offer her.
And Theocritus carefully heightens the poignancy by various means: he
places the singing Polyphemus on the shore, a lone figure staring out to
sea, where presumably his beloved lurks, ignoring him; he gives the
Cyclops a lengthy song, suggesting the extent of his infatuation; he represents him as aware of his ugliness, has him make pathetic attempts to
impress and so on. But at the same time there is much incongruity, which
is a major component of the humour (especially when one bears in mind
the Polyphemus so familiar to us from Homer). For here we have a
monster in love and singing with his great voice a plaintive love song, the
massive and brutal Polyphemus being tender and sensitive and pleading,
and the future cannibal wanting to kiss Galatea's hand rather than eat it.

His song begins with flattery of Galatea's white skin (considered attractive in females in the ancient world):

> 'Why do you reject your lover, white Galatea,
> you vision whiter than cream cheese, softer than a lamb,   20
> friskier than a calf, glossier than an unripe grape?
> Why do you just appear as soon as sweet sleep holds me
> and disappear as soon as sweet sleep lets go of me,
> running away like a sheep that's caught sight of a grey wolf?
> I fell in love with you, girl, on your first visit, when you   25
> came with my mother to pluck hyacinth flowers
> on the hill and I showed you the way.
> Ever since I saw you, from that day to this, I can't stop
> loving you. But, god knows, you don't care at all.

Another major element of the humour is the clumsiness of Polyphemus'
performance. So here he begins with a stupid question, indulges in some
flowery rustic rhetoric in 20f. and includes unflattering comparisons of
Galatea to cheese and a sheep (and by likening himself to a wolf in 24
reminds us of his coming cannibalism). In addition, he is so unsophisticated that he doesn't even understand dreaming (22f.). The tragicomedy
continues in the following lines.

> I know why a beautiful girl like you runs away.   30
> It's because I have one long, shaggy eyebrow
> stretching right across my forehead from ear to ear,

178

and one eye beneath it, and a broad nose over my lips.
But although I'm like that, I have a thousand animals grazing,
and the milk that I get from them to drink is the finest;   35
and I'm never without cheese, not in summer or autumn or at
the end of winter; my cheese-racks are always heavily laden.
I'm a better piper than any of the Cyclopes here, and I
often sing of you and me, my dear sweet-apple,
at dead of night. And I'm rearing eleven fawns for you,   40
each with a collar, and four bear cubs.
Come to me – you'll be no worse off.
Leave the green sea to crash on the shore, you'll get
more pleasure from spending the night with me in my cave.
There are laurels and slender cypresses there,   45
there is dark ivy and a grape-sweet vine,
there is cold water, which well-wooded Etna
sends me from her white snow, a divine drink.
Who would prefer the sea and its waves to all that?
If I myself seem to you too hairy, I have   50
oak-logs and an undying fire under the ashes;
you can sear my soul, and my single eye
as well (and there's nothing dearer to me than that).

After positively drawing to her attention his monstrous face, at 34ff. Polyphemus makes a patent and crude attempt to entice Galatea with items that would in fact hardly attract a sea-nymph, and then cloddishly and tediously repeats the attempt at 38, 40f. and 45ff., ending with the particularly naive 49. There is also unwitting irony in the references to his future blinding at 51-3 (compare line 61 below). In what follows the humour becomes more grotesque.

Ah, if only my mother had born a baby with gills,
so I could have dived down to you and kissed your hand   55
(if you withhold your lips) and brought you either white
narcissus or soft poppies with crimson petals
(one is a summer flower, the other a winter one,
so I couldn't have brought you both at the same time).
But I'll learn how to swim right away, little girl,   60
if only some stranger would sail here, so I can find out
why on earth you nymphs like living in the depths of the sea.
Come out, Galatea, come out and then
forget to go home, as I do sitting here.
I wish you'd agree to look after the sheep with me and milk   65
them and make the cheese set with drops of bitter rennet!
It's all my mother's fault, she's the cause of my trouble,
never saying a single kind word to you on my behalf,
even though she sees me getting thinner day after day.
I'll tell her my head throbs and both   70
my feet: let her suffer, since I am suffering.

The Cyclops' wish for gills (as if he is not monstrous enough already!) actually underlines the incompatibility of Galatea and himself, and he follows that up with an underwater gift of (soggy) flowers, coming across as a rather pedantic Polyphemus at 58f. Then there are the jokes of a son of Poseidon and a sea-nymph being unable to swim, a thin giant, and the Cyclops blaming and running to mother and bizarrely claiming that his feet throb. In the concluding lines he tries to bring himself to his senses, but obviously fails, as we are told that this song was repeated often.

> 'Oh Cyclops, Cyclops, has your mind gone?
> You'd show more sense if you went and plaited some
> cheese-baskets and cut some greenery for your lambs.
> Milk the ewe that's here! Why chase one that runs away?   75
> You'll find another Galatea, perhaps a lovelier one.
> Lots of girls urge me to play with them of a night,
> and they all giggle when I pay attention to them.
> Clearly, on land, I too am seen as a somebody.'

Simultaneously touching and amusing, the last few lines provide a fitting conclusion, with their obvious and inept ploy to make Galatea jealous, the speaker's ineffectual attempt to console himself and the gullibility or deliberate self-delusion in connection with the teasing girls' invitations.[8]

At *Metamorphoses* 13.738ff. (composed just before the birth of Christ) the Latin poet Ovid took this story a little further. He dropped the pathos and played up the grotesqueness and farce, and at the end of his account he reintroduced the Homeric savagery and murderous violence in connection with the Cyclops. For a change we hear now from Galatea herself and see her point of view, as she tells the story, complaining about her monstrous suitor's behaviour. And in place of the imaginary rivals for Galatea in Theocritus we find here (for the first time in surviving literature) a real rival for Polyphemus – the young and beautiful Acis, son of a nymph, and loved by Galatea as much as she hated Polyphemus.

The love-sick monster starts to take pains over his appearance in an attempt to make himself attractive, combing his matted hair with a rake and cutting his shaggy beard with a scythe, and he is so preoccupied with Galatea that he no longer attacks and devours the crews of visiting ships. He also comes out with a love song, making a great din on a real giant's pipe (made of a hundred reeds!); and whereas Theocritus' Cyclops was a rather tragic lone figure on the shore ignored by his beloved, in Ovid Polyphemus is surrounded by his sheep and Galatea is listening, hidden by a rock and lying in Acis' arms (see illustration on p. 177).

The song itself is gigantic too, longer than in Theocritus (and also more uncouth and tiresome). In the *Idyll* the Cyclops began with four comparisons in praise of Galatea; Ovid's giant (who would naturally think that bigger is better) comes out with fifteen such flattering comparisons, and then adds as many again complaining of Galatea's harshness to him (and one imagines that she would have been particularly irritated at hearing that she was crueller than a snake that has been trodden on). Again going one better than Theocritus, Ovid's Cyclops has so many sheep that he does not know their exact number, and he also boasts that the ewes have udders so big that they can scarcely get their legs around them. He can offer the nymph a splendid father-in-law too, the god of the sea himself, who rules over Galatea's own waters. He simply cannot understand why she spurns him and prefers (youthful, handsome, normal) Acis, and he threatens to rip Acis' entrails out, tear him limb from limb and scatter the bits over Galatea's sea (this in a love song!).

After finishing his song the monster stands up, catches sight of Galatea and Acis and bellows with rage. In a panic the nymph leaps into the sea, while the hero Acis runs off, pursued by Polyphemus and shrieking to Galatea for help. Polyphemus flings an enormous chunk of mountainside at him, and although only the very tip hits him, it is so huge that it crushes him completely. The hurling of the mass of rock recalls the *Odyssey*, but there is comic-book violence and exaggeration here, and this time Polyphemus hits the target, with only one shot. Even so he is foiled again, as the nymph uses her divine power to split the boulder, send forth from it a leaping river of water and bring Acis back to life as the god of that river.

There was also a tradition that Galatea returned Polyphemus' love and even had a child or children by him,[9] and for our final spin on this story we will look at the first of the *Dialogues of the Sea Gods* by the Greek writer Lucian (second century AD), which is related to this tradition. Again Galatea speaks and gives us her thoughts on her admirer, but her attitude to him is quite different here, and Lucian also introduces a new figure – the sea-nymph Doris, one of Galatea's sisters. Typically he brings these two divinities down to the human level and presents an entertainingly catty exchange between the two of them, very like the conversations that mortal sisters often have. Doris is teasing and mischievous, constantly trying to score over Galatea, and even rather spiteful, not least because she is apparently rather jealous (of someone having Polyphemus for a lover!). Galatea is on the defensive, and although embarrassed, actually seems a bit flattered (by the attentions of a monster!). There is no pathos or horror here, only light comedy, with several jokes about the Cyclops' eye and eyesight.

DORIS: You've got a handsome lover, mad about you (so I hear), Galatea – this Sicilian shepherd.
GALATEA: Don't you mock, Doris. He *is* Poseidon's son, whatever he looks like.
DORIS: So what? He's hairy, has a wild appearance and (worst of all) he's only got one eye – do you think even being a son of Zeus himself would make him any better-looking?

181

GALATEA: He's not bad-looking. That hairy and (in *your* view) wild appearance is manly. And his eye goes very nicely with his forehead, and he sees just as well as if he had two eyes.

DORIS: All these good things to say for him, Galatea – it looks as if *you* are the lover rather than Polyphemus.

GALATEA: I don't love him, but I don't like the way you're all so critical of him. I suspect it's jealousy. When he was looking after his sheep that day up on his vantage-point and spotted us playing on the shore at the foot of Etna, on that long stretch of sand between the mountain and the sea, he didn't even see you lot; no, he thought that I was the prettiest of us all and kept his eye on me alone. That is what's upsetting you all. It shows that I'm better, that I attract lovers, while he didn't spare a glance for you.

DORIS: Do you imagine that people are jealous of you just because some short-sighted shepherd thought you were pretty? And yet the only thing he could have admired in you was that white complexion, I suppose because he's used to cheese and milk and thinks that everything like them is pretty. Anyway if you ever want to find out what you look like, lean over from a rock and look at yourself in the water when it's calm – you'll see that you are just white skin, nothing more. And that is not considered attractive, unless there's some red to set it off.

GALATEA: Nevertheless, for all my unrelieved whiteness, I've got a lover, even though it's him. None of you has a shepherd or a sailor or a ferryman saying nice things about her. And what's more Polyphemus is musical.

DORIS: Don't mention that, Galatea. We heard him singing the other day, when he came serenading you. Dear Aphrodite! Anyone would have thought it was an ass braying. And what a lyre! The skull of a deer with the flesh scraped off it! The horns, just as they were, served as the instrument's arms, joined together by a bridge, and strings were attached but not wound round a peg! His performance was unmusical and out of tune, with him roaring away in one key, and his lyre accompanying him in another. We couldn't stop laughing at that love song of his. Even that chatterbox Echo was unwilling to respond to his bellowing, ashamed to be seen echoing that barbarous, ridiculous serenade. And lover boy was carrying a pet – a bear cub as shaggy as himself. Who wouldn't envy you a lover like that, Galatea?

GALATEA: Well, Doris, why don't you show me *your* lover, who's obviously more handsome and a better singer and lyre-player?

DORIS: I don't have one, and I don't give myself airs and graces either for being able to attract a lover. Your Cyclops, such as he is, stinks like a goat, eats his meat raw (so they say) and devours visiting strangers. So you can have him, and return his love, in perpetuity.

This dialogue also has its more sophisticated (literary) side and needs to be read with Theocritus very much in mind, as it contains so many twists on *Idyll* 11. In place of a solo love song Lucian presents a bitchy interchange; in lieu of the Cyclops' endearments we find Doris' criticisms; and instead of Polyphemus saying nice things about Galatea we find her saying nice things about him. This applies to minor details too. For example, the compliment about Galatea's whiteness at the start of the

Theocritean song is turned into a dig here. If you compare Lucian with Theocritus you will find that many more minor points have been adopted and cleverly adapted like this.

It is an interesting and illuminating exercise to compare the account of Odysseus' encounter with Polyphemus in Homer *Odyssey* 9.106ff. with Sinbad's experiences in 'The Third Voyage of Sinbad the Sailor' (in *Arabian Nights*). This is the same basic story (a folk tale) told in two different ways, with many striking similarities, and also substantial dissimilarities. Consider in particular how in Homer's version actions and events are more clearly and logically motivated; the characterization of the giant and the hero is more developed; and details not found in the *Arabian Nights* make for added interest, vividness and humour. It is best to read the two tales in translation, but for those without access to translations there is an outline of Homer's narrative at the start of this chapter, and here is a summary of Sinbad's voyage.

During Sinbad's third voyage the ship neared the Isle of the Zughb, where a race of ugly, ape-like dwarfs lived. They swam out to the ship in large numbers, scrambled up the masts, seized the helm and steered the vessel to their island. When they reached it, they deposited all the travellers on the beach and then sailed off, leaving them stranded there.

Sinbad and the rest saw a massive palace with a spacious courtyard, and when they entered it they found a great heap of bones in one corner, and on the far side an oven, roasting-spits and enormous pots and pans. Exhausted after their ordeal, they lay down there and soon fell asleep. At sunset they were awakened by a noise like thunder, and the ground shook, as a huge black giant approached. He had fiery red eyes, a mouth like a dark well, lips that drooped down on to his chest, and ears that hung back over his shoulders; his fangs were as long as a boar's tusks, and his nails were like a lion's claws. As they cowered in terror, the giant felt each of them and finally selected the captain, who was fat. The giant broke the man's neck under his foot, thrust a spit through him, lit a fire in the oven and roasted him. Then he devoured the captain, stretched out and fell asleep.

When morning came, the monster got up and went off. The survivors left the palace, looking for a hiding-place, but could find none, so had to return to it in the evening. That night the giant returned and ate another of them. Next morning when he had gone, they decided that they had to kill him to put an end to his crimes. Sinbad suggested that they needed a raft on which to escape after the killing, so they built one and left it ready on the shore.

In the evening the ogre returned, ate another of the men and fell asleep, as before. Sinbad and the rest got up silently, heated two of the great iron spits in the fire until they were red hot and then plunged the sharpened ends into his eyes, putting all their weight on to them from above to drive them home. The blinded giant groped around for them, but they dodged his clutches. He staggered off, groaning in agony. The men rushed to the beach, launched the raft and began rowing away, but suddenly the giant appeared running towards them, guided by a foul hag of his own kind. When the two of them reached the shore, they stood there hurling curses and threats, and then began hurling massive boulders, one after another, until all Sinbad's companions were drowned except for two. Sinbad and those two soon paddled beyond the barrage and escaped.

APPENDIX

Other gigantic monsters

The Cyclopes were just one race of the various gigantic monsters in ancient myth. Another notable race were the Gigantes (Giants), who were most famous for attacking Zeus and the other Olympian gods. The Gigantes were of incomparable size and almost invincible might, and their appearance was terrifying (e.g. they had snakes in place of legs). In a sudden attack they hurled boulders and burning oaks at heaven. The gods had an oracle to the effect that the Gigantes could not be killed by them alone, but could be destroyed with the help of a mortal. So they called in the superhero Heracles (Hercules) and began a terrific battle with their enemies. He used his bow and arrows to good effect, shooting one Giant in the right eye, while Apollo shot him in the left eye. Zeus hurled his thunderbolt, killing another Giant while he was trying to rape Hera, the queen of the gods. A third Giant was fleeing when Athena flung on top of him the island of Sicily (which tended to slow him down a bit). Finally all the Gigantes were killed.[10]

Some other gigantic creatures called the Aloadae showed a similarly misguided aggressiveness and also attacked heaven. These two sons of the sea-god Poseidon (whose individual names were Otus and Ephialtes) grew every year a cubit in breadth and a fathom in height. When they were nine years old, these precocious children were about four metres broad and seventeen metres tall, and ready for action. They imprisoned Ares (god of war) in a bronze pot, wooed Hera and Artemis (virginal goddess of hunting) and began their assault on heaven by piling Mount Ossa on top of Mount Olympus and then Mount Pelion on top of Ossa, so that they could reach the sky. In some accounts Zeus killed them with a thunderbolt; in others Artemis changed herself into a deer and ran between the pair, who both hurled their javelins at the animal and hit each other.[11]

Another group (the Hecatoncheires = Hundred-handers) are better known for helping Zeus. These three (called Cottus, Briareus or Aegaeon, and Gyges or Gyes) had a hundred arms and fifty heads each, as well as irresistible strength. They fought on the side of Zeus and the other Olympians in their long war against the mighty Titans (primitive deities who were cast down from power by Zeus). Finally in a fierce battle Zeus threw thunderbolt after thunderbolt, making the earth roar and the sea boil, while the Hundred-handers hurled three hundred boulders in rapid succession at the Titans, overwhelming them and sending them down to the land of the dead, where the Hundred-handers guard them in the terrible prison of Tartarus. There is also a quaint story that the other Olympians later rebelled against Zeus and wanted to tie him up, until Briareus was summoned and sat down next to Zeus, intimidating the rebels.[12]

Some giants were brigands and a danger to travellers, like Cacus, Amycus and Antaeus (whom we have already met in this book). Others were rapists. So Orion was said by some to have been shot by Artemis when he tried to rape her or one of her companions. And Tityus also attempted to rape Artemis (or her mother Leto), but was shot by Artemis. As a punishment he was stretched out in the Underworld (covering nine acres of ground), and a vulture devoured his liver, which always grew back again, so that his torment was unending.[13]

Finally at *Odyssey* 10.80ff. there is Homer's account of Odysseus' experience with the Laestrygonians while sailing home from Troy (on which compare pp. 28f.). When the hero and his twelve ships arrive at their land, the rest of his squadron anchor within a natural harbour surrounded by towering cliffs, but he cannily ties up outside the harbour, at the end of a promontory. He sends three of his men off to find out who the inhabitants are, and before too long they find out that the inhabitants are in fact murderous giants, when the local king seizes one of them to eat. The other two Greeks rush back to the ships, pursued by thousands of Laestrygonians, who take up position on the cliffs and hurl enormous boulders down at the ships in the harbour, smashing them, and then spearing the men like fish and carrying them off to make a repulsive meal out of them. Powerless to stop the slaughter, all Odysseus can do is cut the cables of his ship and row quickly away, as the rest of his fleet and the crews are destroyed. This is, of course, reminiscent of the Polyphemus episode in book 9, as again Odysseus loses men to cannibal giants. The links act as a structural device, drawing together these two adventures across separate books. But this is not a pale repetition of the earlier incident. There are significant differences. This time Odysseus himself is not personally involved in the encounter. This is also a much more serious blow, as he is here deprived of many more men and almost all of his squadron. And there is even more impact in the fact that this time even the wily Odysseus can think up no ruse and is worsted by his monstrous opponents.

Notes

Introduction

1. For an interesting survey of monsters in various civilizations see Gilmore (full details of works of scholarship referred to by means of the scholar's name will be found in the Select Bibliography). For a moving and thought-provoking exploration of our fear of and fascination with monstrosity see the film called *The Elephant Man*.

2. On the definition of 'monster' see further Cohen 1996 27f. and Atherton 43ff. Note that a single f. after a number denotes the following page or line (so 27f. = 27 and 28), while ff. denotes more than one following page or line.

3. See e.g. South 351ff. and Williams 107ff.

4. Compare Cohen 1996 6ff.

5. For an interesting and scholarly discussion of real-life monstrosity see Leroi.

6. The book is by Mayor.

7. See further Wilk 93ff.

8. For more on 'the other' in this connection consult Cohen 1996 7ff., Warner 161ff., 217ff., Beal 30ff. and 103ff.

9. See further Dowden 134, 141ff. and Gilmore 14ff.

10. I have touched, but only touched, on monsters in ancient art. This is a topic which is huge enough to merit a book on its own and which lies beyond my own sphere of expertise.

1. Vampires, Werewolves and the Living Dead

1. For interesting investigations of vampires in the ancient world and later see Summers, Copper and Frayling.

2. See Euripides *Hecuba* 543ff. and *Alcestis* 845.

3. See Aeschylus *Agamemnon* 1188f., *Eumenides* 183f., 264ff., 302ff. and *Choephoroe* 577f. The Furies really are terrifying and malformed, and they resemble the monstrous Gorgons in appearance, so I have (tentatively) counted them as monsters. The dividing-line between divinity and monstrosity is often problematical. With characters such as Pan, the Satyrs and Silenus (who were all part goat), triple-bodied Hecate and two-faced Janus I have followed the standard practice of classifying them as deities rather than monsters.

4. On the Keres see especially Harrison 165ff.

5. For more on these three see Rohde II 590ff. and Aristophanes *Frogs* 285ff. Cf. also Warner 23ff.

6. Apollonius also masters an Empusa at 2.4.

7. Compare the ghost stories of M.R. James.

8. Goethe's famous poem *The Bride of Corinth* is based on a Greek ghost story by Phlegon (summarized in Summers 34ff.) and this tale by Philostratus (from which Goethe took the Corinthian setting, the wedding detail and the vampire element).

9. See Virgil *Eclogue* 9.54, Horace *Odes* 3.27.3, Livy 21.46, 62 and Pliny *Natural History* 8.80, 83.

10. Compare also Virgil *Eclogue* 8.95ff. and Propertius 4.5.14, where there are practitioners of magic who are not actually werewolves but can turn themselves into wolves.

11. For further discussion see especially Smith. On later werewolves see Baring-Gould.

12. The tale is also found in Mela 2.14.

13. See Plato *Republic* 565D, Pausanias 6.8.2, 8.6.2, Pliny *Natural History* 8.82, Augustine *City of God* 18.17.

14. See Pliny *Natural History* 8.81f., Augustine *City of God* 18.17.

15. Number 301 in A. Hausrath's 1959 edition.

16. A dead man is also revived like this at Apuleius *Metamorphoses* 2.28ff.

17. Aristophanes *Birds* 1553 and the scholiast ad loc.

18. See Silius Italicus 6.151ff. and Lucan 9.700ff.

19. See Oppian *Halieutica* 1.338ff., Aelian *De Natura Animalium* 17.33, Pliny *Natural History* 8.39, 40, 75, 85, 9.3, 29.66.

2. Impact

1. But don't expect monsters in Greek and Latin literature to be as shocking as those in *Blade II* or *28 Days Later*. Given the nature of the medium, Classical monsters just can't manage the same immediate and powerful visual appeal.

2. The devouring type of monster is common in literature and myth throughout the world: see Warner 23ff. and Gilmore 176ff.

3. For more on the Sirens see Chapter 4 below.

4. See e.g. Virgil *Aeneid* 6.417f., Seneca *Hercules Furens* 783ff.

5. *Thebaid* 1.596ff.

6. For humour as a way of dealing with frightening creatures see Warner 246ff.

3. Laocoon and the Sea Snakes

1. You will also see that Virgil's version of events is more convincing, dramatic and moving than that found in the film *Troy*.

2. The Trojans were blind, but they were actually misled as well, by the skilled liar Sinon (who played on their innocence and kindness) and also by heaven itself (so that they misinterpreted the point to the snakes' assault). That double deceit preserves the Trojans' standing and maintains the pathos (if they had just taken in the horse without the intervention of both Sinon and the serpents, they would have seemed quite ridiculously credulous and stupid, as in the film *Troy*).

3. On such imagery see further Knox in Commager 124ff.

4. It is also instructive to compare and contrast the narrative by the bad poet Eumolpus in Petronius *Satyricon* 89.

4. Sirens

1. So Sirens were a common motif on funerary monuments, where they may be death-dealing or mourning the deceased or acting as escorts to souls. In ancient art we also find bearded Sirens (male, presumably) and many vases depicting Odysseus sailing by the Sirens. See further Gantz I 150, II 708f., Cohen 1995 178ff. and Pollard 137ff.

2. For references for Classical authors in these two paragraphs see under Sirens in the References section in Grimal and cf. also Euripides *Helen* 167ff., Lycophron *Alexandra* 714, Strabo 1.2.12, 5.4.7, 6.1.1, Statius *Silvae* 2.2.1, Servius on Virgil *Georgics* 4.563 and *Aeneid* 5.864.

3. See Servius on *Aeneid* 5.864, Ps.-Heraclitus *De Incredibilibus* 14, scholia B on Homer *Odyssey* 12.39, Eustathius p. 1709 (on Hom. *Od.* 12.47). The prostitute theory was accepted as late as the eighteenth century. Modern scholars explain Sirens as e.g. noonday demons, soul-birds (i.e. souls of the dead in bird form), Muses of the dead, the embodiment of sultry winds or the hidden dangers of a calm sea, a species of oriental owl and even penguins (see further de Rachewiltz 257ff. and Gresseth). Some believe that Homer took them from folktales like those about the Siren of Brittany who sings like an angel and makes hearers forget their families, the Siren near Malta who is wonderfully beautiful, has a glorious voice and presents her victims to the sharks, and the story of the Druids advising travellers in Ireland to close their ears with wax to avoid the fascination of the mermaids (see further de Rachewiltz 276ff.).

4. See further Rahner 328ff. and de Rachewiltz 64ff., who also cite some curious instances of Sirens in a Biblical connection. In Greek and Latin versions of the Old Testament 'Sirens' was used to translate 'jackals' and 'ostriches'. So at *Isaiah* 43.80 (of the coming Messiah) we read: 'the wild beasts of the field will glorify me, the Sirens and the ostriches', and *Micah* 1.8 speaks of idolatrous Samaria 'making a howling like the jackals and a mourning like the daughters of Sirens'. So too St Jerome (who explained Sirens as 'demons or monsters or at any rate large flying serpents with crests') in his translation of Isaiah 13.21 said of the coming destruction of Babylon: 'their homes will be filled with serpents, ostriches will reside there … and Sirens in the temples of pleasure'.

5. With 'modern ones' Douglas is playing on the contemporary use of 'siren' to denote a femme fatale or dangerously fascinating female. Such sirens also figure in twentieth-century literature and cinema. For example, in the 1994 film *Sirens* Hugh Grant is a straight-laced young minister in 1930s Australia who is deeply disturbed by the beautiful naked models (sirens) of a bohemian artist played by Sam Neill. And in Kurt Vonnegut's 1959 novel *The Sirens of Titan* someone called Rumfoord (caught in that well-known galactic phenomenon, the chrono-synclastic infundibulum, and rematerializing at regular intervals) uses a photo of the exquisitely beautiful women (sirens) of Titan to tempt a man named Constant to travel to Titan (a moon of Saturn); Constant accepts the photograph, only to use it in an advert for Moon Mist cigarettes, which subsequently turn out to cause sterility in those who smoke them.

6. Sirens also figure frequently in modern art and music. For example, there are sculptures of them by Rodin and Arp, and paintings by Chagall, Giorgio di Chirico and especially Gustave Moreau (his 1882 watercolour *Sirens* is typically enigmatic, engaging and sensuous; it shows three naked Sirens with pearly flesh tints gazing out to sea with dreamy and rather demented gazes, their long hair wreathed with foliage and coral and coiling serpent-like on the ground). There is also an opera called *La Sirène* by Auber, a symphony entitled *Les Sirènes* by Glière and, most famously, the nocturne *Sirènes* by Debussy, which portrays the innumerable waves and rhythms of the sea, with a haunting wordless melody sung by female voices hovering over them and filled with a languid beauty and tender melancholy. For more on Sirens in modern art, music and literature see de Rachewiltz, South 147ff. and Reid II 1004ff.

5. Other Winged Monsters

1. On Pegasus see especially Hesiod *Theogony* 276ff., 319ff., Pindar *Olympian Odes* 13.63ff., *Isthmian Odes* 7.44ff., Aratus *Phaenomena* 205ff. and Ovid *Fasti* 3.451ff. The horse puts in a (not entirely convincing) appearance in the film *Clash of the Titans*.

2. On the Stymphalian Birds see especially Apollonius of Rhodes 2.1030ff., Apollodorus *Library* 2.5.6, Pausanias 8.22.4ff. and Diodorus Siculus 4.13.2.

3. For more on grifffins in Classical literature see Bolton 62ff. and 83ff. On the origins and later history of the griffin (with useful bibliography) see South 85ff.

4. See Herodotus 3.116, 4.13, 27, Aeschylus *Prometheus Bound* 803ff., Pausanias 1.24.6, 8.2.7, Pliny *Natural History* 7.10.

5. Hence Oscar Wilde's witty description of a lady who merely pretended to be a woman of mystery as 'a sphinx without a secret'. Interestingly enough the same riddle is also found elsewhere, among Mongols, French and Africans (see Frazer I p. 347). There is clever play with the Oedipus myth (and various conventions of Greek tragedy) in Woody Allen's film *Mighty Aphrodite*.

6. Ted Hughes' adaptation of this tragedy (*Seneca's Oedipus*, published by Faber and Faber, London, 1969) is particularly vigorous and hard-hitting.

7. On the sphinx in Greek and Latin see also Hesiod *Theogony* 326ff., Apollodorus *Library* 3.5.8, Diodorus Siculus 4.64.3f. and Pausanias 9.26.2ff. For sphinxes in later literature and in ancient and modern art see South 179ff.

8. For the Harpies in Greek literature and art see Homer *Iliad* 16.148ff., *Odyssey* 1.241, 14.371, 20.66ff., Hesiod *Theogony* 265ff. and Gantz 349ff. For later treatment of them see South 155ff. They make a memorable appearance in the film *Jason and the Argonauts*.

6. A Monster-Slayer

1. For ancient accounts of his career see Diodorus Siculus 4.59ff., Plutarch *Theseus*, Apollodorus *Library* 3.15.6ff. and *Epitome* 1.1ff. Among modern scholars see especially Grimal 445ff., Kerényi 217ff. and Gantz 115f., 248ff., 260ff. and 276ff. References for all the stories about Theseus mentioned in this chapter will be found there. For discussion of their connection with the real world of their era see Ward 97ff.

2. On Theseus in art see Gantz (above in n. 1), Neils and Ward 153ff. and 179ff.

3. On Theseus as the national hero of Athens see especially Walker.

4. For more on typical characteristics of heroes see Dowden 146ff.

5. On this make-over for Theseus see further Ward 25ff. and 143ff.

6. When a king called Croesus asked the oracle if he should invade the neighbouring land, he was told that if he did he would destroy a mighty empire. He promptly invaded and did destroy a mighty empire – his own. It has always amused me that Hannibal's prophet is called Bogus in Silius Italicus.

7. For interesting rationalization of the Minotaur see Plutarch *Theseus* 16 and 19.

8. See e.g. Plutarch *Theseus* 20.

9. Lines 230-1 (in which Theseus rescues the bride) have not been translated because they were not written by Ovid (they are not present in the best manuscripts and are excised by most editors as an interpolation). In any case, even if he did rescue her, that would pale into insignificance beside the fight that he causes.

10. There is much more to say about Theseus but not the space to do so here. I will add that for an interesting discussion of Theseus in literature and art from medieval times to the present readers should consult Ward 188ff.

7. A Good Monster

1. See Callimachus *Hymn* 3.46ff.

2. See Goldhill and Osborne 52ff. and South 225ff. (where there is also discussion of other aspects, such as the Centaurs' origins and types and their later history in art and literature).

3. At *Metamorphoses* 12.210ff. See pp. 86ff. above.

4. See further the interesting discussion of Centaurs in Kirk 152ff.

5. In most accounts the majority of the Centaurs sprang from Ixion and a cloud (formed by Zeus in the likeness of Hera) which he raped, or from Ixion's son Centaurus' intercourse with some mares.

6. The meaning of the lines in Pindar (32ff.) is controversial, but the interpretation offered here seems to me to be the most probable and most pointed.

7. Love, marriage and children occur throughout *Pythian Ode* 9 and also help lighten the mood.

8. With both words I had to opt for just one sense in my translation because there is no English adjective or verb that unites all those meanings.

9. At *Iliad* 20.73.

10. At *Iliad* 24.479 etc. Compare Ovid's line 386.

8. Metamorphosed Monsters

1. These stories can be found at *Metamorphoses* 1.452ff., 3.339ff., 6.382ff. and 10.1ff.

2. See Gantz I 21, 304ff. and J.D. Suther in South 163ff. for Medusa in Classical art and later art and literature, and in particular see Wilk for an interesting book-length study of various representations and aspects of Medusa down to the present day (including parallels from around the world and explanations of the myth). Also of interest is the collection of comments on Medusa in Garber and Vickers. For a grim cinematic version of the killing of Medusa see *Clash of the Titans*.

3. Hesiod *Theogony* 278, Apollodorus *Library* 2.4.3.

4. Note also the piquancy in the whole idea of a monster such as Medusa having lovely hair and being so attractive and the neat twists in 797 and 799 to the motif of not looking at Medusa (put in the mouth of someone who famously averted his eyes from her).

5. On Scylla in Greek art and coins see Cohen 1995 34ff., 175ff.

6. On which see Galinsky 217ff.

7. Cf. e.g. Homer *Odyssey* 10.212ff.

9. Jason and the Argonauts

1. It is readily available in video stores and often appears on TV (a good Sunday afternoon film). For further discussion of the film see Solomon 113ff. (who also covers many others on Classical themes). There is also a stimulating (and demanding) treatment of the quest for the Golden Fleece in Pasolini's 1970 (art house) film *Medea* (in Italian, with subtitles).

2. For more on the intriguing Talos (including explanations of his origins and nature) see Atherton 83ff.

3. When involved with monsters heroines (like Andromeda and Hesione) usually figure as prey for the creature and prize for the hero who defeats it.

4. There is much garbling here as the film mixes in Hercules' (quite separate) loss of Hylas to a water nymph in Apollonius at 1.1172ff.

5. Presumably *Jason and the Argonauts* ends on the high note of the winning of the Fleece and defeat of the skeletons because the film people felt that a return journey would be anticlimactic, but they still wanted to put in the exciting Talos episode, so moved it to the outward leg. But this was also a way of eliminating the awkward Medea from the action here.

6. Line 1364 is a clear reminder for us of her importance.

7. The fighting skeletons were outstanding for their day (this was long before computers). They were the work of the legendary Ray Harryhausen, who took two years over the film's special effects and spent four-and-a-half months over this fight alone. He set up his model of a skeleton and took a frame; then he moved a limb slightly and took another frame; then he repeated that process again and again. This must make him the most patient man in the world.

8. There are more Classical monsters in the 1981 film *Clash of the Titans* (on which see Solomon 116ff.), for which Ray Harryhausen again did the special effects.

10. Fighting with Monsters (1)

1. Out of the gods Apollo famously slew Pytho, a monstrous and prophetic snake which lived at a spring not far from Delphi and killed animals and people in large numbers, until shot by his arrows.

2. There is a helpful study of such combat myths in Fontenrose, and particularly interesting is the list of various recurring themes on pp. 9-11. My own analysis goes beyond his and has a different thrust. For combats with monsters see also Atherton 19ff. and Gilmore 11f., 27ff.

3. See Propp. Valuable work with his 'functions' is to be found in Dundes 1964 and 1965 209ff. and Jason and Segal. I employ a modified version of this approach that takes into account recent refinements of Propp (e.g. by Scholes 96ff., Bremond and Greimas 222ff.). For such 'functions' in modern horror narratives see Carroll 97ff.

4. The Classical myths are those of Medea vs the dragon (Apollonius of Rhodes 4.123ff.), Talos vs Medea (Ap. Rhod. 4.1635ff.), Theseus vs Minotaur (Apollodorus *Epitome* 1.7ff., Catullus 64.52ff.), Pollux vs Amycus (Valerius Flaccus 4.133ff.), Trojans vs Harpies (Virgil *Aeneid* 3.209ff.), Dioscuri vs Harpies (Apollodorus *Library* 1.9.21f., Ap. Rhod. 2.176ff.), Alpos vs Dionysus (Nonnus *Dionysiaca* 45.169ff.), Damasen vs monstrous serpent (Nonn. *Dionys.* 25.451ff.), Apollo vs Pytho (Apollod. *Lib.* 1.4.1, Ovid *Metamorphoses* 1.438ff.), giants vs gods (Apollod. *Lib.* 1.6.1f., Claudian *Gigantomachia*), Typhos vs Zeus (Hesiod *Theogony* 820ff., Aeschylus *Prometheus Bound* 353ff., Ovid *Met.* 5.321ff., Nonn. *Dionys.* 1.145ff., Antonius Liberalis *Metamorphoses* 28, Apollod. *Lib.* 1.6.3), Perseus vs Medusa and the sea-beast (Ovid *Met.* 4.614ff., Manilius 5.539ff., Apollod. *Lib.* 2.4.2f.), Bellerophon vs Chimaera (Apollod. *Lib.* 2.3.1f., Hyginus *Fabulae* 57), Cadmus vs dragon (Ovid *Met.* 3.26ff., Apollod. *Lib.* 3.4.1), Odysseus vs Polyphemus (Homer *Odyssey* 9.193ff.), Heracles vs the Molionides (Apollod. *Lib.* 2.7.2) and Cacus (Virg. *Aen.* 8.185ff., Ovid *Fasti* 1.543ff.) and the Nemean Lion (Apollod. *Lib.* 2.5.1, Diodorus

Siculus 4.11.3f.) and the mares of Diomedes (Euripides *Alcestis* 481ff., Diodorus Siculus 4.15.3) and the Hydra (Apollod. *Lib.* 2.5.2, Diod. Sic. 4.11.5f.) and Geryon (Apollod. *Lib.* 2.5.10) and the Hesperides' dragon (Apollod. *Lib.* 2.5.11, Diod. Sic. 4.26.2ff.) and Cerberus (Apollod. *Lib.* 2.5.12) and Hesione's monster (Apollod. *Lib.* 2.5.9, Diod. Sic. 4.42.4ff., Val. Flacc. 2.451ff.) and Antaeus (Apollod. *Lib.* 2.5.11, Diod. Sic. 4.17.4, Lucan 4.593ff.). The non-Classical myths (from a variety of periods and cultures) are those of Ragnarok, St George, Marduk vs Tiamat, Thor vs Hrungnir, Tahoe vs Ong, Coyote vs Wishpoosh, Beowulf vs Grendel and Grendel's mother and the dragon, Sigurd vs Fafnir, the Yellow Emperor vs Ch'ih Yu and Susanowo vs the monstrous snake.

5. For the references for all myths discussed in this chapter see n. 4 above.

6. See Apollodorus *Library* 2.4.2 and Manilius 5.571.

7. Nearest to him are Medea and Perseus, who appear in two combats each.

8. *Library* 2.5.10.

9. Only comparable are the multiple combats in the battle between the gods and the giants, in which Heracles is heavily involved.

10. There are also the apt associations of Hercules' own descent to the Underworld to fetch Cerberus, as various scholars have noted.

11. In Lucan 4.593ff.

11. Fighting with Monsters (2)

1. For links between Typhos and oriental mythology see Graf 91f., Reinhold 69ff., Edmunds 177ff., Walcot 9ff., Burkert 7ff. and Fontenrose 122ff., 177ff.

2. For versions in which Zeus experiences such difficulties see Apollodorus *Library* 1.6.3, Antoninus Liberalis *Metamorphoses* 28, Nonnus *Dionysiaca* 1.137ff. and Ovid *Metamorphoses* 5.321ff. (discussed below). For general surveys of ancient literature on Typhos see Fontenrose 70ff. and Celoria 178ff.

3. Some have doubted that Hesiod actually wrote this passage, but there are good grounds for considering it authentic, and even if it is an interpolation it does perform this role (see West 381f.).

4. We cannot tell for sure if the tragedy or Pindar's poem was the earlier of the two.

5. Compare Burton 92f., Murgatroyd 91f.

6. Intriguingly there is a still more outrageous and amusing possibility – that the unnamed Muse telling Minerva the story was herself an unreliable narrator and misrepresented the actual ending of her enemy's song. Certainly in partisan fashion she abbreviates the woman's account and quotes only part of it, while quoting all of Calliope's (very long) response.

7. Ovid's version was probably composed before Manilius' account, although absolute certainty over relative dating is impossible. Ovid's *Metamorphoses* was complete by AD 8. Manilius in book 4 of his *Astronomica* alludes to Tiberius as the current emperor (he was emperor AD 14-37), but it is possible that the digression on Andromeda in book 5 was in part or in whole an earlier composition which was subsequently inserted.

8. Both authors have JOURNEY, ARRIVAL, MOTIVATION, PHYSICAL APPROACH, FIGHTING, DEATH, VICTORY and EXPLOITATION OF VICTORY. Ovid includes at the end two functions not found in Manilius – CELEBRATION OF VICTORY and SACRIFICE.

9. For more on Ovid's gentle mockery of Perseus in this episode and the surrounding ones in the *Metamorphoses* see Otis 346ff., Glenn 1986 52ff. and Mack 121ff.

10. In the *Astronomica* (reasonably enough, as this is a digression on the

constellation of Andromeda) she dominates the opening all the way down to 566, still figures strongly at 567ff., when Perseus first turns up, is certainly not forgotten when the monster appears and the battle begins (there is focus on her at 587ff. and 605ff.) and also receives mention when the fight is over. In the *Metamorphoses* the focus is initially on Perseus, and once the battle starts she disappears entirely until it is finished.

11. The Latin word *ilia* in 734 can mean 'guts', but 'groin' is a much more common sense for the word and is more in keeping with the humour elsewhere in these lines.

12. Polyphemus

1. For the different types of Cyclopes, and for theories about the origins and meaning of their myth, see Glenn 1978 and Rautenbach.

2. For variants on this folk tale found throughout the world and over many centuries see Page 1ff. and Glenn 1971. On different perceptions in the *Odyssey* of the Polyphemus incident see Atherton 1ff.

3. For Polyphemus in shorter accounts and fragmentary remains down to the time of Virgil see Glenn 1972.

4. See below and note also that there is none of the humour found in Homer (and Euripides). The *Aeneid* was not finished when Virgil died, and he will have intended to revise this episode (e.g. line 640 is incomplete), but it is still variously effective.

5. They begin in book 6, with Aeneas' trip to the Underworld, followed by the great war in Italy (books 7-12).

6. For more on Achaemenides see Ovid *Metamorphoses* 14.160ff.

7. Compare *Aeneid* 3.273.

8. For more on Polyphemus and Galatea in Theocritus see *Idyll* 6. Also of interest is *Eclogue* 2, in which Virgil took over and assigned to a human shepherd much of the material in *Idyll* 11, playing down the humour and increasing the pathos.

9. See e.g. Propertius 3.2.7f., Appian *Illyrians* 2.3, Nonnus *Dionysiaca* 6.300ff.

10. See Apollodorus *Library* 1.6 for this battle.

11. See Apollodorus *Library* 1.7.4.

12. See Hesiod *Theogony* 617ff., Homer *Iliad* 1.396ff.

13. On Orion and Tityus see Horace *Odes* 3.4.71f., 77ff., Virgil *Aeneid* 6.595ff. and Apollodorus *Library* 1.4.1,5. On Classical and later giants in general see South 293ff.

Select Bibliography

I list below only those works which are cited in the text and which I have found particularly helpful in the writing of this book. For additional bibliography see esp. South xxiii ff. and 375ff.

Adriano, J.D., *Immortal Monster* (Westport, Connecticut, 1999).
Atherton, C. (ed.), *Monsters and Monstrosity in Greek and Roman Culture* (Bari, 1998).
Baring-Gould, S., *The Book of Werewolves* (London, 1865; reprinted 1995).
Beal, T.K., *Religion and its Monsters* (New York and London, 2002).
Bolton, J.D.P., *Aristeas of Proconnesus* (Oxford, 1962).
Borges, J.L. and Guerrero, M., *The Book of Imaginary Beings* (New York, 1970).
Bremond, C., 'The Logic of Narrative Possibilities', *New Literary History* 11 (1980), 387-411.
Burkert, W., *Structure and History in Greek Mythology and Ritual* (Berkeley and Los Angeles, 1979).
Burton, R.W.B., *Pindar's Pythian Odes* (Oxford, 1962).
Carroll, N., *The Philosophy of Horror or Paradoxes of the Heart* (New York and London, 1990).
Celoria, F., *The Metamorphoses of Antoninus Liberalis* (London, 1992).
Cohen, B. (ed.), *The Distaff Side* (Oxford, 1995).
Cohen, J.J., *Monster Theory: Reading Culture* (Minneapolis, 1996).
Commager, S., *Virgil. A Collection of Critical Essays* (Englewood Cliffs, New Jersey, 1966).
Copper, B., *The Vampire in Legend, Fact and Art* (London, 1973).
de Rachewiltz, S., *De Sirenibus* (New York and London, 1987).
Dowden, K., *The Uses of Greek Mythology* (London, 1992).
Dundes, A., *The Morphology of North American Indian Folktales* (Helsinki, 1964).
Dundes, A., *The Study of Folklore* (Englewood Cliffs, New Jersey, 1965).
Edmunds, L. (ed.), *Approaches to Greek Myth* (Baltimore and London, 1990).
Fontenrose, J., *Python: A Study of Delphic Myth and its Origins* (Berkeley, Los Angeles and London, 1980).
Frayling, C., *Vampyres: Lord Byron to Count Dracula* (London, 1991).
Frazer, J.G., *Apollodorus The Library* (Cambridge, Mass., 1976).
Galinsky, G.K., *Ovid's Metamorphoses: An Introduction to the Basic Aspects* (Berkeley and Los Angeles, 1975).
Gantz, T., *Early Greek Myth* (Baltimore and London, 1993).
Garber, M. and Vickers, N.J., *The Medusa Reader* (London and New York, 2003).
Gilmore, D.D., *Monsters, Evil Beings, Mythical Beasts, and All Manner of Imaginary Terrors* (Philadelphia, 2003).
Glenn, E.M., *The Metamorphoses: Ovid's Roman Games* (Lanham and London, 1986).

Select Bibliography

Glenn, J., 'The Polyphemus Folktale and Homer's Kyklopeia', *Transactions of the American Philological Association* 102 (1971), 133-81.

Glenn, J., 'Virgil's Polyphemus', *Greece and Rome* 19 (1972), 47-59.

Glenn, J., 'The Polyphemus Myth: Its Origin and Interpretation', *Greece and Rome* 25 (1978), 141-55.

Goldhill, S. and Osborne, R., *Art and Text in Ancient Greek Culture* (Cambridge, 1994).

Gould, C., *Mythical Monsters* (London, 1886).

Graf, F., *Greek Mythology: An Introduction* trans. T. Marier (Baltimore and London, 1996).

Greimas, A-J., *Structural Semantics: An Attempt at a Method*, trans. D. McDowell, R. Schleifer and A. Velie (Lincoln and London, 1983).

Gresseth, G.K., 'The Homeric Sirens', *Transactions of the American Philological Association* 101 (1970), 203-18.

Grimal, P. *The Dictionary of Classical Mythology*, trans. A.R. Maxwell-Hyslop (Oxford, 1985).

Harrison, J., *Prolegomena to the Study of Greek Religion* (repr. Princeton, New Jersey, 1991).

Jason, H. and Segal, D. (eds), *Patterns in Oral Literature* (The Hague and Paris, 1977).

Kerényi, C., *The Heroes of the Greeks* (London, 1974).

Kirk, G.S., *Myth: Its Meaning and Functions in Ancient and Other Cultures* (Cambridge, 1970).

Leroi, A.M., *Mutants* (London, 2003).

Lum, P., *Fabulous Beasts* (New York, 1951).

Mack, S., *Ovid* (New Haven and London, 1988).

Mayor, A., *The First Fossil Hunters: Paleontology in Greek and Roman Times* (Princeton, 2000).

Murgatroyd, P., *Melpomene: Translations of Selected Greek Lyrics with Notes* (Amsterdam, 1989).

Neils, J., *The Youthful Deeds of Theseus* (Rome, 1987).

Otis, B., *Ovid as an Epic Poet* (Cambridge, 1970).

Page, D., *The Homeric Odyssey* (Oxford, 1955).

Pollard, J., *Seers, Shrines and Sirens* (London, 1965).

Propp, V., *Morphology of the Folktale*, trans. L. Scott (Austin, Texas, 1968).

Rahner, H., *Greek Myths and Christian Mystery*, trans. B. Battershaw (London, 1963).

Rautenbach, S., 'Cyclopes (I)', *Acta Classica* 27 (1984), 41-55.

Reid, J.D., *The Oxford Guide to Classical Mythology in the Arts, 1300-1990s* (Oxford, 1993).

Reinhold, M., *Past and Present: The Continuity of Classical Myths* (Toronto, 1972).

Rohde, E., *Psyche* (New York, 1966).

Scholes, R., *Structuralism in Literature: An Introduction* (New Haven and London, 1974).

Smith, K.F., 'An Historical Study of the Werewolf in Literature', *Publications of the Modern Language Association of America* IX,1 (1894), 1-37.

Solomon, J., *The Ancient World in the Cinema* (New Haven, Connecticut, 2001).

South, M., *Mythical and Fabulous Creatures: A Source Book and Research Guide* (New York, 1987).

Summers, M., *The Vampire in Europe* (London, 1929).

Twitchell, J.B., *Dreadful Pleasures: An Anatomy Of Modern Horror* (Oxford, 1985).

Select Bibliography

Walcot, P., *Hesiod and the Near East* (Cardiff, 1966).

Walker, H.J., *Theseus and Athens* (Oxford, 1995).

Ward, A.G. (ed.), *The Quest For Theseus* (New York, 1970).

Warner, M., *No Go the Bogeyman* (London, 1998).

West, M.L., *Hesiod. Theogony* (Oxford, 1966).

Wilk, S.R., *Medusa: Solving the Mystery of the Gorgon* (Oxford, 2000).

Williams, D., *Deformed Discourse* (Montreal and Kingston, 1996).

Index

This book covers all the major and most famous monsters of Classical mythology (for lesser ones consult Frazer and Grimal). In this index numbers refer to pages in the book, and italicized words after an entry direct you to the italicized name (i.e., for more on Aegaeon look under Hecatoncheires).